D1595947

EARLY CHRISTIAN INTERPRETATIONS
OF HISTORY

THE BAMPTON LECTURES OF 1952

EARLY CHRISTIAN INTERPRETATIONS OF HISTORY

BY

R. L. P. MILBURN

FELLOW AND CHAPLAIN OF WORCESTER COLLEGE
OXFORD

HARPER & BROTHERS PUBLISHERS

NEW YORK

PREFACE

'The historical', it has been said, 'is what we understand least and what concerns us most'; and such a subject may scarcely be neglected at any rate by the Christian Church, which claims to derive its doctrines less from abstract thought than from the contemplation of certain historical facts. It seems, therefore, that an enquiry, even though short and tentative, concerning the nature of history need not be regarded as alien to the apologetic purposes for which the Bampton Lectures were founded, especially if it takes the form of allowing the historians of the early Church to speak for themselves.

The scope of the investigation is, I trust, made clear in the first lecture. It remains only to add that 'history' has been taken to include both the historical process, as to some extent revealing the purposes of God, and historical method also. The necessarily curtailed treatment of the doctrine of the Assumption seemed to invite fuller discussion of its historical evidences in an appendix.

My debt to previous writers will, at least in part, be manifest from the names mentioned in the notes. Several kind friends have helped in the work of verifying references, and to them I express my gratitude, as also to the editor of the *Church Quarterly Review* who gave permission for the use of extracts from an article which appeared in that journal, in March 1938. My wife kindly undertook the task of preparing the index.

It would be agreeable if one could share the hopeful feelings expressed by the Bampton Lecturer for 1787: 'I have only to beg the favour of the intelligent reader to peruse these discourses and the annexed annotations with an inclination to be satisfied, and in that spirit of candour and impartiality with which he will find them to have been composed'. But, in any case, it is proper to conclude by echoing, albeit in a minor key, the prayer 'Domine Deus, quaecunque dixi de tuo, agnoscant et tui; si qua de meo, et Tu ignosce et tui'.

R. L. P. M.

WORCESTER COTTAGE, OXFORD
Nov. 30, 1953

EXTRACT FROM THE LAST WILL
AND TESTAMENT OF
THE REV. JOHN BAMPTON
CANON OF SALISBURY

'. . . I give and bequeath my Lands and Estates to the Chancellor, Masters, and Scholars of the University of Oxford for ever, to have and to hold all and singular the said Lands or Estates upon trust, and to the intents and purposes hereinafter mentioned; that is to say, I will and appoint that the Vice-Chancellor of the University of Oxford for the time being shall take and receive all the rents, issues, and profits thereof, and (after all taxes, reparations, and necessary deductions made) that he pay all the remainder to the endowment of eight Divinity Lecture Sermons, to be established for ever in the said University, and to be performed in the manner following:

'I direct and appoint, that, upon the first Tuesday in Easter Term, a Lecturer may be yearly chosen by the Heads of Colleges only, and by no others, in the room adjoining to the Printing-House, between the hours of ten in the morning and two in the afternoon, to preach eight Divinity Lecture Sermons, the year following, at St. Mary's in Oxford, between the commencement of the last month in Lent Term, and the end of the third week in Act Term.

'Also I direct and appoint, that the eight Divinity Lecture Sermons shall be preached upon either of the following subjects—to confirm and establish the Christian Faith, and to confute all heretics and schismatics—upon the divine authority of the holy Scriptures—upon the authority of the writings of the primitive Fathers, as to the faith and practice of the primitive Church—upon the Divinity of our Lord and Saviour Jesus Christ—upon the Divinity of the Holy Ghost—upon the Articles of the Christian Faith, as comprehended in the Apostles' and Nicene Creed.'

CONTENTS

EARLY CHRISTIAN INTERPRETATIONS
OF HISTORY

CHAPTER I

THE HISTORIAN'S TASK

Do not interpretations belong to God? Gen. xl. 8

In the course of his address to the Dauphin, Bossuet declared that history is a subject eminently suitable for study, since, as he put it, 'whatsoever part of ancient history you read all will turn to your advantage. No fact will pass but you shall perceive its consequences. You will admire the train of God's counsels in the concerns of religion; you will also note the complexity of human affairs and thence become aware with what great care and foresight they must be governed.'[1] And these words of the bishop serve but to repeat the ancient doctrine that history 'regulates our lives'[2] or is, at any rate, a 'philosophy that teaches, by examples',[3] the value of right belief and right conduct.

In its earliest stages, history may minister chiefly to the profound instinct of curiosity and wonder which is man's natural reaction to the marvellous fashioning of the world which he is called upon to inhabit, and we scarcely need Cicero[4] to remind us that a feeling of lively pleasure is properly aroused by any colourful and varied narrative. But as, with Herodotus, fabulous and mythical history yields to the attempt, still poetic in tone, to trace the relationship between the nations and examine the deep causes of strife, so the conviction grows that story-telling is not enough, and the historian joins with the moralist in drawing clear-cut lessons out of what Lord Chesterfield called a confused heap of facts.[5] Thucydides, with his stern contempt for unreliable fable-mongers who 'composed their works more to please the ear than to tell the truth',[6] saw to it that his record of the Peloponnesian War was so constructed that soldiers and politicians of the future would find in it a never-failing store of practical wisdom, while Tacitus speaks for many a Roman historian when he declares that the impulse which drove him on to write was the desire 'that noble actions should not pass away in silence, and that dread of disgrace might deter

I

men from knavery in word and deed'.[7] The historian's task has often been similarly interpreted in the modern age. Lord Acton, for instance, notes that 'the knowledge of the past, the record of truths revealed by experience, is eminently practical as an instrument of action and a power that goes to the making of the future', and he adds that 'if the past has been an obstacle and a burden, knowledge of the past is the safest and surest emancipation'.[8] The principle thus laid down echoes the homelier accents of the mediaeval chronicler who declared that 'it is every man's duty to be daily learning how he ought to live by taking the heroic figures of the past as his model and profiting thereby'.[9]

Nevertheless, the view that history should educate as well as amuse was not accepted by all even in the purposive atmosphere of the Victorian Age. Thackeray's method of studying history consisted of lying in the heather with an odd volume of the *Spectator* or *Tatler* in his hand whereat 'the England of our ancestors is revivified, the Maypole rises in the Strand, the beaux are gathering in the coffee-houses'[10] and the whole colourful panorama of a past age is conjured up by means of casual, uncritical browsing. Landor, again, had proclaimed that 'History, when she has lost her Muse, will lose her dignity, her occupation, her character, her name',[11] just as, years later, Augustine Birrell laid it down that 'history is a pageant, not a philosophy', and dismissed educative maxims with the words 'the less we import their cheap wisdom into history the better'.[12] But such light-hearted approaches were roundly condemned by men like Sir John Seeley as 'the old literary groove, leading to no trustworthy knowledge'. 'Break the drowsy spell of narrative', Seeley added, 'ask yourselves questions,' for history 'should not merely gratify the reader's curiosity about the past but modify his view of the present and his forecast of the future.'[13] In other words, though a few *dilettanti* or literary stylists may stand apart, most historians have felt themselves able to detect a certain pattern and reliability in events which allows the past to provide a reasonable ground for future expectations and even to display the unmistakable impress of an 'enduring Power which makes for righteousness'.[14]

But the more extensively purpose and meaning are imported into history, so much the greater becomes the temptation to mould it in accordance with the assumed principles of morality. Polybius, adopting the detached and passionless view of an agnostic, exiled from his country and composing a world-history under the patronage of self-consciously broad-minded men of culture, put the matter as concisely as anyone. 'A knowledge of history', he writes, 'is the most satisfactory training and education for affairs',[15] but he goes on to add that spurious history is without any value: 'just as, when a living creature loses its eyes, its body is rendered entirely useless, so what remains of history when it is bereft of truth is nothing but a worthless fable'.[16] But it is easier to pay lip-service to this principle than to act upon it. Cicero, for instance, declared it to be a generally acknowledged axiom that 'no historian would dare to utter an untruth or to suppress what was true: his writings must display no trace of partisanship or spite'.[17] 'History', he explains, 'is a storehouse containing all the countless lessons of the past', and it is acclaimed as 'witness of the ages and light of truth, giving life to remembrance, the guide of human existence and messenger of antiquity.'[13] Yet, in the course of his letter to the historian Lucius Lucceius, Cicero hints that Lucceius should treat the incidents of the civil war 'with considerable freedom' as has been his custom, in order to stigmatize 'the disloyalty, the intrigues and the treachery' of which Cicero's opponents have been guilty, whilst, at the same time, the 'great variety of material' supplied by Cicero's own experiences is to be worked up into a narrative 'charged with a sort of pleasurable interest, which could powerfully grip the reader's attention'.[19] Frankness of this kind is formally canonized in the suggestion which Cicero makes elsewhere that 'orators are allowed to tell lies in their historical works, so that they may be able to speak with more point',[20] and which leads on to St. Jerome's blunt declaration that 'people are sometimes compelled to say not what they know to be right but what necessity dictates'.[21]

Zeal and, to a lesser degree, vanity have commonly proved themselves the greatest enemies of historical truth, even though sombre warnings abound that attempts to serve a good cause by dishonest narrative tend sooner or later to result in disaster. For the urge to sharpen the lessons of history, and to display events as they ought to have happened rather than as they in fact occurred, not seldom masters the instinct for sincerity and for scholarship alike, since, as Bossuet put it, 'the greatest intellectual failing is to believe things because we should like them to be so and not because we have seen that they actually are so'.[22]

The Oxford scholar who declared that 'the Christian religion is a daily invitation to study history'[23] was but repeating in a pointed and arresting manner the commonplace that Christianity, unlike many other religions, is primarily a religion of history in that it speaks in terms less of ideas than of events. The content of Christian mission-preaching was a series of happenings which, though no doubt they served to illustrate the perduring relationship between nature, man and God, invited judgement not merely as speculations but in the cold light of historical truth. Two somewhat inconsistent suspicions have from time to time been harboured against those who set down the primitive Christian records; that they found their history already prepared for them in the prophecies of the Old Testament, which had necessarily to be fulfilled by the Messiah and his followers if the claims of the Church were not to be dismissed as ridiculous, and, secondly, that their gaze was directed away from facts in the expectation that, at any moment, the Lord might return in glory to bring the temporal order to a close. The writings of the New Testament have been repeatedly examined and discussed with anxious and minute care. During these lectures, therefore, no attempt, save for an occasional backward look, will be made to go over that ground once more. The aim will rather be to consider what Christian writers from the second to the fifth century thought about the method and stuff of history, in the attempt to discover whether their approach to such matters was in fact vitiated by a casual heedlessness or by doctrinal interests, and in the hope that their achievement may throw some light on the historian's task, its risks and opportunities.

The Christian historians owed a double debt to predecessors.

4

On the one hand they were composing their works in an Empire still informed by the Classical spirit in thought and culture, a dominant trait of which was a certain gravity and weight that scorned rhetorical vulgarity or antiquarian prying and caused the more respectable writers of Greece and Rome to offer, in history, 'something useful to those who desire to obtain a clear picture of events and to forecast similar events which may, in all human probability, be expected to occur.'[24] This balanced and practical outlook, bounded by a sense of responsibility and respect for truth, is carefully analysed by Polybius. 'The peculiar function of history', he writes, 'is, in the first place, to ascertain what words were actually spoken and next to find out the reason why what was done or said resulted in failure or success.'[25] For the historian's task is not looked on merely as a matter of conscientious reporting; rather it is held to demand all that a man possesses of delicate judgement linked with accuracy. St. Augustine noted that 'it is one thing to record events, quite another thing to teach people what they ought to do. The task of history is to record events faithfully and in a serviceable manner.'[26] 'To record events faithfully'—such is the first essential condition; nevertheless it was well understood that bald narrative is not enough and that some deeper view is required which shall link events together by a study of causation, in accordance with the pronouncement of Sempronius Asellio that 'it is not sufficient for us to proclaim fact; we have to set forth the purposes and reasons which underlie events'.[27]

In the ancient world, therefore, a certain scorn exists for the armchair historian, on grounds that Montaigne later summed up in the words, 'the only good histories are those which have been written by the Persons themselves who commanded in the Affairs whereof they write or who have participated in the Conduct of them, or, at least, who have had the Conduct of others of the same Nature. . . . What can a man expect from a Physician who will undertake to write of War, or from a mere Scholar treating upon the Designs of Princes?'[28] But more important than this insistence that the writer of history shall avoid the peril of being 'Deep-versed in books and shallow in himself'[29] is the awareness of what

John Buchan called 'the fundamental irrationality of a large part of Clio's domain'.[30] Buchan was commenting on Sainte-Beuve's dictum that 'history seen from a distance undergoes a strange metamorphosis; it produces the illusion—most dangerous of all—that it is rational', and some who might suppose that the French essayist had made his epigram at the price of exaggeration may yet accept Buchan's own judgement that history is not exempt from 'the stubborn nodules of the unrelated and inexplicable which everywhere confront us'. When Byron spoke of 'Livy's pictured page',[31] he was not only paying tribute to the principle that the historian must be an artist as well as an artisan but was also approaching that 'classic' estimate of history which refuses to assign to it as its function merely the endless stringing together of facts but claims for it virtues of grace and perception which cause it to become, in Quintilian's words, 'the near ally of poetry and a kind of epic freed from the shackles of metre'.[32] The requirement that historians shall use gifts of insight as well as application entitles them, according at any rate to the opinion of Diodorus Siculus, to enjoy the honour of being 'servants of the divine providence', while their craft is acclaimed as 'the utterance of truth and a sort of mother-country of the whole of philosophy'.[33]

The Biblical approach, on which Christian writers were even more closely dependent, was differentiated from classical theories by its insistence on the unity of all history. The great contribution of the Hebrew people to the philosophic thinking of the world had no doubt been their passionate adherence to the doctrine that 'the Lord our God is one Lord',[34] guiding the destinies of empires as well as controlling the operations of nature. Along with this conviction that the power behind events is a unity went the belief, to which such stories as that of the tower of Babel[35] bore witness, that there had been an original oneness underlying what later came to be a diversity of languages and cultures. This ideal unity was re-established at Pentecost when the variety of tongues served only to testify to the oneness of the family of the children of God, joined together in the new Israel that drew its members from every race under the sun. On this reckoning, the book of Acts does not merely set forth an apology for the Christians as law-abiding citizens but is also designed to show that prophetic hopes had been fulfilled by this re-establishment of the primitive unity, which had been early broken by the follies and failures of mankind. St. Paul's sermon at Athens, the centre of the civilized world, where Herodotus had read his history out aloud and Thucydides had sketched the outlines of his 'possession for all time', points the moral of the tale. 'The Lord God', he proclaimed, 'made of one blood all nations of men for to dwell on the face of the earth',[36] and this ideal unity will be matched by the judgement of the whole world on one appointed day by one Redeemer, in whom, as Paul elsewhere explains, 'all things are summed up'.[37] Gregory of Nazianzus later noted that 'each of the three synoptic Gospels was written for one of the nations whose language appeared on the inscription set at the top of the cross—Hebrew, Greek and Roman—while the Gospel of St. John was written for all',[38] in the sense that, throughout the Johannine prologue, the Word of God is set forth as including the whole of mankind in the appeal of its one, all-embracing act of charity.

Pagan wisdom had investigated the beginnings of history while the Jews redeemed it from vanity by assigning to it a meaningful end, one that defies the desperate pessimism of the eternal circle of events: 'that which hath been is that which shall be, and that which hath been done is that which shall be done, and there is no new thing under the sun'.[39] The Christian Church added the claim that the whole varied course of history gains full significance only when considered in the light of a central happening wherein God matched his initial creative impulse with a uniquely valuable outburst of redemptive activity. From one point of view history appears as a great parable which many 'seeing may see and not perceive and hearing may hear and not understand'.[40] It has, for instance, frequently been observed that the rise and fall of empires drives home the lesson of the transience of human achievement and represses human arrogance. 'Ye have built houses of hewn stone', proclaimed the prophet, 'but ye shall not dwell in them: ye have planted pleasant vineyards but ye shall not drink the wine thereof',[41] a sombre trumpet-call to Israel which the Preacher later echoes in the minor key: 'I hated all my labour wherein I laboured under the sun; seeing that I must leave it unto the man that shall be after me. And who knoweth whether he shall be a wise man or a fool . . . this also is vanity.'[42] But over against the chronic inconstancy of human affairs is to be perceived by the faithful the 'empire of the Son of Man, the empire that is to stand amidst the ruin of all others and to which alone eternity is promised'.[43]

Treating history on a large scale and concerned primarily to demonstrate this oneness centred on God, most Biblical writers lacked that whole-hearted regard for logical method which led J. B. Bury to claim that 'history is a science, no less and no more'.[44] For when God is brought into the picture, the neat and friendly forms of thought in which man is content to take his refuge tend to be overlaid by something of majesty and mystery, and the scientific historian, in his ambition to classify the past and arrange future events, is sometimes thwarted by an unmanageable Providence. The Jewish historians, who were pledged rather to declare the mighty works of the Lord than to manage Providence, wrote with a purpose more consistent and obvious than that of their classical counterparts. 'For the Jew,' observed Dean Inge, 'faith always clothed itself in a historical dress. The truth is that which was or that which shall be.'[45] On this view the historian's task is not to discover illustrations of general laws but to trace the development of a unique story, a story which appeared to Thomas Aquinas to 'flow along in the manner of some noble poem'.[46] Bishop Butler once observed that 'the general design of Scripture, considered as historical, is to give us an account of the world, in this one single view as God's world',[47] and the vivid conviction of its writers that events held a significance which it was their duty to reveal led them to be concerned more with the broad outlines of history than with its minute particulars. Concerning the book of Kings, for example, it may be an exaggeration to say that 'we have less a history of Kings than a commentary upon Yahwe-worship',[48] but few could quarrel with these words of one who would have

8

claimed to offer a conservative exegesis: 'We cannot fail to observe that this book is dominated throughout by the aim of making the history a vehicle of moral and religious teaching. Interwoven with the narrative is a perpetually recurring strain of comment and application, the avowed purpose of which is to point out the great lessons which were seen to be exemplified in the past history of the people. And when we read the book in the light supplied by these comments, we find that nearly everything it contains is subservient to the main end of impressing those lessons on the minds of the readers.'[49] And the chief of these lessons, of course, is the 'principle of retribution—the truth that fidelity to Yahwe is rewarded by national prosperity and unfaithfulness punished by national misfortune', an emphasis, when viewed from the secular standpoint, on the doctrine *l'union fait la force* to the truth of which all history concurs in testifying.

It must not, however, be assumed that Jewish historians were necessarily indifferent to the claims of scholarship and exact record. A clear tendency towards self-conscious objectivity is to be found at any rate in the writings of the savant Josephus who was enabled to view events from outside as a favourite of men whose nation had crushed his own. 'And I am so bold as to say,' runs the epilogue to his *Antiquities*, 'now that I have completely perfected the work that I proposed to myself to do, that no person, whether he were a Jew or a foreigner, could for all his good intentions have so accurately delivered these accounts to the Greeks as I have done.' Elsewhere he makes a spirited attack on Greek historians who 'knew nothing on good foundation when they set about writing, but merely jotted down their own conjectures as to facts'.[50] He attacks them for desiring to make a display of their fine powers of writing and their over-emphasis on the artistic side of the historian's task: 'We must indeed yield the palm to the Greek writers for eloquence and literary skill, but certainly not as regards the truth of ancient history'.[51] Yet Josephus himself falls below the standards of strictest accuracy. When the account that he gives in the *History of the Jewish War* is compared with the record of the same events in his autobiography, he stands convicted of inconsistencies too marked to be attributed merely to careless-ness. Moreover, his pro-Roman feelings make him an apologist for Titus, as, for instance, in his account of the deliberations before the burning of the Temple in A.D. 70. Josephus makes Titus declare that he would in no circumstances destroy so magnificent a work,[52] whereas the fourth-century historian Sulpicius Severus, who is here probably reproducing a lost section of Tacitus' *Annals*, records that 'a number of people, including Titus himself, thought that whatever happened the temple ought to be thrown down, so that the religion of the Jews and the Christians might be more completely destroyed'.[53]

Human frailty may cause Josephus more than once to leave the straight path of perfect accuracy. Nevertheless, he holds himself aloof, along with Thucydides and Polybius, from the conventions of ancient and mediaeval history-writing in that all three viewed events, from exile, with a sophisticated detachment and a pre-cocious reverence for bare fact which were neither desired nor attained by the great majority of historians, whether classical or Biblical. For such historians were, as a rule, less closely concerned with scholarly research than with the aim of illustrating a theme. Caesar and Sallust, for instance, wrote as apologists, the one for his own actions, the other for his party. Similarly the author of Acts eagerly proclaimed that Christianity was, and deserved to be, officially tolerated in the Roman Empire. And we have been reminded often enough that the Gospels are not primarily bio-graphies but concise records of events the consideration of which makes a man wise unto salvation. Such purposes need not neces-sarily imply any distortion of narrative, except such as derives from selection and stress. So at least St. John puts it in the concluding verses of his Gospel: 'Many other signs did Jesus in the presence of the disciples, which are not written in this book; but these are written, that ye may believe that Jesus is the Christ, the Son of God'.[54] There is here no academic trifling with such a theory as Croce's that it is impossible to grade historical events in a scale of importance. Rather is it held that events gain meaning and value only in so far as they illustrate the fulfilment in history of a truth that 'transcends the limits of the external, objective world'.[55]

Just as the Christian Church became the legatee of Greece and Rome besides claiming to inherit the Hebrew Scriptures, so its historians were grounded in these two allied, yet distinct, traditions. Their classical and Biblical predecessors alike wished to make narrative serve the end of instruction, but, while the former pressed home political lessons, the latter concerned themselves primarily with the less tractable affairs of religion. According to Polybius, all historians agree that 'the study of history is the surest training and education for political affairs',[56] whereas, for the writers of the Old Testament, to contemplate the varied course of events leads rather to the exclamation: 'Who is like unto thee, O Lord, among the Gods? Who is like thee, glorious in holiness, fearful in praises, doing wonders?'[57] The Biblical writers were therefore untroubled by problems of causation, and habitually speak in terms less of sequence than of purpose: 'that it might be fulfilled' rather than 'it so happened'. Their assurance contrasts with the hesitant questionings of the classical historians, both on the side of formal attempts to distinguish between remote and immediate causes and in matters of more popular interest. To pagans who sought to learn whether the destiny of mankind is ruled by stern fate, wise providence or capricious fortune various explanations were offered, but they amounted in the end to little more than Tacitus' answer, '*in incerto iudicium est*',[58] we really do not know.

Nevertheless, a study of causes and an attempt to interpret facts are the characteristic functions which mark off the historian from the chronicler. While falsehood and exaggeration in the record of events are to be condemned not merely as knavish but as shortsighted folly, differences of interpretation may be expected to occur, in accordance with the insight, presuppositions and skill of the craftsman. The emperor Frederick the Great observed that truth must always clasp the pen of history,[59] but he offered no such answers to the earlier question: 'What is truth?' as his countryman Wilhelm von Humboldt attempted to provide. Von Humboldt laid down the rule that 'the task of the writer of history is to state what happened. The more purely and comprehendingly he succeeds in this, the more completely has he discharged his duty.'[60] Yet von Humboldt realized that to set out a bare list of facts does not adequately 'state what happened'. When the task of collecting his materials and investigating them critically has been accomplished, the historian, it is noted, must, like the poet, use his imagination in joining isolated events to form a living whole. He needs what von Humboldt describes as 'a dominating idea' if things are to be held together.

It has, then, to be asked whether the circumstance must be deplored that the early Christian writers can scarcely claim to have looked at events in a completely neutral and detached manner or to have resembled that select group of dispassionate historians, with Ranke as perhaps their most notable modern representative, who not only exclaim, with the author of 'Coningsby': 'What wonderful things are events, the least of them are of greater importance than the most sublime and comprehensive speculations',[61] but who self-consciously seek to marshal their facts in critical and colourless fashion. This question can perhaps be answered with a confident affirmative only when it has been established that pure objectivity in history-writing is both possible and to be desired. It would, of course, be ridiculous to deny that this is frequently the case. It may be the historian's task to determine the relation between imports and exports during the sixteenth century, or to compare the organization of local government at the present time with that of the Georgian period. He then deals with the material for an academic monograph which demands, and which will attain the highest possible success through, the strict application of the scientific method. But on one definition a man who 'records a miscellany of isolated facts' is a diarist. He becomes an historian only when he is granted 'the right of judging his own data'.[62] And this delicate task of interpretation admits of human fallibility as well as skill, above all when the subject to be interpreted is such a complexity as the life of a man or the life of a nation.

It would seem, indeed, that there are several reasons why even the scrupulous historian must find it hard to confine his exuberant material within the straitened bounds of scientific procedure. In the first place, although man may be able in some sense to stand outside the course of time and judge the panorama of events, he is also involved in their continual flow and movement and can never claim, in a measureless universe, to have fixed knowledge within precise and final limits. History is, therefore, ever viewed through a 'shimmer of relativity', since

> 'Last year's words belong to last year's language
> And next year's words await another voice.' [63]

Moreover, people cannot depersonalize themselves. Whether they like it or not, their view of what is important and worth chronicling is conditioned by their training and charactetrisics. The story is well known of the Shah of Persia—or if not Persia, then somewhere else—who, whilst on a state visit to England, was entertained to a classical concert at Queen's Hall. When the music was over, equerries enquired whether his Highness had enjoyed himself, to which the reply was understood to be that he had failed to appreciate anything except the first item. Murmurs instantly arose round the prince as his satellites politely denounced the whole programme except the opening *scherzo*—'such colour, such tonal balance'—until, outside the hall, it came to be realized that the only thing which had pleased him was the tuning-up of the instrumentalists. And the point is this: no doubt the English musical critics wrote, each to his own paper, a learned and correct appreciation of the concert; but one may be sure that not even the fullest account would even have referred to the squeaks and scrapings which preceded the appearance of the conductor. Yet, if the Shah had been required to do the reporting, *his* education and perceptions would have impelled him to use up his column in a description of those—to us—random irrelevancies, to which the Brahms and the Schubert were, in his view, but a tedious epilogue.

The matter may be illustrated from one of the classic comparisons in historical method, that between Livy and Polybius. Livy is a true representative of republican Rome in that he saw in history 'a national work, a school of citizenship, and an instrument of government'. Like Polybius, he felt that history is of practical utility in furnishing examples 'from which you may select what is worthy of imitation by yourself and your country, and learn to avoid what is disgraceful both in conception and in result';[64] but, unlike Polybius, he is rather an artist whose aim is worthily to expound his theme—the pre-eminent majesty and glory of Rome—than a critic who begins by suspecting everything. Not that Livy is so easily duped. 'I know', he says, 'that history is perverted by funeral orations and falsified inscriptions as each family grabs for the honour of great and famous achievements',[65] but he is more concerned to be an apologist for the orthodox dogma of his time— *Tu regere imperio populos, Romane, memento*—than to waste his energy on critical minutiae. A distinguished French scholar judged his work to smack of 'revolting partiality',[66] and it is impossible to deny that there is some excuse for this violent condemnation, since Livy's firmly-held belief in the divine right of Rome and of senatorial government at Rome makes him do less than justice to his national and political opponents. Yet such a colourful description of the rise of Rome may in some respects give a truer portrait than the desiccated rationalism and photographic analysis of Polybius, particularly since Livy, just because he is a Roman and proud of the fact, sometimes records events, omitted by Polybius, that illustrate with notable clarity the nature and thoughts of the Roman people. To take one instance, Livy's account of the Second Punic War[67] includes a number of notices of religious importance, accounts of hackneyed phenomena like showers of blood-red pebbles or of such hysterical manifestations as the burial alive of Gauls and Greeks in the Forum Boarium. He tells of the dissatisfaction that a populace, affected by the stress of prolonged hostilities and subject to the disturbing influences of alien immigration, felt with the formalism of the conventional Roman rites, and he mentions the often remarkable efforts, culminating in the importation of the goddess Cybele in the form of a black stone, which were made to allay fears and strengthen morale. Such superstitious details are passed over by Polybius in dignified silence. His attitude towards the stuff of religion was that adopted many years later by

William Robertson, a Presbyterian minister of liberal views, who became principal of Edinburgh University in 1762 and gained international repute by his biography of the emperor Charles V. Robertson, who made it his laudable aim to 'preserve the dignity of history', thought that this end would best be secured by neglecting religion in its more exuberant aspects. 'The wild adventures', he wrote, 'and visionary schemes in which Loyola's enthusiasm engaged him equal anything recorded in the legends of the Romish saints, but are unworthy of notice in history.'[68] No writer can entirely efface his opinion from his work. Acton's comment, 'the strongest and most impressive personalities project their own broad shadow upon their pages',[69] is true not only of the strong and impressive but of all persons. And Polybius was, naturally enough, impelled to avoid strict historical impartiality, in the easiest way, by choosing out for narration such events as accorded with his own interests and rejecting what seemed unimportant to his prejudices. The words of Dio Cassius might not unfairly be put into his mouth: 'I read more or less everything that anyone has ever written in these matters; I did not, however, record everything, but such things as I selected'.[70]

Yet some such task of compression appears to be an unavoidable element of the historian's responsibility. For, according to Hume,[71] history is a collection of facts which are multiplying endlessly, and, if they are to be made intelligible, they must in some way be abridged. And it is this 'painful labour of abridgement',[72] this separation of the relevant from the unimportant, which seems to demand of the historian gifts of insight which rise above, or are at any rate complementary to, the pursuit of truth by strictly scientific means.

The craft of the historian may then be thought to resemble that of the portrait-painter rather than the photographer, since the greater value normally assigned to a painting is a tribute to the importance of right interpretation: 'a mere copier of nature', said Sir Joshua Reynolds, 'can never produce anything great'.[73] It is not the case that the subject is distorted by eccentric additions, but by passing through the alembic of an artist's brain it is transformed in such a way that its hidden beauties and deeper meaning become manifest to those whose untutored gaze would have failed to detect them. Brute facts are not the whole truth. They need to be interpreted by persons whose work is compared, in the Talmud,[74] to the hammer-blows which awaken the sparks slumbering in a rock, and who should be of such quickened perception that they can rise to what St. Jerome called the 'comeliness of spiritual understanding'.[75] 'Facts', it has been observed, 'are ventriloquists' dummies. Sitting on a wise man's knee they may be made to utter words of wisdom: elsewhere they say nothing, or talk nonsense, or indulge in sheer diabolism', and the principle which Aldous Huxley[76] thus vigorously enunciates may be clearly demonstrated when any biography is in question. There is the vexatious circumstance that a series of patently true events in a man's life may, when recorded unqualified, sometimes give an essentially untrue picture, whereas an impression of the man, created with little regard for strict accuracy of detail but by one who knew him and sympathized with his motives, will approximate closely to the truth.[77] To take an extreme case: a man who has devoted himself to avaricious and hard-hearted money-grabbing may, in the mellower moments of his life, have performed half a dozen generous actions. If these latter are faithfully recorded and all else left unsaid, the reader will gain from these perfectly true events an opinion of the man's character that is almost entirely false. Similarly, there are few lives, however saintly and heroic, which do not exhibit patent instances of folly or hypocrisy, and, when cynical biographers stress such peccadilloes but discreetly slur over the nobler incidents, they, again, produce a picture in which the details are as accurate as the whole is mendacious. Sympathy alone cannot be guaranteed to make a man a good biographer, but without such a quality it is hard for him to succeed.[78] For, failing to understand his subject's aspirations, hopes and fears, he will, almost of necessity, present a hard, 'external' sort of picture, and may even reach the position described in a recent American novel when one 'forgets the genius, the inner fire; beholds only the outer shell, uncouth, pulpy, nauseous to the senses'.[79]

Students of Lytton Strachey's entertaining life of Dr. Thomas Arnold will find no difficulty with the source-criticism of that work. If it be read side by side with Stanley's classic biography of Arnold, the method of its composition becomes immediately obvious. There is no pretence of original research. Considerable portions of Stanley's book have been incorporated by Strachey in his essay, partly by word for word transcription, partly in the form of a compressed précis. But much that is solid and sensible has been left out, while the more ludicrous occurrences are skilfully stressed so that Arnold may appear, like most eminent Victorians, to be slightly pompous and absurd. Yet suppression of truth is no more pardonable than to suggest falsehood. In the course of a violent attack on Hume, Macaulay wrote, 'Hume is an accomplished advocate. Without positively asserting much more than he can prove, he gives prominence to all the circumstances which support his case and glides lightly over those which are unfavourable to it.'[80] A homelier example of the same process may be drawn from Mark Pattison's memoirs, where mention is made of a female relative who 'having no imagination and being scrupulously truthful as to the most minute details' tried, when telling of her achievements, 'to produce the heightening effect by suppression of the less flattering tones'.[81]

It may indeed be asked how the historian can hope to present the characteristic impression made by a man or nation, when that impression is effected through a multitude of actions, each, perhaps, in itself trivial enough. Can a method claim even to be strictly scientific when it leaves out some facts uncompensated, or should there be, to make up for the omissions, some special stress and emphasis laid on those events which are recorded, just as the skilful portrait-painter darkens the hard lines round the mouth or lets the lip hang a shade more feebly than in real life, in order the more clearly to draw out truths of character that lie behind the momentary expression?[82] In historical writing exaggerations of this kind must no doubt be avoided, because of the risk that they will minister not so much to a disclosure of hidden truth as to empty panegyric or caricature and will cause what Thomas Fuller described as 'slanting and suppositive traducing of the records',[83] but it may yet be held that isolated true facts often require consideration in the light of subsequent facts before the story can possibly be told in its fullness. The man who is involved in events can seldom see with any clearness the pattern of their fashioning: it is the backward glance through the arches of the years that reveals the form and coherence of history.

Examples can be drawn from the New Testament to illustrate this principle, and the story of the Annunciation may be thought as suitable as any. A photographically accurate picture of this incident, occurring in a Palestinian village during the reign of Herod the Great, would perhaps reveal a Jewish peasant-girl in a condition of trance. That scene would make a record true so far as it goes but scarcely adequate if the Church is right in its estimate of the importance of the occasion, which is then more faithfully represented by the picture, admittedly fanciful in certain details, of a beautiful maiden kneeling at her prie-Dieu, a pot of lilies at her side and the brilliant figure of the archangel Gabriel confronting her. Similarly, if the tradition of the Church has any value, to show forth Christ as merely a Galilean carpenter, though accurate enough in some respects as a photographic record, would be so woefully incomplete a portrait as actually to convey falsehood. If it be right to detect a considerable difference between the presentation of Christ in St. John's Gospel and that which is to be found in the record of the Synoptists, it may be pertinent to enquire not so much whether the Johannine portrait is a permissible, though somewhat unhistorical, refinement but whether this interpretation of character in the light of subsequent events—in the light of the Resurrection and the religious experience of the early Church—is not a fuller (and thus in many respects a truer) picture than any eye-witness account could have afforded. It may perhaps be so, if the Christian doctrines are valid. And the fact that such questions can even be asked would seem to imply that history has ceased to be 'a science no less and no more' in the sense that in all its ranges it admits of neat and logical proof.

Historians, no less than artists, may be called upon both to interpret and to embody and to make their aim 'not reproduction but translation'.[84] The Russian philosopher Berdyaev used to complain that 'those who read a history text-book are bound to feel that the history and culture of ancient peoples have been utterly emptied of all soul and life, leaving nothing but a sort of superficial photograph or sketch'.[85] In this outburst Berdyaev sought to condemn those historians whose prime desire is to present an objective, passionless record and who forget that the photograph not only can lie but, in a sense, must lie if only because it has no power to look before and after. 'The least philosophic form of history', a French scholar has recently recorded, 'is always interpretative, since it is obliged, if it is not to degenerate into a shapeless compilation, to furnish us with the Ariadne thread without which we should lose ourselves in the labyrinth of facts',[86] or, in the words of a German critic, 'to separate interpretation from narrative is like trying to separate a man from his shadow'.[87] But such considerations tend to remove the historian's craft from the comfortable range of accepted certainty. Edwyn Bevan once declared that 'in action there is no possibility of safety in the sense of security from turning out in the end to have been mistaken',[88] and the historian, as well as the man of action, may not claim to be continually exempt from the necessity of choice and the possibility of error. For upon many historians a twofold obligation would seem to be laid. They must indeed employ the scientific method, but must balance it with that sympathetic intuition which enables them to read the heart of the nation or individuals whose fortunes they are describing, just as a portrait-painter needs vision as well as technical ability. And if this is true, it is profoundly unsatisfactory to an age impatient of 'dusty answers', since qualities of insight, or faith, are thereby demanded in order to arrange and explain the facts which scientific research has painstakingly garnered.

The early Christian historians acted upon such principles confidently enough. They did not make the mistake, so roundly condemned by a modern novelist turned philosopher, of 'identifying the world of science, a world from which all meaning and value have been deliberately excluded, with ultimate reality',[89] nor, in striving for a simple solution, did they forget the danger of which Coventry Patmore later gave warning:

> 'Beware, for fiends in triumph laugh
> O'er him who learns the truth by half.'[90]

Well aware of the intractable and bizarre elements in history that result from the incalculable pressure of the Divine on human affairs, and aware also of the rule summed up in the words 'while we gain exactness we lose contact with reality',[91] they were on occasion tempted to mould facts to suit their presuppositions. Nevertheless, the most responsible and influential of their number had sufficient feeling for scholarship and integrity to preserve the delicate balance that has to be maintained between interpretation and chronicle, and to shrink from mishandling a record of events in history whereby God displayed to mankind a portion of his Truth.

CHAPTER II

THE USE OF HISTORY IN EARLY APOLOGETIC: CLEMENT OF ROME TO IRENAEUS

Great is truth, and stronger than all things. I. Esdras iv. 35

The writers of the Gospels, with their keen sense of urgency and stress, had little inclination to indulge in any theorizing about the nature of history. Whether they looked for an almost immediate close of the whole historical process, when the Lord would come as a thief in the night, or whether they thought rather of the work of Christ as there and then bestowing upon men the gift of an eternal life which freed from the tyranny of time and circumstance, their prime concern seems throughout to have been practical rather than speculative. Moreover, a strain of novelty and even revolution in the Christian message led to a certain depreciation of past history and scorn of the Pharisees and Sadducees who represented the old, established order. On the other hand, by contrast with the Jewish religion of hopeful expectation, Christianity was based upon accomplished fact in which the mighty working of the divine providence was to be discerned. And, since God 'remains ever true to his nature', the events of the Gospel story were necessarily in accord with such intimations of the full truth as had been vouchsafed to the prophets of old, or, to put the matter in reverse order, Old Testament prophecies found their fulfilment, sometimes with an unexpected twist to it, in the life of Christ and the origins of the Christian Church. The death and resurrection of the Lord were therefore from the first preached as 'according to the Scriptures'[1] and correspondences were eagerly noted between inspired forecasts on the one hand and, on the other, the course of events that marked the decisive utterance of the Word, made flesh. Nor was it only a matter of prophetic forecasts, since the historical incidents of the old dispensation were, in St. Paul's phrase, 'written for our admonition, upon whom the ends of the ages are come'.[2]

21

This view of history as fulfilment, which recurs with varying emphasis throughout the course of Christian thought, appears to be based on the words and deeds of Jesus Himself. For the claim to Messiahship involved the performance of deeds accepted as Messianic; and when Jesus entered Jerusalem 'lowly and riding upon an ass',[3] as Zechariah had foretold, and cleansed the court of the Gentiles in the Temple which, when the Messianic Age arrived, was to become 'a house of prayer for all the nations',[4] even the simple folk whom St. Matthew describes as children could hardly fail to realize that now was the time exultantly to cry 'Hosanna to the Son of David'.[5] Similarly, by the use of Scripture texts, Jesus was able to forewarn his disciples and strengthen them for the ordeal which they would have to face when the inevitable clash occurred with the Jewish authorities or the Roman civil power. He assigned to Himself the mysterious role of 'a man of sorrows and acquainted with grief'[6] who should indeed 'see of the travail of his soul and be satisfied'. His life would be offered as 'a ransom for many',[7] yet his followers were never to forget God's assurance, given through the prophet Hosea, that 'after two days He will revive us: on the third day He will raise us up and we shall live before Him'.[8] This message of combined solemnity and hope had necessarily to be given in terms of the educational and cultural background of those who were to receive it, that is, in accordance with the Scriptures; and, in so far as Jesus satisfied the expectations of Scripture, He established, for the guidance of the early Church, the truth of the principle of prophecy and fulfilment whereby the Old Testament came to be recognized as prefiguring a fuller reality.

History estimated in terms of salvation is history seen in the light of myth, if the word myth be indeed rightly chosen to express the simplifying interpretation which has to be called in to explain advanced and complex structures. There is nothing more mythical about an explanation of history offered in terms of prophecy and fulfilment than there is in ideas of progress or of cyclic growth and decay, and myth of some kind has to be invoked if order is to be imposed upon the vast heap of facts which must otherwise remain unsifted and in chaotic disarray. Where Christian myth differs from most other interpretations is in the confident presumption that limits the really decisive element in history to a few notable persons and events which stand out from the general background of facts as alone possessing crucial importance. On this view history may indeed be highly valued as a parable in which the workings of God's providence can be discerned in obscure and partial fashion, but, in addition, the 'scandalous' claim is put forward that the imperfect records of a few generations of Hebrews bear a significance for judgement and salvation which is denied to countless ages without a name. Celsus,[9] the pagan opponent of Origen early in the third century, had some witty and telling observations to make on the folly of Jews and Christians whose pretensions to the divine favour resembled, in his opinion, the empty croaking of a concourse of frogs huddled round a pond; and the Voltaires of every age have not been slow to elaborate this theme. Yet, if God is to be inevitably driven on, by the charity which is his nature, to the supreme act of condescension whereby He meets men on their own ground, this Incarnation is presumably bound to occur at a particular time and in a particular place. Even though He 'will gather all nations and tongues and they shall see his glory',[10] the Lord must answer to the expectations of a 'peculiar people chosen unto Himself' and must initially state his message and carry out his mighty acts in terms which this favoured generation can understand.

The explanation of history in terms of prophecy and fulfilment caused the Christians to take careful account of their relationship with the Jews. The position was a paradoxical one, since the Jews were responsible for the crucifixion of the Master and had been in the habit of 'stirring up a persecution' against the leaders of the Church, while, on the other hand, their Scriptures and their history were charged with unique importance as being the momentous presage of Christ. St. Paul succeeded in achieving a theoretic justification for what had already been accomplished in fact, and tore the Church away from Jewry by his recasting of the older doctrine of the Remnant in the simile of the olive-tree.[12] The holiness of the Patriarchs, explained Paul, ensured the consecration

23

of the Israelites and the unswerving favour of God, and, as faithlessness caused the Jewish branches to be broken off in disgrace,
so by a mysterious operation 'contrary to nature' the branches of
the Christian wild olive were grafted in to inherit the blessings
promised to Abraham and his seed for ever.

This line of thought is worked out with great polemic vigour
and with none of St. Paul's affectionate backward glances in the
Alexandrian treatise that goes under the name of the *Epistle of
Barnabas*. It is assumed by the writer that Sacrifice, together with
such cognate institutions as the Temple and the Sabbath, have been
abolished in favour of 'the new law of our Lord Jesus Christ',[13]
and the utter failure of the Jews is emphasized by the explanation
that one reason for the coming of the Son of God in the flesh was
that He might 'complete the total of the sins of those who perse-
cuted his prophets to death'.[14] The author added that the Jews who
originally received the covenant had been deprived of their position of privilege as the reward of their iniquity in turning to idols,[15]
while the examples of Jacob supplanting Esau and of Jacob blessing
the younger son of Joseph before the elder are adduced in support
of the significant promise made to Abraham that he was to be 'the
father of Gentiles who believe God in uncircumcision'.[16] The
deduction that the Christian Church is the only heir to the promises of God was, according to 'Barnabas', made perfectly clear
by the action of Moses when he came down from Mount Sinai
and, in horror at the iniquity of his people, flung the tables of the
Lord's covenant out of his hands so that they were smashed in
pieces: 'Moses received the Covenant but [the Israelites] were not
worthy, and the Lord gave it to us, as unto a people of his inheritance, by suffering on our behalf'.[17] The complete breach between
Judaism and Christianity is thus emphasized and, with the help of
a vigorously allegorical exegesis, it is demonstrated that both prophecies and history are, so far as concerns the Jews, mere figures
or outlines which acquire their true meaning only when they are
realized and fulfilled in the church of Christ. A somewhat similar
claim had earlier been implied in the opening chapter of the Acts
of the Apostles. For, according to that record, the first corporate

action of the Church after the Ascension of Christ was not to decide its constitution or debate its proper attitude towards the Temple authorities and Roman governor but to elect the twelfth Apostle, thus showing that the new, and true, Israel was based upon twelve men as prefigured by the old, fallible Israel which had been composed of twelve tribes.

The theme of prophecy and fulfilment, which recurs frequently enough in the speeches attributed to Peter and Paul, is thus accepted as an element of importance in such thoughts about history as were entertained by the early Church. But two other notes are sounded in the Acts of the Apostles which will be heard echoing from time to time in the succession of Christian literature, whether the writings are formally classed as history or not. The first is the claim, made by implication right at the beginning of Acts, with its reference back to the prologue of St. Luke's Gospel, to present an accurate and orderly account of what in fact happened, so that those who came to the Church for instruction might know 'the certainty concerning such things'.[18] In the second place, the triumphant spread of the Gospel from Jerusalem to Rome is used to support the claim that the Church was in fact the new Israel which, according to prophecy, should be 'for a light to the Gentiles' and for 'salvation unto the end of the earth'.[19] It gave colour also to what later became a familiar apologetic *motif*, that the Christians were law-abiding and indeed desirable citizens of the Empire who became involved in trouble and commotions only through the malevolent activities of the Jews. In addition, Acts seems to touch on a more purely theological interpretation of history, whereby the pattern of events is seen to be wrought not by any necessary principle of cause and effect but by the intimate and incalculable pressure of the Spirit of God.

It is sometimes alleged against the early Christians that their lack of historical sense is demonstrated by the way in which, after a first tentative approach in the Acts of the Apostles, they failed to compose anything that could properly be described as 'Church-history' until, in the triumphant days of Constantine, Eusebius of Caesarea felt impelled to trace the stages which had led to the victory of the

Faith. One reason for this state of affairs is that, in their anxiety to spread abroad or to defend the Gospel, churchmen during the first three centuries concerned themselves more with practical apologetic than with history as a subject of academic study or as a diversion. And though it is true that, so far as our knowledge goes, no Christian between A.D. 100 and 300 wrote a formal history of his own times, interest in and speculation about the nature and meaning of history was seldom far absent from the Scriptural commentary and the doctrinal or political apologies which are the characteristic literature of this period. Apocalyptic vision and hopes of the speedy return of Christ might jerk the gaze heavenwards and cause 'Maran atha', 'Come, O Lord',[20] to be the heartfelt cry wrung from the congregation at the climax of the liturgy; but systematic attacks by opponents of the Faith caused the uplifted eyes to be drawn quickly back to earth and to find their assurance in hard facts. For the Church at first, as perhaps continuously throughout the centuries, was poised uneasily between two menacing yet opposed tendencies. On the one hand some, in a mood described by Irenaeus as empty-headedness,[21] looking merely at the outward, everyday aspect of the Saviour, and refusing to accept it as true that He 'taught', and indeed acted, with 'authority and not as the scribes',[22] were content to explain Him as but one in the long line of Hebrew prophesiers, and leave it at that.

There is nothing unfamiliar to us in this approach to the New Testament but, in the second century, the more urgent danger seemed to come not from those who would depreciate the person of the Lord but from a misplaced reverence which sought to raise Him above the changes and chances of finite existence and denied the reality of the human nature and the human flesh which He assumed in the performance of his 'mighty work'. The cultured Gnostics recoiled in horror from the scandal of a true Incarnation and strove to convert historic fact into edifying and ingenious romance. For instance, in the so-called Acts of John, a work which dates from about A.D. 150, we read that, shortly before the Passion, John the Apostle and certain companions engaged with Jesus in a kind of ritual dance during which mysterious, secret knowledge was imparted to them. 'Having thus danced with us the Lord went forth. And we, as men gone astray or dazed with sleep, fled this way and that. I, then, when I saw Him suffer, did not even abide by his suffering, but fled unto the Mount of Olives, weeping at that which had befallen. And when He was crucified on the Friday, at the sixth hour of the day, darkness came upon all the earth. And my Lord, standing in the midst of the cave and enlightening it, said: John, unto the multitude below in Jerusalem I am being crucified and pierced with lances and reeds, and gall and vinegar is given Me to drink. But unto thee I speak, and what I speak hear thou. I put it into thy mind to come up into this mountain, that thou mightest hear those things which it behoveth a disciple to learn from his teacher and a man from his God.'[23] In treatises such as this the Gnostic writer has exchanged the cautious interpretation of fact, which is the historian's craft, for fantasy that makes no serious claim to be related to actual events.

Ignatius, bishop of Antioch, when on his way to martyrdom at Rome under the emperor Trajan, left as his most urgent appeal, in letters which he wrote to the churches of various cities of Asia Minor through which he passed, the plea that they would never abandon belief in the humanity of Jesus and in the historical events connected therewith. 'He suffered all these things for our sakes, that we might attain salvation, and He truly suffered even as also He truly raised Himself up, not, as some faithless persons say, that his Passion was a matter of semblance, whereas it is they who are mere semblance. Things will assuredly turn out for them in accordance with their opinions; they will find themselves disembodied and phantasmal.'[24] Or again: 'There are some who ignorantly deny Him, or rather have been denied by Him; since they are advocates of death rather than of the truth. They are the people whom neither the prophecies nor the law of Moses have persuaded, nor yet the Gospel until now. . . . What does anyone profit me if he praises me but blasphemes my Lord, refusing to confess that He was clothed in flesh? The man who speaks in this way has denied Him absolutely, and is but a living corpse.'[25] The vigour of Ignatius' language is perhaps justified as revealing his determination to safeguard the principle that Christianity depends upon historic fact. There is, as von Hügel used to point out,[26] a world of difference between Ought-ness and Is-ness, and the Church, not wholly unaware of the stubborn difficulties involved, based its faith upon truth declared in history rather than upon speculations about what might have happened or ought to have happened.

It may, then, be in place to consider the views held on the subject of history by certain of the early churchmen who were primarily concerned with practical apologetic rather than with history as a subject of formal study. Right at the beginning of the second century the pastoral letter from the Church of Rome to the Church of Corinth that goes under the name of the First Epistle of Clement touched on several of the points which were frequently to recur in subsequent writings. 'Clement' is concerned to show the horrors of faction and jealousy and, by contrast, the blessedness of humble submission to the will of God, and the Corinthians are reminded of the jealousy of such persons as Cain, Dathan and Abiram, while Noah, Abraham, Jacob, Moses and David are put forward as patterns of virtuous conduct: 'The humility and obedient submission of so many famous persons have served to improve not only ourselves but also the generations before us, those who received the oracles of the Lord in fear and truth.'[27] In such words as these the author repeats the Pauline idea that God educates mankind by making history provide examples from which successive generations, if they will view events in a spirit of receptiveness and dependence, may be able to take advantage. The fate of Lot's wife, for instance, is thus described: 'She became a pillar of salt unto this day, so that it might be realized by all that those who are double-minded and who are doubtful concerning the power of God are used as an example of judgement and as a warning to all generations.'[28] On the other hand, such noble figures as the apostles Peter and Paul were reckoned to be edifying examples of a more recent age,[29] and it was understood that, in the providence of God, pagan biography also was capable of affording lessons of the highest value: 'Many kings and rulers, when a time of pestilence has set in, have obeyed the advice of an oracle and given themselves up to death so that they might deliver their subjects by their own blood. Many have departed from their own cities, so that civil strife might come to an end.'[30] History is, in fact, looked on as a collection of examples which awaken in men the realization of right and wrong, and thus lead to improvement through knowledge. The general standpoint resembles that of the mediaeval scholar who declared that: 'The human mind will assuredly be directed in a virtuous course for the future by its researches into the annals of the past',[31] or, in Sir Walter Raleigh's words: 'We may gather out of history a policy no less wise than eternal; by the comparison and application of other men's forepassed miseries with our own like errors and ill deservings'.[32] But, along with the conception of history as possessing practical utility and educative value, the author of the First Epistle of Clement reintroduces the New Testament theme of fulfilment whereby God's word is proved to be true not only in its appeal to the heart but as certified in fact. 'All glory and enlargement were granted to you,' writes 'Clement' to the Corinthians, 'and the text was fulfilled "My beloved ate and drank and was enlarged and waxed fat and kicked"; wherefore there arose jealousy and envy and strife and faction, persecution and disorder, warfare and captivity.'[33] Here the event—the turbulent envy of those who waxed fat and kicked—shows the validity of the forecast of such happenings, that is made in Deuteronomy.[34] The inspired utterances of Holy Writ, it is implied, will ring true down the ages, and will display their divine authority by the fact that strict observation shows them to occur in the course of history. Incidentally, the odd circumstance that the Christians are heirs to the sacred books of the renegade Jews is thus explained without difficulty. 'You have studied the Holy Scriptures which are true and given by the Holy Spirit',[35] we read, and it is understood that this same inspiring Spirit, against which the Jews have hardened their hearts, is poured forth afresh in the New Israel, bearing witness to the unchangeable nature of God, yet with enhanced freedom and power.

The author of I Clement, then, would maintain that history is one of the means ordained by God for training the morality no less than the intellect of the human race, since his enduring principles are shown forth by the approval or disapproval with which He visits the deeds of mankind: 'I will set my glory among the nations, and all the nations shall see my judgement that I have executed'.[36] 'Clement' does not bother himself with any general theorizing, but takes acknowledged facts and interprets them to show that they are edifying and full of meaning. He acts, indeed, in accordance with a precept of Polybius to the effect that the historian's task is first to state what happened and then to supply reasons. 'The mere description of an occurrence', Polybius puts it, 'may interest us, but it confers no benefit. When, however, the cause is added, the study of history becomes fruitful.'[37]

It is not necessary even for those who accept his main contentions to agree with every detail of the picture as 'Clement' paints it. His thought is to a large extent influenced by the Pauline antithesis of 'flesh and spirit', so that he becomes impatient of the gentler shades of colour, and likes to depict the struggle between the presbyters of Corinth and their factious gainsayers in the sharply contrasting opposition of black and white. The men who 'in pride and contentiousness are the instigators of loathsome jealousy'[38] stand out less as real men than as typical examples in the age-old struggle of light against darkness. Persecution of the pious by the wicked is seen, in accordance with the fifty-third chapter of Isaiah, to be an expected part of the course of events, while Psalm-texts are skilfully invoked to show that 'deceitful lips which speak iniquity against the righteous' will no doubt afflict the just for a time but will assuredly meet with punishment at the hand of God. 'Clement' may perhaps be excused if, in distressful times, his interpretation lacks precise and cautious balance and if, in the interests of simplicity, he states good as good and bad as bad without any attempt at qualification or finesse. In so doing, he is but carrying into Church history principles which had been axiomatic with the prophets of the Old Testament. There is here no toying with ideas of history as perpetual recurrence or as governed by blind necessity. Rather it is a straight, or perhaps spiral, line running from the origin of things to their consummation and, according to 'Clement', God guides his people, throughout history, by chastisement as also with mercy: 'for He is a good Father and chastens us, so that we obtain mercy through his holy chastisement'.[39]

The theme of prophecy and fulfilment was taken up, with wider elaboration, by the apologist Justin Martyr, who wrote about half a century later than 'Clement'. It is held to apply not merely to the Scriptures of the Old Testament, which the Church arrogated to itself in consequence of the failure of the Jews, but also, with the help of the conception of the 'Word', to Greek pagan literature as well. In notable fashion Justin declares: 'We have been taught that Christ is the first-begotten of God and we have shown that He is also the Word, in which the whole human race has received a share. And those who have lived in conjunction with this Word are Christians even though they have been described as atheists, that is to say Socrates and Heraclitus and people like them among the Greeks or, among the rest of mankind, Abraham and Ananias and Azarias and Misael and Elijah and many others.'[40] This same thought is amplified in the Second Apology: 'Every noble utterance and discovery of philosophers or lawgivers they have worked out by research and contemplation, with the aid of a partial influence of the Word. But because they did not recognize the Word, which is Christ, in its fulness, they have frequently spoken in contradictory terms.'[41] Justin, like others before him, is here affirming that Christianity represents a completion of what has been previously shadowed forth; but the basis has been widened: the Greek philosophers, no doubt unwittingly, play their part in preparing the way for the full manifestation of truth, and the prehistory of the Church is not confined to Palestine but extends to any age wherein men have freely spoken with the understanding granted to them from on high. 'All writers', observed Justin in another passage of his Second Apology, 'through the seed of the implanted Word which is in them, have been able to perceive the truth even though dimly',[42] with the result that 'whatsoever has been nobly said by anybody really belongs to us Christians', since, in the words of a later poet:

'All truth is from the sempiternal source
Of light divine.'[43]

It is not to be supposed that, in Justin's opinion, there is no difference between the inspiration accorded to the Hebrew prophets and
that bestowed on the Greek philosophers. The same inscrutable
choice of God, which causes Israel to be selected as the instrument
of his purposes, is shown also when the prophets receive the free
flow of the Word while in pagan philosophers its operation is partial and less personal. 'The prophets alone,' we read, 'who have
perceived the truth and announced it to mankind, without hesitation or fear of anybody, without desire for glory but simply
speaking the things which they saw and heard, were filled by the
Holy Spirit.'[44] All honest men possess the 'seeds of truth'[45] within
them; but a fuller knowledge is reserved for the prophets as well
as for their Christian hearers who discover the message of salvation
triumphantly vindicated in the events recorded by the New Testament writers. Justin speaks in the same strain when he claims that
it is above all things necessary to 'pray that the gates of light may
be opened to you; for no one can see or understand if God and his
Christ do not give him understanding'.[46] Such acts of faith need
not imply credulity, for, as Justin is careful to explain, Christians
do not 'believe empty fables or stories without foundation'.[47]
Indeed, those who yield themselves to the guidance of the divine
Reason may be required to make a bold stand against convention,
since 'Reason prescribes that those who are truly pious and philosophic shall honour and love only what is true, refusing to follow
ancient traditions, if these be worthless'.[48] It is rather a question of
difference of mood, whereby one historian may regard events in
isolation, and with no connecting thread of purpose, while
another agrees with Browning[49] that:

'This world's no blot for us
Nor blank: it means intensely and means good:
To find its meaning is my meat and drink.'

Another argument is adduced by Justin in a somewhat naïve
manner which shows, however, a keen sense of the worth of

historical chronology, when the claim is made that the Scriptures are proved by their greater antiquity to be superior to the work of the Greek philosophers. Plato, for instance, is declared to have drawn his doctrine of the creation of the world 'from what had been expressly taught by Moses',[50] while the Stoic view that the world should finally be consumed by fire had been anticipated by the message of Deuteronomy:[51] 'A fire is kindled in mine anger, and burneth unto the lowest pit, and devoureth the earth with her increase'. With such examples to support it, the general principle is laid down: 'it is not the case that we hold the same opinions as others do, but that all men imitate and repeat our discoveries'.[52]

Throughout Justin's writings there echoes a note of toleration and universalism. 'Jacob served Laban', he wrote, 'for the spotted and speckled cattle, and Christ endured service, even to the cross, for men of varied colour and appearance from every nation.'[53] Similarly, it is maintained that God created the world for the sake of the human race and 'He takes pleasure in those who imitate his qualities, but is displeased with those who embrace what is worthless either in word or deed'.[54] The failure of the Jews, who are held to have 'forsaken God',[55] provides a warning that God is not mocked, in the spirit of the prophet's lament: 'for our sins and for the iniquities of our fathers, Jerusalem and thy people are become a reproach to all that are round about us'.[56] But it also gives the opportunity for the establishment of the world-wide Church, growing up harmoniously within the Roman Empire. In this 'Church Universal' every attempt to discover and proclaim truth is honoured, and all history is relevant, in greater or less degree, to the 'one far-off divine event'[57] towards which and from which the story of the world radiates. Yet Justin is preserved from the visionary vagueness which breadth of outlook may sometimes induce by having his feet firmly planted amongst the brute facts of Old Testament narrative, which it was a prime Christian duty to accept and interpret 'in the light of the knowledge of the glory of God'.[58]

Writing in the year 1897 concerning the early growth of the Christian Church, Dr. Gilbert Murray explained that 'the world, mistrusting Reason, weary of argument and wonder, flung itself passionately under the spell of a system of authoritative Revelation, which acknowledged no truth outside itself and stamped free enquiry as sin'.[59] There are, however, grounds for disputing this view. The centuries of anxious controversy which attended the formulation of Christian doctrine give little indication of weariness in argument, while St. Justin, at any rate, thought of the Logos, God's outspoken Word of Reason, as the key to the riddle of existence, and, so far from restricting his appreciation of the truth, strove to show forth Christianity as the heir to the discoveries of the ages. In one notable respect, however, he diverged from the standards of rationalism. Instead of taking as his motto, 'Many marvels there are, but nothing more marvellous than man',[60] he saw the whole course of history as reflecting not merely the vagaries of human endeavour but also the constant purposes of the Almighty.

'Fragile are the flowers', remarked Seneca, 'that grow only in the sunny valley',[61] and one of the beneficial results of the fact that Christianity grew up amidst the opposition of heretics was the fact that churchmen were forced to interest themselves in the exact study of history in so far as they recognized the urgent necessity of supplying chronological tables and, in particular, orderly lists of bishops. In this respect the Church was merely adapting to its own uses what had for some time been a fashionable form of erudition. The scholarly Eratosthenes, who was appointed librarian at Alexandria by Ptolemy III in 245 B.C., is celebrated not only as the founder of scientific geography but also as having composed a laborious chronography, based on accurate arithmetic. Taking as his framework lists of the rulers of various countries, he offered a scheme of historical tables, systematically arranged, that served as a pattern to many imitators later on. The Jews also concerned themselves keenly with chronological argument in their desire to prove that Hebrew culture is older than classical culture, while Jews and Christians alike ridiculed the fantastic Oriental chronologies of Alexander Polyhistor and his successors, as well as those sham 'Chronica' which recorded the events of pagan saga and, with sly pedantry, fabricated a complex series of dates for the exploits of gods in whom no one believed.

Early in the third century Julius Africanus put together the first detailed chronology written from the Christian point of view. Rather before his time such apologists as Tatian and Clement of Alexandria had become involved in disputes concerning the exact date of Moses, and it was the aim of Africanus to settle this and other questions by means of a complete synopsis that should relate the events of sacred history to their contemporary setting in the Hellenic world. But, beside the general desire to show the antiquity of Old Testament origins, orthodox Christians were faced with the need to defend their doctrines against the speculations of heretics; and, in the course of this controversy, a simple, if rather specialized, type of chronological argument was invoked. This took the form of tracing lists of bishops of the principal sees back in the direct line to the Apostles themselves and thus to Christ. It was the boast of the orthodox that, by contrast with the short and dubious successions of heretical bishops, their lines of succession from the Apostles guaranteed the tradition of pure and uncorrupted truth. The matter is put, in a rudimentary way, by 'Clement' of Rome himself,[62] when appeal is made to the 'Apostles who received the Gospel for us from the Lord Jesus Christ' and who then, in the course of their missionary tours, 'appointed their first converts to be bishops and deacons', in accordance with Isaiah's prophetic forecast, 'I will establish their bishops in righteousness and their deacons in faith'.[63]

But it is in the writings of Irenaeus, bishop of Lyons towards the end of the second century, that this anti-heretical *motif* is clearly worked out for the first time and applied to successions not only of bishops but, occasionally, to those of presbyters also. 'We are in a position', Irenaeus claims, 'to reckon up those who were by the Apostles instituted bishops in the churches, and to show the successions of these men to our own times, persons who neither taught nor knew anything like the ravings of these heretics.'[64] 'It would', he continues, 'be tedious to reckon up the successions of all the churches', so he concentrates on that of Rome and produces

35

the famous list—Linus, Anencletus, Clement and the rest—that formed a chain running straight back to the 'blessed Apostles who, having founded and built up the church, committed into the hands of Linus the office of the episcopate'. In answer to the claim of the heretics to have 'discovered unadulterated truth', Irenaeus declares that 'by this order and succession the tradition of the Apostles in the Church and the preaching of the truth have come right down to us';[65] and he drives home the point, in controversial fashion, by adding 'eighth from the Apostles' or 'tenth from the Apostles' when referring to Bishop Hyginus or Bishop Anicetus. Similarly the fiery Tertullian, speaking for North Africa, declared that 'the churches in general produce men to look after them who were instituted into the office of bishop by the Apostles and were transmitters of the apostolic seed',[66] while 'no other teaching will have the right of being received as apostolic than that which is at the present day proclaimed in the churches of apostolic foundation'.[67] Irenaeus and Tertullian are not primarily concerned with any theories about the nature of episcopacy; their chief aim is to show that the ordered succession ensures soundness of doctrine.

Another example of this line of argument is provided by Hegesippus, a contemporary of Irenaeus and vigorous opponent of Gnostic speculations. He visited a number of Christian communities and was gratified to discover that the bishops with whom he conversed all taught the same doctrine: 'I abode with the Corinthians many days during which time we found refreshment together in the true doctrine. But when I was at Rome I made for myself a succession-list going as far as Anicetus, whose deacon Eleutherus was; and from Anicetus Soter received the succession and, after him, Eleutherus. Now, in every succession and in every city, things are in accordance with the preaching of the Law and the Prophets and the Lord.'[68] It is not so much a matter of succession as of successions, in that the various sees which could claim a line of bishops descending from apostolic times are united in declaring the essentials of sound doctrine. Human frailty might lead to deviations from this common tradition, but they would stand self-condemned as being eccentric and out of accord with the original deposit of the Christian faith. Later apologists tended to go further and assign to each of the early bishops exact dates which probably have little value other than as conjectures, but the fact remains that, impelled, it may be, rather by missionary zeal than by any hunger for abstract truth, Christian writers as early as the second and third centuries A.D. were setting down in sincerity chronological records that deserve praise for their accuracy and well-ordered arrangement. Nor was the thought of prophecy and fulfilment entirely absent from such compositions. Hippolytus, for instance, the first Roman antipope,[69] who met a martyr's death in the lead-mines of Sardinia, seems to have compiled, along with lists of rulers in the various countries, a sequence of patriarchs, prophets and high priests who present an inner, purposeful succession of persons leading up, by way of the Old Testament, to the fulfilment of God's plan of salvation in Christ. In correspondence with this series of 'strangers and pilgrims' who 'saw and greeted the promises from afar',[70] lines of bishops are traced, by way of the Apostles, from Christ, whose message they transmit to the world. This double stream, like some mosaic from Ravenna, leads up to, and proceeds from, the central event 'after which things can never be quite the same again'; and exact chronological study is found to be no enemy of religious insight but rather gains acceptance as providing the framework of hard fact without which all speculation must drift over into formless fantasy.

CHAPTER III

ALLEGORY AND MYSTERY: ORIGEN

> The Most High declares the things that are past and the things
> that shall be, and reveals the traces of hidden things.
>
> Ecclus. xlii. 19

On the tomb of Bishop Butler, in Bristol Cathedral, there is to be seen a long inscription composed by the poet Southey. It concludes with a description of Butler as 'finding in outward and visible things the type and evidence of those within the veil' and appends a quotation from the *Philocalia* of Origen:[1] 'He who believes the Scriptures to have proceeded from Him who is the author of nature, may well expect to find the same sort of difficulties in them as are found in the constitution of nature'. In other words, the Georgian bishop, no less than the scholar of Alexandria, realized that the strange complexities of the natural world, in which may be discerned something of the manifold patterns imposed upon that world by its Creator, are matched by the fascinating yet elusive structure of history; since history is no mere catalogue of events, but offers to the enlightened interpreter

> 'A sense sublime
> Of something far more deeply interfused,'[2]

bearing, as it does, the mysterious impress of God's handiwork.

The author of Psalm 136, when inviting the assembled congregation to 'thank the Lord of all lords', gives a list of the works of the Almighty which invite the exultant response 'for his mercy endureth for ever'. Jehovah is praised not merely for the heavens, the earth, the sun and the moon made by his 'excellent wisdom', but also for the display of power whereby his mighty hand and stretched-out arm led the people of Israel, against all the odds, through the Red Sea waters and into the promised land. History thus joins with nature in reflecting his glory, and both are pages in the book 'which heavenly truth imparts'.

John Keble's well-known hymn goes on to explain that

> 'Two worlds are ours; 'tis only sin
>   Forbids us to descry
> The mystic heaven and earth within,
>   Plain as the sea and sky;'

and, if the author had wished to maintain the Biblical view entire, he would have added that 'Sin fractures the vision, not the fact',[3] that it is only the dullness of human perception which fails to detect similar evidences of the divine power operating in the whole course of history. On this estimate, history is valued less because of its own intrinsic interest than as a means whereby God manifests Himself and gives hints alike of his unchanging laws and of his incalculable majesty.

Foremost among those who have stressed the interpretation of history as essentially symbolic of a fuller, supernatural truth stands Origen, who became head of the Christian school at Alexandria in A.D. 203. Origen united in himself the gift of poetic insight with a rare combination of scholarly sensibilities, practical good sense and missionary zeal, and it has throughout the ages been claimed as the privilege of the poet and the mystic that he may 'look behind language, behind the visible world apprehended by mind and senses to another secret language, a secret world known only to the initiate'.[4] On Origen's view, history seemed to present itself as 'a vast ocean of mysteries',[5] to the understanding of which, however, a clue was provided. John Keats, like others before and after him, found the key to the riddle of existence in the recognition and love of the fine craftsmanship of God or man:

> ' "Beauty is truth, truth beauty,"—that is all
>   Ye know on earth, and all ye need to know'.[6]

But Origen, preferring morality to aesthetics, discovered the answer to his mysteries rather in God's unselfish Providence, whereby the Omnipotent displayed, in the processes of history, not only justice and power but also the condescension of loving-kindness. It must therefore be premised that Origen restricted his field of interest. He anticipated in some sort the claim of Leibniz that 'the only use of history, apart from the pleasure it gives, is that the truth of the Christian religion is thereby shown forth: an end which can be secured only with the help of historical study'.[7] For Origen, therefore, significant history meant Biblical history. He was perfectly ready to do as he advised his pupil, Gregory the Wonder-worker, and 'spoil the Egyptians' by drawing from pagan learning so much as might serve as a preparatory course of study leading up to the Scriptures,[8] but he has little sense of the dignity of historical research, except in so far as it prepares for and comments on the unique truth of the Gospel. It was, however, on Origen's view, by no means the case that any such revelation was offered in facile or clear-cut manner to the casual glance.

Again and again in his works Origen sounds a note of vehement warning against uncritical acceptance of the Biblical record. He held this kind of approach to be not merely inadequate but dangerous, and to be, in some degree at least, the cause of the characteristic failure of both Jews and Gnostics to comprehend the knowledge that makes men wise unto salvation. Thus, in his commentary on St. Matthew's Gospel, he indicates that prophecy and narrative alike have their true and full meaning remorselessly squeezed out of them when they are crudely understood *au pied de lettre*. 'Every one', he observes, 'who has received instruction in the teaching according to the letter of the law is called a scribe; that is to say, you may interpret the words "Woe unto you, scribes and Pharisees, hypocrites" as being directly addressed to everyone who confines his knowledge to the letter.' Such a scribe is, in fact, one of the scribes who will neither enter the Kingdom of Heaven himself nor suffer others so to do, whereas the scribe made a disciple of the Kingdom of Heaven is one who, after acquiring rudimentary knowledge through the letter of the Scriptures, 'ascends to spiritual things—in other words the kingdom of the heavens.'[9] Again, starting from the text 'The King's daughter is all glorious within', Origen points out that the investigator of Biblical history must never dismiss the narrative of Scripture as 'merely the ornate composition of feeble human eloquence' but must remember that 'the treasures of divine meaning are enclosed within the frail vessel of the common letter'.[10]

What Origen dreaded was the bleak inadequacy of a barren literalism which failed to see the course of scriptural history transfigured in the light of Christian devotion whereby new wonders should continually be drawn out from what might, to the uninitiated, often seem a pedestrian record. 'Let us without hesitation,' said Cassiodorus three centuries later, 'let us without hesitation rise up to the study of Holy Scripture by means of the invaluable expositions of the Fathers, as though by a ladder of vision, so that, borne along by their genius, we may be found worthy to attain effectively to the contemplation of God. For that is perhaps the Jacob's ladder by which the angels ascend and descend, and on which the Lord relies as he stretches out his hand to the wounded and supports the weary steps of those who clamber upwards.'[11] And Origen, in somewhat similar fashion, seems to indicate that history is like a ladder, where literal facts are the lowest rungs.[12] Again, when the obscurities of early Israelite history are being discussed, he remarks: 'If anybody requires of us clear and distinct declarations on these points we must reply that it was the design of the Holy Spirit, in those portions of Scripture which seem to relate the history of events, rather to cover and conceal. . . . The Kingdom of Heaven is like a treasure hid in a field, and the soil and surface, so to speak, of Scripture—that is to say, the literal meaning—is like a field, thick with plants of all kinds, while the deeper and more profound "spiritual" meaning is in truth the invisible and hidden treasures, for the finding out of which divine help is needed.'[13]

Origen, for all the scientific temper of his mind, as shown in his critical and scholarly attempts to discover the true text of the Scriptures,[14] yet realized that, for the apprehension of full truth, reason is not enough. Like the mathematician Pascal, whose learning was based on the rigid application of logical method, he knew that God is sensible to the faithful heart as well as to the enquiring intellect. Again, like Pascal, he realized that 'few of the great things of life are amenable to rigorous demonstration'[15] and that students of Biblical history, indeed of most history, require something more than a capacity for the patient collection of facts. With this in mind, Origen divided his Christian contemporaries into 'bodily' and 'spiritual' persons, according as they contented themselves with the obvious meaning of phenomena or probed, restlessly and deeply, beneath the surface of things in their search for truth. Sometimes the classification of believers is threefold, to match the psychological distinctions of body, soul and spirit, as in a well-known chapter of the *de Principiis*: 'The more simple individuals may be edified, so to speak, by the body of Scripture, that is to say by the common or historical sense, while those who have begun to make reasonable progress and are able to see something rather more advanced, are assisted by what you might call the soul of Scripture. Those, again, who are perfect will be edified by the spiritual law itself.'[16]

Origen might perhaps have felt some slight sympathy for Macaulay's vigorous pronouncement: 'Facts are the mere dross of history; it is from the abstract truth which interpenetrates them and lies latent among them like gold in the ore that the mass derives its value',[17] but he was well aware also of the principle summed up in the philosopher's maxim that 'history without truth is a body without life',[18] and he aimed not so much to depreciate the events of Biblical history as to proclaim that their significance was richer and fuller than an uncomprehending analysis would allow. He declares that the evangelists were chiefly concerned not with stories or mere narrative, but with mysteries,[19] or again, 'all the narrative portion of Scripture which seems to deal with marriages or the begetting of children or battles of various kinds . . . must surely be regarded as nothing other than the forms and figures of hidden and sacred things'.[20] Origen is convinced that a veil hangs over the whole of Scripture—narrative, prophecy and law alike—and that the man who sees the veil of Scripture rent in twain from the top to the bottom and detects what has been contained therein is filled with the true knowledge.[21]

In adopting this allegorical[22] mode of interpreting the Biblical record, Origen was following the tradition of his native Alexandria. In particular, the Jewish *savant* Philo had shown himself to be, in the words of a friendly critic, 'rich in his language, broad in his thought, and sublime and elevated in his opinions'[23] because of his skill in taking over and applying to the Hebrew Scriptures methods devised by such early critics of Homer as Theagenes of Rhegium in their attempt to harmonize mythology with reason and to maintain old and honoured truth side by side with the ideas of a newer age.[24] The Greek scholars had described this kind of allegorizing as $\theta\epsilon\rho\alpha\pi\epsilon\acute{\iota}\alpha$ $\mu\acute{\upsilon}\theta\omega\nu$ [25]—'restoring the myths to health'—and as the only antidote to false and impious opinions. Similarly Philo declared that Homer, Hesiod and the rest often wrote in a 'physiological' manner, by which he meant that these poets clothed their doctrine about the true nature of things in a cloak of mythology which only the initiate knew how to unwrap.[26] On this view, the Greek gods do but personify the powers of nature or symbolize abstract virtues. So, when considering the Scriptures, Philo expressed no little scorn and blame for those who study the text merely in its obvious and literal sense. 'In a superficial way,' he remarked, 'they follow only what is external and concrete', thus presenting an unfortunate contrast to the allegorizers, who are led by the spirit of the Bible. In his comments on the Pentateuch, Philo makes it clear that he thought of these books primarily as an allegory of the experiences of the human soul. Adam represents Mind, to which Sense-perception, that is Eve, is united as a helpmeet.[27] It is the task of Adam to tend the Garden of Eden, or, as put in more rational terms, Mind is required to concentrate on the cultivation of Virtue,[28] the four rivers of the Garden standing for Prudence, Courage, Self-control and Justice.[29] Pleasure, in its tortuous and variegated course, is aptly represented by the Serpent,[30] and the fact that there are pleasures which bring death to the soul is expressed by the incident recorded in the book of Numbers:[31] 'And the Lord sent fiery serpents among the people, and they bit the people; and much people of Israel died'. 'How then', Philo continues, 'is their suffering cured? It is when another serpent is made, opposite in kind to that of Eve, I mean the principle of self-control. For self-control is something quite opposite to pleasure, a manifold virtue standing over against a manifold affection and repelling pleasure as its foe. God therefore commands Moses to make the serpent that denotes self-control and says "Make for thyself a serpent, and set it upon a standard". You see that Moses makes this serpent not for anybody else but for himself, since God's bidding is "make it for thyself", whereby you may realize that self-control is a possession not of every man but only of the man beloved of God.'

Philo is not the only exegete to interpret the serpent metaphorically as pleasure, feeding on what is but dust by contrast with the heavenly manna. But whereas, for instance, in the Book of Wisdom[32] the story of Moses and the brazen serpent is treated as an historical event which gains enhanced value as a symbol of redemption, for Philo the historical element appears to be unimportant, indeed unreal, and fact is wholly transformed into allegory. In his desire to save the credit of the Scriptures and to make them prefigure all that was best in Greek philosophy, Philo sought to avoid all possible occasions of stumbling. Conscious that the sacred words, when understood in their literal sense, sometimes strain the credulity and are often trivial, he regarded it as inevitable that they should conceal some underlying thought (ὑπόνοια) which patient meditation, aided by God's grace, could not fail to extract.

Philo's device of explaining away difficulties and reconciling awkward discrepancies by a free and flexible use of allegory was soon adopted by some of the apologists for Christian doctrine. Even in his own day the Therapeutae, whom Eusebius, at any rate, took to be Christians, 'were accustomed to make their interpretations of the sacred writings figuratively by means of allegories. For the whole law appears to these men to be like a living creature. The spoken ordinances are its body, but its soul is the invisible sense underlying the statements. It is this hidden sense that the sect has begun especially to contemplate, so that in the mirror of words it sees reflected surpassing beauties of thought.'[33] Philo's influence is to be clearly discerned in the works of Justin Martyr as well as in the Epistle of Barnabas, the tenth chapter of which provides a typical example of 'Alexandrian' reasoning: 'Now in that Moses said "Ye shall not eat swine, nor an eagle nor a hawk nor a crow nor any fish which lacks scales"[34] he comprised three points of doctrine in his understanding. . . . The commandment of God is not concerned with abstinence from eating, and it was in the spirit that Moses spoke. Now he mentioned the swine for this reason: thou shalt not associate, he means, with men who are like swine, that is to say, when they are living luxuriously, they forget the Lord but when they are in want they recognize Him, just as the swine when it is eating does not know its master but when it is hungry it calls out and then after getting its food returns to silence.' The commandment not to eat the eagle, hawk, kite or crow is similarly interpreted as being a reminder not to associate with greedy and covetous persons, while the injunction 'Thou shalt not eat the lamprey nor the octopus nor the cuttle-fish' is explained as a warning that 'thou shalt not associate with or become like the sort of men who are utterly impious and already condemned to death, just as these fish alone are accursed and float about in the deep water, not swimming freely like the rest but dwelling deep down at the bottom of the sea'.

In his Alexandrian background, therefore, Origen had ample precedent for treating historical documents, sometimes capriciously, as symbols of a deeper truth. But just as, in Christian doctrine, no speculations, however noble and refined, had the least chance of acceptance unless they were buttressed by a text of Scripture, so, in Christian exegesis, it was to the Scriptures that men turned for guidance. Origen, at any rate, chose St. Paul rather than Philo as the justification for his allegorizings. It was Paul who had declared 'we have this treasure in earthen vessels'[35] and Paul who had made enquiry and answer, concerning the Deuteronomic precept 'Thou shalt not muzzle the ox when he treadeth out the corn', 'Is it for the oxen that God careth or saith He it altogether for our sake? Yea, for our sake it was written.'[36] Again, it was Paul who had explained the rock from which the Israelites in time of need drew their water to drink as prophetic of Christ,[37] and who rebuked the Galatians for failing to perceive the hidden meaning that underlay the account of Abraham and his two sons. Origen notes that: 'Paul upbraids certain individuals who imagine that they read the Law but yet fail to understand it because they ignore the fact that an allegorical meaning underlies what is written'.[38] The authority of the Apostle was paramount, but Origen, in his role of philosopher, never shrank from defending the faith that was in him. He maintained that allegory was needful just because visible things are merely symbols of the invisible world, our apprehension of the truth clutches but at the shadow of Truth as God sees it, our everyday reality is no more than a fallible and imperfect representation of all that may rightfully claim to be described as real.[39]

In his majestic commentaries, as well as in his one formal exposition of Christian philosophy, Origen again and again alludes to the aim which he sets before himself, 'to discover in every expression the hidden splendour of doctrines veiled in common and unattractive phraseology'.[40] Thus, in the fourth book of the *de Principiis*, he explains that 'when we read of the construction of the tabernacle, we hold it as assured that the written descriptions are figures of certain hidden things, though to adapt these appropriately may well be an exceedingly difficult, if not impossible, task'.[41] It is understandable that, in the hostile judgement of the Neoplatonist philosopher Porphyry, Origen and his followers are said to 'boast that the things said plainly by Moses are riddles, treating them as divine oracles full of hidden mysteries, and bewitching the power of critical judgement by means of nonsense and obscurity'.[42]

Origen is not unaware of the hazards of his bold attempts to remove the scandal of difficulties and inconsistencies in Scripture. Sometimes, however, he magnifies these difficulties unduly, as when the minute scrutiny which he applies to the text draws him on to be over-subtle or, in contrast with his professed principles, inclines him to a pedestrian exegesis which verges on the ludicrous. Thus, after pointing out the folly of taking all the precepts of the Law at their face value, he goes on to indicate passages in the Gospels also which cannot be taken literally. 'How', he asks, 'can the order be observed that, when one is smitten on the right cheek one should present the left cheek also, since everyone who strikes

with the right hand smites the left cheek first? Moreover, this precept also of the Gospel must be reckoned an impossibility that, if
the right eye offend thee, it is to be plucked out—for how shall it
seem appropriate that, when both eyes have the power of sight,
the responsibility for the 'offence' should be confined to one eye
and that the right one?'[43]

But Origen's methods of Biblical interpretation open up the
way to profounder dangers than undue nicety in verbal juggling.
St. Jerome gave it as his opinion that 'Origen surpassed himself in
his book on the Song of Songs',[44] but it is perhaps in this commentary that Origen has his feet least firmly placed on a secure
foundation of brute fact. He devotes much discussion to the verse,
'My beloved is like a roe or a young hart: behold he standeth
behind our wall, he looketh in at the windows, he glanceth
through the lattice',[45] and interprets it as follows: The house in
which the Church is dwelling is the Holy Scripture of the Law
and the Prophets. Christ at first stands behind the wall of the Old
Testament and therefore remains unseen by those inside. But in
due time He shows himself at the window and summons the
Church, who is seated within, to leave the house and join Him:
'His call and invitation therefore is to pass from the fleshly to the
spiritual, from things visible to things invisible, from the Law to
the Gospel.'[46] But the spiritual Gospel here opposed to the Law is
no robustly historical account of a life lived in Palestine 'when
Pontius Pilate was governor of Judaea'. There is a certain edging
away from that element of the Christian doctrine which has always
savoured of difficulty and paradox—the claim that a God who is
ex hypothesi raised beyond and above the limitations of time
makes use of historical events at particular times for purposes of
self-revelation. Origen presses the point home elsewhere in the
same commentary when he once again touches on the theme of
the inferiority of the Law. For this time it is not a matter of the
contrast between the Law and Christ on earth, but rather that
between the Law and Christ who had 'entered not into a holy
place made with hands . . . but into heaven itself'.[47]

In Platonic fashion Origen goes on to note that 'the invisible and incorporeal things that are in heaven are true, but the visible and corporeal things that are on earth are said to be "copies of the true things", not true'.[48] On this line of argument it is not so much a contrast between two historic revelations, God's promise in the Old Covenant and his performance in an Incarnation, as a corporeal, earthly hint standing over against eternal, heavenly truth. In face of such refined speculation, the claim that 'the Word was made flesh' might seem jarring and crude. Yet the point must not be pressed too hard. Origen may have felt that the high importance of the Gospels lies in the spiritual truth which they communicate rather than in the value of their historical details; nevertheless he defends the general validity of the Gospel record and declares that 'the passages which are historically true are far more numerous than those which contain a purely spiritual meaning'.[49] He would, no doubt, have accepted the views on Biblical history-writing recently expressed by Professor C. H. Dodd:[50] 'The broad rhythms of the history stand out firm and clear, and we may without misgiving follow the sweep of events . . . from age to age, recognizing our records as a true representation, in general terms, of what actually took place'.

Origen at any rate sums up the matter in similar fashion when, in his Apology to Celsus, the representative of the cultured pagan world, he writes thus:[51] 'The man who deals sensibly with classical history and who wishes to keep himself free from error in such matters will exercise his judgement in deciding what he is going to accept and what he will take in a figurative sense, investigating the intention of those who composed such accounts; and certain statements he will decline to believe on the ground that they were set down in order to gratify somebody or other. And this is the object I have had in mind throughout the whole of my enquiries into the Gospel concerning Jesus, not inviting men of ability to a simple and unreflective faith, but wishing to indicate that those who propose to examine such matters will need to avail themselves of common sense and prolonged investigation and, if I may so put it, insight into the intention of the authors.' This all has a fairly up-to-date ring, and may be compared with a somewhat bolder passage that is to be found in the Homily on Leviticus:[52] 'You must be prepared to recognize that the narratives of Holy Scripture are "figures" (*figurae*), and for that reason you must consider them in a spiritual rather than a carnal fashion, and thus grasp their purport. For, if you take them in a carnal manner, they harm you and fail to nourish. You get cases in the Gospels of the "letter which kills"; for it is not only in the Old Testament that the "letter which kills" is discoverable, but in the New Testament also occurs the "letter which kills" the man who does not apply a spiritual interpretation to what is recorded.' What Origen really intends to point out is that only the quickened perceptions of the faithful heart will detect the full riches of Gospel truth; or, to use his own striking image, that understanding of the Gospels is granted to none but those 'who recline on Jesus' breast'.[53]

In his commentary on St. John, Origen goes so far as to express himself thus:[54] 'I do not condemn the Evangelists even if they sometimes modified things which to the eye of history happened differently in the interests of the mystical aim which they had in view, so that they speak of a thing which happened in one place as if it happened somewhere else, or of what took place at one time as if it had happened at another time, and introduce certain changes into the words actually spoken. Their intention was to speak the truth where it was possible both materially and spiritually and, where it was not possible to do both, they preferred the spiritual to the material. Indeed spiritual truth was often preserved in what might be described as material falsehood.' Elsewhere Origen points frankly to the discrepancies that may be found in the Gospel narratives. Thus, when commenting on St. Matthew's Gospel, he notes the varying narratives of Christ's anointing by the woman and decides that either Christ was anointed by three or four different women—which he regards as improbable—or that some error must have crept in because the evangelists were attempting to draw out the general significance of the event and paying little regard to particular details. His conclusion is that such discrepancies can be reconciled and the dignity of the Gospel record maintained only through the help of allegorical interpretation.[55]

Origen's aim, therefore, is far from being a destructive one. Rather he feels it his mission to explain what he calls the 'disharmony of history'[56] which is bound up with the fallibilities of human perception and the variable attempts to interpret such truths as elude nice definition. With his customary poetic touch, Origen declares the whole Scriptural record to be God's symphony, wherein the inexpert listener may think he perceives jarring notes while the man whose ear has been well trained realizes the fitness and grace with which the varied notes are worked up into one harmonious composition.[57] In his Homily on Jeremiah Origen makes use of a different picture and explains that spiritually-minded readers must be like botanists whom careful study has rendered capable of distinguishing between the various species of plants and knowing which ones are of medicinal value and how they have to be prepared in order to effect their cures.[58] Again, such enlightened critics are compared to anatomists who understand that each member of the body has been created by God to perform a particular function, though the value and utility of certain members may remain quite unperceived by persons whose knowledge is superficial.

In other words, plain facts need someone to point out their significance. But, in historical as in artistic interpretation, excess is more disastrous than defect. Even though the lament may be justified that commonplace chronicling takes the heart out of history, yet unchastened interpretation produces mere caricature. Origen's methods 'determined the character of a large part of the patristic and mediaeval exegesis'[59] and it must be allowed that churchmen showed little restraint in grasping at the chances which allegory afforded to them of seeing the whole of history as a parable, designed to illustrate the events of the Christian dispensation. At the beginning of the seventh century, Bishop Isidore of Seville was pointing out to the members of his flock how the events of the Old Testament serve but to proclaim the glories of the New Covenant and how, in their turn, the smallest details of the Gospel narrative are rich in moral and ecclesiastical truth. 'Eve', he tells us, 'signifies the Church established through the mysterious water which proceeded from the side of the dying Christ just as Eve proceeded from the ribs of a sleeping man.' 'Abel, shepherd of the flock, signified Christ, who is the true and good shepherd as He Himself says "I am the good shepherd and lay down my life for my sheep".' So, in the moralizing rather than in the prophetic strain, Isidore uses the Gospel incident of the demoniac and the Gadarene swine: 'Now the swineherds who fled in order to report to the people in the city all that had been done represent the rulers of wicked nations who, while they flee from the faith of Christ, yet stand amazed at his miracles and proclaim them'. Similarly, the man with the withered hand signifies the synagogue, or perhaps the soul that is unfruitful in works of mercy; in the latter case, the words 'stretch forth thy hand' are to be taken as advice always to stretch forth the hand in almsgiving to the poor.[60]

Isidore lays down the general principle that the books of Scripture resemble a harp with strings of infinite resonance, while later on the motto of the Schoolmen, in their investigations of Biblical history, came to be 'the letter teaches you what happened: allegory teaches you what it all means'.[61] It was thus maintained that the Biblical records put forward bare facts which could be transmuted into saving doctrines only by a symbolical mode of interpretation; and the exuberant impressionism of allegory, colourful and exciting as it was, led inevitably to fantasy and a forgetfulness of truth.

Even those writers who possessed a natural inclination towards accuracy, such as Bede, came under the spell of the Origenistic alchemy whereby the most ordinary incidents of the Scriptural record could be claimed as 'full of mysteries and figurative value'.[62] Moses, declares Bede, did not write 'merely because he had an interest in history'[63] and the literal sense is but a stepping-stone[64] which leads to deeper meaning or, in other words, the veil[65] that must be stripped off if the 'full value of spiritual truth' is to be discovered. God's message to mankind resembles precious spices in that it yields its gracious fragrance only when it has been well pounded and sifted.[66] Literal interpretations, on Bede's view, smack of a barren Judaism, which fails to perceive the 'fair harmony of things'[67] or 'marvellous sacramental accord'[68] whereby nature and history alike supply types and indications of fuller truth. Yet his balanced and scholarly temper warns Bede 'not to abandon the obvious meaning of history when you allegorize'[69] and not to imagine that allegorical speculations can always take the place of a careful examination of texts and sources.

In spite of its great and recognized dangers, the allegorical method helped Origen and his successors to safeguard much that the earliest generation of Christians had unselfconsciously accepted. It enabled them to avoid the error of those who, like the dualist Marcion, would set the stern justice of the Law in opposition to the loving-kindness of Christ, thus preserving for the Church the Scriptures of the Old Testament, and pinning the revelation of God to earth instead of allowing it to dissipate in the clouds of idealism. Through allegory the fierce saga of Eastern sheikhs and the trivialities of Mosaic legislation found an honoured place in the preparation for the Gospel, and one which did not disgrace the Holy Ghost who had inspired the authors of the sacred books. Origen puts the matter thus in his Homily on Numbers:[70] 'There now follows the account of the inheritance of Reuben, Gad and the half tribe of Manasseh; and, as I undertake the task of commenting on this theme, I wish first of all to ask my hearers to be careful and to raise their minds to the level of spiritual understanding. One has to weigh what is said not merely by the content of the utterance but one must certainly take into account who the speaker is. . . . Now the narrator of these events which we find in Scripture is not a boy nor is he a man of any sort; indeed—not to waste words—he is no angel or heavenly power either, but, as established tradition maintains, he is the Holy Spirit.' 'Therefore', as Ambrose later put it,[71] 'when things in their literal acceptance appear to teach what is unseemly, you must tear off the mysterious veil and explain them in a spiritual fashion.'

But it is easier to state this principle than to put it unerringly into practice, as Origen frankly allowed when he declared: 'Even the simplest of believers who accept the doctrine that the Holy Scriptures are no human composition but written by the Holy Spirit must admit that there are certain mystical economies indicated therein. But what these are and of what kind he who is right minded and not overcome with the vice of boasting will scrupulously acknowledge himself to be largely ignorant.'[72] There were, of course, what Origen called the 'chaste and honourable doctrines of the Church'[73] to assist the puzzled enquirer. 'That alone', he declares, 'is to be accepted as truth which differs in no respect from the tradition of the Church and the Apostles.'[74] But Origen had too questing a mind to sink back happily upon an *imprimatur*, and he nowhere clearly relates the 'pattern of sound words', which the Church of the third century accepted, to his own discoveries and speculations.

The sum, then, of what Origen learnt and taught was that history, like nature, is a sacrament, where outward and visible signs serve to mediate a full richness of inward and spiritual truth to receptive minds; and, in any doctrine of sacraments, the precise relationship between objective facts and the faith which transfigures is not easily expressed in the clear-cut formulae of logic. Origen, however, was not disheartened by this circumstance. Adopting the view which Augustine later summed up in the statement that 'things easy to understand are commonly held of little account',[75] he explained that 'certain stumbling-blocks, as it were, and offences and impossibilities were introduced into the midst of history' 'in order that we may be drawn on to search out that truth which lies deep down and demands very careful investigation'.[76] On this reasoning, those who find Clio a hard taskmistress may console themselves with the thought that all her caprice and vagary serve but to draw men on through tantalizing half-lights and obscure byways to find their rest, at the last, in the City of God.

CHAPTER IV

STRAIGHTFORWARD CHRONICLE: EUSEBIUS

Men shall speak of the might of thy marvellous acts. Ps. cxlv. 6

For all the contempt of the world and eager watch for its dissolution which marked out the early generations of Christians as leading a 'life unlike other men's'[1] and even as displaying a certain 'hatred of the human race',[2] they yet retained something of that lively interest in history which characterizes the Biblical view of life. Nevertheless churchmen were at first primarily concerned, by means of a gradual and systematic working-out of their doctrines and apologetic, to relate their new-found faith to contemporary thought; and it was not until the beginning of the fourth century that a backward glance over three hundred years of widespread progress and development induced Eusebius, bishop of Caesarea, formally to compose an *Ecclesiastical History*.

For this task Eusebius was well equipped alike by temperament and opportunity. Little is known of the early history of his life beyond the facts that he was born about 262 and brought up at Caesarea where he was ordained presbyter. Though his interests were broadened by travel to such places as Jerusalem, Tyre and Antioch, he had no need to go beyond Caesarea in search for the inspiration which earns for him a place beside Herodotus, on Croce's estimate, as the 'father of modern history-writing'.[3]

Herod the Great's magnificent harbour-town offered to the impressionable two striking lessons. In the first place, the Christian Church there, with its memories of Philip the Evangelist, of Cornelius and his household visited by the Holy Ghost in testimony that Gentiles should be baptized,[4] and of St. Paul's trials before Felix and Festus, had prospered side by side with those obvious marks of the power of Rome that were appropriate in a city which was the residence of the provincial governor. Eusebius was thereby reminded of the good order and political stability which had favoured the growth and expansion of the missionary Church. To these benefits he alludes near the beginning of his *Ecclesiastical History* when, after declaring that 'Tiberius devised no evil against the teaching of Christ', he explains: 'It was Providence on high which, by a divine dispensation, put such thoughts into the emperor's mind, in order that the word of the Gospel might be without hindrance in its first stages and so run abroad throughout the earth in all directions'.⁵ Secondly, the rootless and generally uncertain state of the numerous Jews at Caesarea appears to have reminded him continually that 'Jerusalem is ruined and Judah is fallen; because their tongue and their doings are against the Lord, to provoke the eyes of his glory'.⁶ Eusebius mentions that he himself had seen the Romans cultivating part of Mount Zion as a market garden, and he comments on the piteous spectacle of stones from the Temple of Jehovah being gathered together for use in the construction of pagan temples and theatres.⁷ 'Jerusalem,' he observes, 'the once renowned city of the Jewish race, with her glory and her fruitfulness in God, is now bereft of her holy citizens and pious men.'⁸ Here, as in the providential occurrence of the peace bestowed by the Roman Empire, were to be discerned traces of God's control over history in the interests of the salvation of mankind, a theme which was to underlie all Eusebius' work as historian and apologist.

Besides all this, Caesarea had enjoyed a reputation for scholarship since the time, some thirty years before Eusebius' birth, when Origen, after a jealous rebuff from his bishop, settled there and devoted himself to the cause of Christian education, crowning his labours with a martyr's constancy in the persecution stirred up by the emperor Decius. And, perhaps more important for Eusebius than any reputation or atmosphere, there was the presence of Pamphilus. This devoted scholar had left his native city of Berytus in order to study at Alexandria and then, impelled no doubt by respect for Origen's memory, had come to Caesarea, where his ample means allowed him to establish a library and employ a body of students in the collection and accurate transmission of manuscripts. Eusebius testifies to the 'consummate learning'⁹ shown by Pamphilus in things human and divine and compares him, in the fulsome, 'Byzantine', manner to 'a luminary which shines by day among the glittering stars, conspicuous among them all in dazzling splendour'.[10] 'For', continues Eusebius, 'he had embraced in no ordinary degree those studies which the Greeks admire; and in those connected with the divine doctrines and the inspired Scriptures he had so trained himself that none of his contemporaries could be said to have done the like.' Eusebius proceeds to testify to the God-given intelligence and wisdom which Pamphilus used to display, as well as to his generosity: 'What scholar was there who did not find a friend in Pamphilus? If he knew of any such persons being in want of the necessaries of life, he freely supplied whatever he could. He used most readily to provide copies of the Holy Scriptures, not merely as a loan but even as a gift, and that not only to men but to women also, if he saw that they were given to reading.'[11] Eusebius was destined to become bishop of Caesarea and, later, to transcend all local limits as the recognized embodiment of statesmanlike moderation and the loyal recipient of imperial patronage, but the most notable work to which he directed his abilities, the composition of his *Ecclesiastical History*, was undertaken, it is fairly safe to say, at the instigation of Pamphilus, his 'master',[12] his companion in many a scholarly enterprise and 'of all my friends the one whose memory to me is dearest'.[13]

Eusebius' talent was thus moulded in the direction of critical and painstaking yet generous and practical learning, and his natural inclinations appear to have been in sympathy with this approach to things. He found himself unable to engage with fervour in any narrow partisanship and, in the disputes about doctrine which vexed the empire during the reign of Constantine, preserved a conservative and non-committal attitude which enabled him to be claimed as a supporter by Orthodox and Arians alike But it would be misleading to consider him merely as an erudite trimmer, well practised in the art of accommodating his beliefs to the varying currents of opinion in Church and State. He was, indeed, accused by Potammon, a fiery Egyptian delegate to the Synod of Tyre held in A.D. 335 under Eusebius' presidency, of having betrayed his faith in the stress of persecution, and he so resented the charge

that he promptly brought the session to a close; but this Council
was a turbulent affair in which allegations were lightly bandied
about, and it is most unlikely that, if Eusebius had lapsed discredit-
ably at a time when Pamphilus and others stood firm, he would
have been elected to the bishopric of Caesarea a few years later.
Moreover, his writings indicate that he made no secret of his sym-
pathies but freely visited his Christian friends in prison, was an
eye-witness of martyrdoms at Tyre[14] and in Egypt and, apparently,
suffered a term of imprisonment himself.[15] These experiences
served to equip him for the composition of history in a manner
which satisfies the demand that a man should have personal knowledge of the kind of subjects with which he proposes to deal.

The first draft of Eusebius' great *Ecclesiastical History*, neatly
arranged in seven books, told the story of the growth of the Church
from apostolic times down to the year A.D. 303.[16] But three further
books, together with the tractate on the *Palestinian Martyrs*, were
added as supplements at various times during the next twenty
years or so. The scale of these is altogether different, and great
movements of contemporary history pass unnoticed in favour of
anecdotes and personal reminiscences of the final persecutions. To
feel himself actively concerned in what seem to be events of decisive importance is a heady experience for the sensitive man. The
poet Goethe, after playing a very insignificant and undramatic part
in a campaign in Flanders, addressed himself thus in his diary:
'from today starts a new epoch in the history of the world, and
you can say that you were there'.[17] Similarly, but perhaps with
rather more reason for his enthusiasm, Eusebius took a particularly
keen interest in what he proudly called 'the conflicts that took
place in our own day'.[18] But, before he set about the task of pro-
ducing a full Church history, Eusebius had prepared the skeleton
by making use of a fashionable type of scholarship and setting out
chronological tables in a systematic form.

The 'Libyan philosopher',[19] Julius Africanus, had anticipated
him in this task by some eighty years and had attempted to bring
Jewish and Christian history into close relation with the traditions
of paganism. It had been declared that 'God made of one blood

CHRISTIAN INTERPRETATIONS OF HISTORY

all nations . . . to dwell on the face of the earth'[20] and Africanus, not unmindful of the principle that 'chronology is the eye of the historian',[21] wished to demonstrate history as an entity in which no parts are irrelevant and where the whole acquires meaning as bearing the impress of the divine purpose. Of the five books which make up this *Chronographia* the first two are concerned only with the Biblical records, from the Creation down to the time of Moses, but the three later books trace the parallel courses of sacred and secular affairs as far as the year A.D. 221.[22] Eusebius made ready use of this compendious treatise, in which Biblical and classical dates were set out for easy comparison, and praised it as being 'worked out with zeal and precision'.[23] But he greatly extended the range of his enquiry, investigating, with the painstaking method which is his sovereign characteristic, the work of numerous historians in the endeavour, which he put before himself, 'to establish the exact chronology of every people according to its own reckoning'.[24] Florence Nightingale is said to have found statistics 'more enlivening than a novel'[25] since she 'loved to bite on hard fact', and Eusebius of Caesarea seems to have shared her taste for the meticulous arrangement of carefully collected material.

In constructing his *Chronicle*, before he embarked on his larger work, Eusebius was obeying a profoundly sure instinct. For, as a recent critic has observed, 'Chronology is the backbone of history. Absolute chronology is the fixed central core around which the events of nations must be grouped before they may assume their exact positions in history and before their mutual relationships may be properly understood.'[26] Eusebius recognized the limitations imposed upon his efforts and felt sure that the words 'It is not for you to know times and seasons, which the Father hath set within his own authority' are intended by the Lord to apply 'not merely to the final cataclysm but to all times'[27] in order that human arrogance may be repressed; but he was not for that reason deterred from attempting the task to the best of his ability.

The arrangement which he adopted was a double one. In the so-called *Chronography*, he puts forward a bare outline history of those five nations of the world which appeared to him to have been most significant for the history of mankind—the Assyrians, Hebrews, Egyptians, Greeks and Romans. He tabulates the reigns of their kings and offers critical discussions of their systems of reckoning dates. This piece of research is summarized and extended in the '*Canons*', a series of parallel columns, one for each great empire. The Hebrews, of course, separate into Israel and Judah for the duration of the divided monarchy, just as the events of Greek history are noted under several headings, at one time Sicyon and Argos, later on Corinth, Sparta and Athens. Medes eventually supersede Assyrians, while Lydians and Macedonians are included for the appropriate periods. The calculation of dates is made from the birth of Abraham, here reckoned as the year 2017 B.C., and with this series of years the Greek Olympiads, which seemed to Eusebius to mark the commencement of authentic Greek history, are duly correlated from the year 776. The absorption of other nations by the Roman Empire enabled the whole plan to be set out in much simpler fashion, but, even when there were eight or nine columns to look at, it could be seen at a glance which kings were simultaneously on the throne, and the length of their respective reigns. The names of Jewish high priests and Christian bishops also occur, and short reminders of notable events were added in the margin.

This *Chronicle* was, for a thousand years and more, the chief source-book[28] used throughout the Christian world by those who concerned themselves with the accurate presentation of past events. Translated by Jerome into Latin and by others into a number of Oriental languages, it exercised a wide and uninterrupted influence. 'The historian', observed Taine at the beginning of his work on *L'Ancien Régime*, 'may be permitted the privilege of the naturalist. I have observed my subject as one might observe the metamorphosis of an insect', and it is worthy of note that the first, formal attempt at reconstructing the history of the Church from its beginnings was this early essay, dry but precise and dependable, in the scientific method. But in undertaking all this labour, congenial though it might be, Eusebius was actuated by something more than the passion to discover and record facts in their most concise and impersonal form. He wrote, as a believer, in the assurance that Christian truth is best demonstrated by the appeal to logical argument which, for Eusebius, was not a matter of abstractions but had, as its proper theme, the variegated stuff of history. 'I have read through very many books of ancient history,' he remarks in the preface to his laborious work, 'and I have thought it in place—or rather extremely useful and necessary—to arrange all the matter in a small compass.' The history of the world is thus shown forth in compressed and unified fashion, but it is related throughout to the decisive events which are detailed in the records of the Chosen People, beginning with Abraham, since to him 'and his seed for ever' were the promises made.

Eusebius wrote much, and most of his works may be described as built up on the foundation of the *Chronicle*. In the treatise which he entitles 'The Preparation of the Gospel', he reviews, with careful quotations from original sources, the more prominent religions, mythologies and philosophies of paganism, in order courteously to point out the superiority of the Old Testament revelation. Then, in his 'Demonstration of the Gospel', he answers the objectors, who maintain that those who reverence the Hebrew Scriptures should observe the forms of religion there inculcated, by pointing to the character of Judaism as preparatory to the Christ whose coming the prophets had foretold with ever-increasing clarity. He goes on to declare God's use and control of history, and to discuss the providential appearance of Christianity at the precise moment when the world was best adapted to receive and disseminate its teachings. Proceeding onwards from these apologetic works, Eusebius directed his efforts to the composition of his *Ecclesiastical History*, 'the most important monument', as one scholar has described it, 'of ancient Christian literature'.[29] Its heavy and unattractive style cannot conceal the vast learning nor deaden the note of triumph as Eusebius traces the rapid growth of the Church, to fulfil a glorious destiny and vindicate the claim that its Master should be the 'expectation of the nations'.[30]

Eusebius makes clear, in a preface, what he proposes to do, and describes the plan of his work under five heads. In the first place he will narrate 'the number and character of the affairs which are said to have been transacted in the history of the Church', devoting particular attention to the 'successions of the holy Apostles' and the work of those who were 'leaders and presidents' in the more distinguished communities. The influence of the *Chronicle* is obvious enough in this arrangement; indeed the themes which Eusebius emphasizes throughout the *Ecclesiastical History* reflect the interests of the earlier work. His plan is next, by way of contrast, to expose the heretics who 'through a passion for novelty fell into the most grievous error . . ., ravaging the flock of Christ unsparingly like grievous wolves.' He intends, moreover, to point out the disasters which deservedly overcame the Jews and to give an account of the persecutions inflicted by the 'heathen' upon 'noble men' concluding with the martyrdoms that took place in his own times.[31]

Eusebius was well aware of the difficulties which were likely to meet him in the execution of his self-appointed task, and, after outlining what he proposes to do, he 'craves the leniency of kindly persons' on the ground that he could not hope to fulfil his promises 'completely and without omission'. Speaking as one who is the 'first to travel along a desolate and untrodden path', he explains that it will be necessary for him to make judicious extracts from a number of varied sources, 'plucking as it were from the meadows of literature suitable passages from authors of long ago'. His aim is declared to be the practical one of filling an obvious need with his composition which he trusts will 'prove of the highest value to those who are eager for the useful learning which history affords'.[32]

It is, then, as the first systematic and purposeful narrator of the events which marked the expansion of the Christian Church that Eusebius stands before us. His aim is laudable enough, and he very reasonably combines confidence in his abilities with the realization that it is hard for the historian to range widely and yet be always accurate in detail. The mood in which he undertakes his task is that expressed by the Venerable Bede at the beginning of his great *Historia Ecclesiastica*: 'If any reader finds things set down in my writings that are contrary to truth, let him not lay this to my charge. For I have always tried, in accordance with the unvarying rule of history, to gather together the substance of what is reported and set it down straightforwardly for the instruction of future generations.' But, since he aims high, Eusebius must submit to comparison with others who have worked at history-writing on a large scale. In the year 1834 Ferdinand Christian Baur, one of the great scholars of his day, wrote a complete treatise in which he compared Eusebius with Herodotus, the father of history with the father of Church history, but Josephus seems to provide a nearer parallel. Both writers concern themselves with the story of a nation, Josephus with the people of the Hebrews, Eusebius with 'a race neither little nor weak, and not established in some obscure corner of the earth, but the most populous of all nations'.[33] Both write with an apologetic motive. For Eusebius' desire to manifest the 'antiquity and divine nature of Christianity'[34] is matched by Josephus' clear intention, in the *Jewish War* to show that the interests of Rome and Judaism need never have clashed but for the machinations of fanatics, in the *Antiquities* to interpret Judaism to the Gentile world. Both were eye-witnesses of some part of what they record, and both pique themselves on their painstaking accuracy; indeed Josephus declares that he was impelled to write his account of the *Jewish War* because the earlier narratives were either 'casual and contradictory stories based on rumour'[35] or else distorted by partiality. Both make careful use of documents, but whereas Eusebius usually allows his quotations to speak for themselves, Josephus not infrequently interlards his Biblical sources with Rabbinic legends, such as the curious stories connected with the birth of Moses,[36] and has no hesitation about inserting long, rhetorical speeches composed on the Thucydidean principle: 'the words run in the fashion I should suppose each speaker to have necessarily used in the circumstances, following as closely as possible the general tenor of what was actually said'.[37] Eusebius, in his *Ecclesiastical History*, austerely refrains from any such practice. He shows no desire, in this work, to display virtuosity in the composition of such supposed speeches, a task which. according to

Dionysius of Halicarnassus,[38] 'some people regard as the supreme test of an author's skill'.

It must indeed be allowed that Eusebius entirely failed to concern himself with the literary graces. In the course of a spirited passage forming part of what still remains the best appreciation of Eusebius in the English language, Bishop Lightfoot observes: 'his gigantic learning was his master rather than his slave . . . his style is especially vicious'.[39] But the charges made by Lightfoot and others against his method of composing history, that it is desultory and full of repetitions, appear to have less substance. Eusebius, in the *Ecclesiastical History*, writes as an annalist, and does not pretend to do anything else. Adopting the method which had been successful in the case of the *Chronicle*, he arranged his material in blocks, taking the reign of each emperor as his unit of time. A subordinate scheme was provided by the bishops of the most important sees, notice of their successions being given in one or more short paragraphs under the respective reigns. Within each of the periods thus delimited Eusebius set down the matter which he judged appropriate to the topics which he had undertaken to discuss, adding also a note of the main productions of Christian literature. Naturally enough, he is sometimes driven by the intractable nature of his material, or even by the human failings of carelessness and fatigue, to diverge in certain details from his rigid scheme. Moreover, like most other people, he sometimes makes mistakes, as when he, on occasion, muddles up the similar and easily confused names of the emperors and princes of the Antonine house. Such faults, which have in recent years suffered persistent and somewhat pettifogging criticism,[40] may be regarded as venial enough, the most serious defect in the *Ecclesiastical History* being a certain lack of easy continuity, caused, in particular, by the way in which the biographies are interrupted. To take the example most often cited, that notable apologist and martyr St. Justin receives, as is right and due, fairly full notice from Eusebius. But the account of his life and work is broken up into three separate sections in order that each may appear neatly under the heading of the appropriate emperor.

Eusebius, however, compensates for all that he lacks in charm and continuity by providing a storehouse of material carefully chosen and arranged, without which our knowledge of the first three Christian centuries would have indeed been scanty. In answer to de Quincey's complaint that the great scholars of the eighteenth century were 'poor as thinkers', Mark Pattison declared that 'thinking was not their profession',[41] and then went on to explain that their duty was to collect and critically to edit the sources from which history is built up. This is more or less the duty which Eusebius imposed upon himself. At the cost of making his *Ecclesiastical History* somewhat jerkier to read than it need have been, he liberally sprinkles its pages with quotations drawn from the original authorities. Nearly two hundred and fifty extracts, of which about half would otherwise have been totally unknown, are transcribed word for word, and to these must be added about another hundred summaries or approximate quotations which Eusebius appears to have jotted down from memory and without exact checking. Even the transcribed passages are not always free from errors, due, it would seem, either to defective texts or to the work of enthusiastic but incompetent assistants in the school at Caesarea, and Eusebius himself does not exhibit unfailing judgement in deciding where to begin or end a quotation. But the value of his collection of documents cannot be gainsaid, and no allegation that he made dishonest use of them is seriously to be upheld. Indeed, the reliability of Eusebius is demonstrated wherever his work can be checked. Just as the discovery at Athens of a fragment of the text of the quadruple alliance made between Athens, Argos, Elis and Mantinea proves that Thucydides was careful and precise when reproducing diplomatic documents,[42] so Eusebius was shown to be equally exact when there was found at Arycanda, in 1892, an inscription which records the petition of the provincials of Lycia, who gratified Maximin by professing zeal for the persecution of Christians, together with the emperor's reply.[43]

In writing his history with the hope that it would educate, Eusebius was following a tradition that prevailed for many centuries. The Thucydidean principle that history should present a record of practical utility,[44] though it had to compete with the opinions of those who likened the historian's task rather to the craft of fiction or to oratorical display, continued to appeal to the serious-minded as giving point and dignity to their work. Following his self-conscious and academic fashion, Polybius, for instance, declared that it was his aim to produce 'not so much an encomium upon the Romans or Carthaginians'[45] as a narrative replete with serviceable lessons for the generations to come, on the ground that 'past events make us pay particular attention to the future'.[46] The obscure hotch-potch of contemporary happenings will, in fact, probably have less value for instruction than events of long ago, when these are seen in the clarity of perspective, and, as the twelfth-century chronicler Henry of Huntingdon put it, 'history mirrors to us the past as though it were present; it indicates the course of future events by bringing the past before our mind's eye'.[47] Dr. Arnold made the same point when he declared the study of ancient history to be 'not an idle enquiry about remote ages and forgotten institutions but a living picture of things present, fitted not so much for the curiosity of the scholar as the instruction of the statesman and citizen'.[48]

Eusebius shares this implied sense of the historian's responsibility. His aim, in part, is to edify, and this fact has led hostile critics to be sometimes unfair to him. One example may serve to illustrate this. Near the beginning of the eighth book of the *Ecclesiastical History* occur the words: 'We shall add to the general history only such things as may be profitable, first to ourselves and then to those that come after us',[49] a passage which draws from Gibbon the typical comment: 'Eusebius indirectly confesses that he has related whatever might redound to the glory, and that he has suppressed all that could tend to the disgrace, of religion'.[50] It is, of course, the historian's delicate task to choose out the significant incidents from the vast array of facts that may often lie to hand, and Gibbon, in his zealous onslaught, has overlooked the circumstance that, only a few lines above, Eusebius has frankly admitted the faults and failures of the Church at the end of the fourth century: 'As the result of greater freedom, our affairs suffered a change towards vanity and sloth. We fell to envy and fierce railing against one another and, as it were, made war upon ourselves, when occasion offered, with weapons and spears formed of words. . . . In our blindness we took not the least care to render the Deity well-disposed and favourable towards us but, like some kind of atheists, and imagining that our affairs passed all unnoticed and unperceived, we kept on adding one wickedness to another.' Eusebius then interprets the outbreak of severe persecution at the hands of the emperor Diocletian as a deserved, even as a merciful, dispensation of God. There is not much special pleading here, and he may surely be said to vindicate himself from the charge of 'speaking smooth things'.[51] Indeed some critics have gone precisely to the other extreme and accused him of emphasizing the sombre colours overmuch in order to contrast with them the happiness and light which God was to bestow by his gracious choice of Constantine as his agent in remodelling the destinies of the world.

Such high appreciation of the first Christian emperor is converted into exuberant panegyric in the treatise known under the somewhat misleading title of *The Life of Constantine*. This is really less a biography than a funeral oration, and follows the form proper to such works at the beginning of the Byzantine age. The learned critic Otto Seeck used to describe it as a 'book of lies',[52] but he later saw fit to modify this harsh judgement, and it is now generally held that Eusebius, however jarringly his fulsome praise of the emperor may sound in some ears, offers information which is partisan and enthusiastic rather than deliberately false, and that he provides extracts from genuine documents. We, in our day, may perforce subscribe ourselves as 'yours sincerely' at times when we would gladly hide our innermost feelings, or even use the words 'your obedient servant' to persons in whose presence we feel no emotions of servility or even of deference; but Eusebius, for all his natural reticence and terseness, obeyed a more flamboyant convention, according to which Constantine is described as 'flashing forth the rays of his sacred light to the very ends of the whole world, even to the most distant Indians. . . . People honoured him with pictures and the dedication of statues in their respective countries, and Constantine alone of all emperors was acknowledged and acclaimed by everyone.'[53] He is compared with Cyrus, Alexander and Moses. His appearance at the Council of Nicaea resembled that of 'some heavenly messenger of God',[54] for 'his piety and godly fear were indicated by his downcast eyes and the blush of his countenance' while 'he surpassed all those about him in stature as well as in youthful beauty, majestic and dignified presence, and the vigour of invincible strength. These qualities, united to a gracious manner and that gentle modesty which befits kingship, pointed to an excellence of understanding that was above all praise.'

There is much in this strain, but it would be a mistake to discuss it as hypocritical or, in the words of the historian Socrates, as 'laudatory grandiloquence'.[55] Eusebius, like many another, was captivated by the figure of Constantine who seemed to stand forth as a kind of incarnation of the glorious hope of a New Age. 'Would it not be shameful', he says, 'that the memory of Nero and other impious tyrants . . . should meet with diligent writers to embellish the account of their worthless deeds with elegance and charm and that I should be silent, to whom God Himself has vouchsafed such an emperor as all history records not, and has accounted me worthy to see him, to know him and to enjoy his society?'[56] Moreover, Eusebius is not wholly uncritical in his view of Constantine and can, for instance, allow that the confidence which the emperor placed in insincere and unprincipled men 'sometimes led him on to conduct unworthy of himself'[57]; but as a rule he writes frankly as an admirer, and the *Life of Constantine* often smacks of hero-worship rather than of the more sober ranges of history. Nevertheless, the portrait thus produced mirrors the fashion of its times. The same tale is told, for instance, by Constantine's coinage, with its revival of the type struck by Alexander six centuries earlier, and showing the emperor as a pattern of youthful grace, with gaze upturned to receive the inspiration of God. 'How much power of divine faith', notes Eusebius, 'was sustained in his soul anybody might learn by reflecting how on his gold coinage he represented his very own image in the form of someone eagerly looking up towards God in prayer.'[58]

In general, however, Eusebius is little inclined towards credulity. It has been held against him that, in the *Ecclesiastical History*, he accepts with uncritical alacrity the story of letters that passed between Christ and King Abgar of Edessa, 'a most illustrious potentate of the nations beyond the Euphrates',[59] or that he reproduced as genuine the letter of Antoninus Pius[60] to the Common Assembly of Asia, which is clearly an imaginary composition designed to show how easily the Christians came to enjoy the favour of benevolent and respected emperors. But these examples of error simply show that Eusebius, in consulting hundreds of documents, misjudged one or two of them. It is, moreover, notable that he almost entirely disregards the vast literature of apocryphal Gospels and Acts, and this suspicion of the miraculous and bizarre continually shows itself in smaller matters also. For instance, he gives a long extract from the genuine and interesting account of the martyrdom of Polycarp, bishop of Smyrna, in A.D. 156. But, when he reaches the description of the martyr's death, he makes two changes. Polycarp had been condemned to be burnt at the stake but, according to the narrative, 'the fire made a wall about the body of the martyr, and it was in the midst, not as burning flesh but as a loaf of bread being baked or as gold and silver refined in a furnace'.[61] Eusebius excises the homely reference to the baked loaf and then, shortly afterwards, makes a more significant omission. We read in the *Martyrdom* that, after a while, the executioner approached in order to stab Polycarp with a sword, 'which when he did, there came out a dove and a quantity of blood'. Eusebius, in quoting this passage, leaves the story, with its reminiscence of the nineteenth chapter of St. John's Gospel, intact in all particulars except that he cuts out any reference to the dove. This word[62] has been the subject of desperate emendations by modern critics, but most probably it is part of the original text and symbolizes the happy departure of Polycarp's soul to receive its heavenly reward. Eusebius, however, with his strict approach to historic fact, refused to admit what seemed to him an unnecessary and miraculous adjunct.

This almost sceptical temper pervades even the hero-worship of the *Life of Constantine*. The celebrated account of Constantine's vision of the cross of light 'in the very heavens, set above the sun, and bearing the inscription "Conquer by this"' is declared by Eusebius to be 'not at all easy to accept if it had been related by any other person'.[63] 'But since', he goes on to say, 'the victorious Emperor himself declared it to me long afterwards . . . and confirmed his statement with an oath, who could hesitate to believe the story, particularly since the course of time has borne its witness to the truth of the narrative?' Eusebius treats his sources fairly and quotes from them even when they appear difficult, adding, however, a note of scholarly caution. Thus, after recording an improbable speech by Constantine's hostile colleague Licinius, in which Christ is challenged to demonstrate his power over the ancient gods of Rome, Eusebius adds the note: 'These then were the words which he addressed to those present, and some of the people who heard what was said informed the writer of this history not long afterwards'.[64] Again, he treats in almost apologetic fashion the account of the resolute and the timid standard-bearer, according to which the one who ran away was slain but the brave man was preserved from danger amidst a hail of arrows. 'This story', Eusebius notes, 'is none of mine, but once more it was the emperor himself who related it in my hearing.'[65]

For instruction, as well as for artistic effect, the expression of history in terms of warring opposites is well adapted. Herodotus had interpreted history as a struggle between East and West, while Thucydides exalted the opposition of Athens and Sparta into the principle of the strife of liberal freedom against rigid authoritarianism. Eusebius worked on an even grander scale. For him, as for the prophet Daniel, events on earth represent, and play some part in, the mighty, cosmic struggle between the forces of good and evil. The Christians are thought of as a nation, 'a new nation that has suddenly appeared at the due and secretly appointed time',[66] a nation that is 'indestructible and invincible since it even receives the help that comes from God'. Although 'devils' and 'invisible adversaries'[67] had been waging a perpetual war against it, they seemed to have suffered a spectacular and final rout when the Christian Empire was established under Constantine. Not all observers shared Eusebius' triumphant joy over the capitulation of State to Church: Jerome, for instance, tartly notes that 'as the Church increased in influence it decreased in Christian virtues'.[68] But for Eusebius the turn that events had taken was no doubtful issue, and was best described, as he explained during the course of his famous oration in the church at Tyre,[69] in Isaiah's words: 'Be glad O thirsty desert; let the desert rejoice and blossom as a lily; yea, the desert places shall blossom forth and rejoice'.[70] For 'those who, like giants, engaged in battle against God have brought upon themselves utter destruction, while the result of the godly endurance of her who was desolate and rejected by men was such as we have seen with our own eyes'.

So definite a view of the God-directed destiny of the Church made Eusebius show on occasion less than justice to certain of her declared opponents. Since the early heretics are regarded as the devil's agents, employed 'for the destruction of souls and as ministers of perdition',[71] the notices about them in the *Ecclesiastical History* are scanty and culled, in a somewhat arbitrary manner, from the works of such orthodox opponents as Irenaeus. The historian Sallust took the view that Rome continued in good health so long as she was being harried by Carthage, but Eusebius overlooks the value of opposition for ensuring full development, and passes over most of the activities of the abhorred heretics in scornful silence. More remarkable is the change in the language used about Licinius. For while Licinius is Constantine's fellow-emperor, he is 'honoured for understanding and piety'[72] or even 'most dearly beloved of God',[73] but after he had 'fallen into madness'[74] and set himself against both Constantine and Constantine's God, he becomes 'an infamous master of intrigue'[75] and a 'drunken scoundrel',[76] distinguished by 'innate wickedness'[77] and 'insatiable rapacity'.[78] Nevertheless, despite the horror that Licinius' change of heart had caused him, it is to be observed that Eusebius had enough sense of historical propriety to leave unaltered his earlier encomiums. For, in writing his history of the Christian people, Eusebius had taken as his model the methods and standards of the most reputable historians of the ancient world. The manner in which he suppresses his own personality, even when he is dealing with events that concerned him nearly, points to a conscious attempt to secure an unbiased view of things; and this deliberate search after truth, guiding his precise and scholarly temper, enables him to produce a classic narrative of the strivings and triumph of the early Church. Many in East and West continued the story, but, for centuries, none attempted to supersede Eusebius' far-famed record which indeed bears favourable comparison with the pagan writings of his age. Only Ammianus, perhaps, rivals him in careful and objective composition, while the authors of the more nearly contemporary *Augustan History* are content to portray the reigns of the successive emperors in terms of *chronique scandaleuse*. It is fortunate indeed that the most influential Church historian should have made it clear by precept as by example that the cause of religion is best served by the resolute and candid attempt to ascertain and present 'things as they actually happened'.

One final charge against Eusebius has to be met. It is sometimes alleged that, while the book has the advantage of compactness, it presents a colourless, feeble picture of the historical process. 'Without heights and without depths,' observes one critic, 'without power and without force, events trail along, and fatiguing they certainly are in their uniform monotony.'[79] What is thus condemned in somewhat exaggerated fashion is that Eusebius obstinately refuses to bother about proximate causes or to demonstrate in the course of his history how that 'earthly happenings spring from earthly causes and lead to earthly results'.[80] He may use a variety of sources, some Christian, some pagan, but he welds them into one Church history to which, it is maintained, he imparts a 'savour of holiness'[81] by interpreting events in terms of God's immediate touch. All that this objection amounts to is that Eusebius writes in his somewhat annalistic fashion without making any minute search into the complexities of causal connexions. He thus carries over into his narrative the 'Biblical' point of view, according to which God rules in history and decides the destiny of nations and individuals, 'bringing', as Amos put it, 'the Philistines from Caphtor and the Syrians from Kir' as well as the Israelites out of the land of Egypt.[82] Eusebius reproduces also the Biblical doctrine that 'the eyes of the Lord are over the righteous' but 'the countenance of the Lord is against them that do evil'.[83] For Constantine, as for Eusebius, 'righteousness exalteth a nation'[84] and the surest guarantee of national prosperity is to be found in the offering of such sincere and united worship as is God's due. It was the opinion both of the emperor and of the bishop of Caesarea that all heretics and schismatics, who 'with witless levity presume to rend the religion of the people into a variety of sects',[85] stand condemned not so much for doctrinal irregularity as because they lead the way to that disharmony which invites the divine chastisement. The principle implied throughout Eusebius' works, and sometimes expressly stated, is that by a dispensation of divine justice good fortune follows upon piety while wickedness receives its due reward of misfortune, so that, as it is put in Constantine's remarkable letter to the Persian king Sapor II,[86] 'abundant thanksgiving is owed to God since through his good providence all men who observe his holy laws rejoice and exult in the peace that is granted to them'.

This vindication of God's justice is confirmed, surprisingly enough, by James Anthony Froude, an historian who can hardly be accused of bias in favour of any of the traditional expressions of religion but who felt constrained to admit 'that the world is somehow built upon a moral foundation, that in the long run it is well with the good, in the long run it goes evil with the wicked'.[87] And for the view that God is the deciding force in history, Eusebius would have the support of a host of witnesses. Miss Evelyn Underhill, for instance, declares that 'it is the prerogative of religion to discover this (divine) action informing every small event of our inward and outward existence, and thus giving significance to the bewildering mesh of circumstance which hems us in';[88] an affirmation which was in some sort anticipated by the French historian a century earlier: 'I see God in the laws which regulate the progress of the human race as clearly, nay, much more clearly present than in the movements of the stars'.[89] Even Ranke, though proposing to offer a methodical and passionless review of events, had no scruple in declaring that 'in all history God dwells, lives, is to be seen. Every deed displays Him, every moment preaches his name, but mostly, it appears to me, the content of history.'[90] It may be that here the confines of faith have been touched on rather than those of exact demonstration. But, if so, the example of Ranke, as of Eusebius in the circumstances of an earlier age, would seem to show that there is nothing incompatible between the strictly scientific attempt to record facts and a more mystical approach which would seek to interpret them, reverently and with hesitation, as reflecting the purposes of God.

CHAPTER V

GOD'S JUDGEMENT IN HISTORY:
AUGUSTINE, OROSIUS AND SALVIAN

He shall judge the world with righteousness, And the peoples
with his truth. Ps. xcvi. 13

'History', declared Augustine Birrell, 'is a pageant, not a
philosophy. To keep the past alive is the pious function of
the historian.'[1] Yet, side by side with those whose prime duty is
straightforward narrative, a place may be found for men of more
reflective temper whose concern is not so much to record as to
explain, and to indicate, amidst the particularities of history, its
universal, guiding principles. The early Church could boast a
number of such speculative writers, amongst whom Augustine,
together with Orosius and Salvian, exercised the most widespread
and permanent influence. Though circumstances sometimes
tempted them to assess history, in the fashion later adopted by
Gibbon, as 'little more than the register of the crimes, follies and
misfortunes of mankind',[2] they never forgot, even in distressful
times, that

> 'The years, like great black oxen, tread the world,
> And God, the herdsman, goads them on behind.'[3]

Augustine's interpretation of history may be considered from
three points of view. First there is his attitude towards Biblical
record, and his nice blending of accuracy with the power to draw
out from Scripture the living word that should appeal to his generation. Next to be noted is his confidence in the progress of
history towards a goal, as shown by the manner in which he takes
over and enriches the idea of the six ages of mankind correspond-
ing to the six days of creation; and, linked with this, is the opinion
which Augustine formed about the history of his own times, as
displaying, though sometimes in a glass darkly, the purposes of
God. Augustine's approach to Scriptural history is in accordance

74

with the methods which had been hammered out during the three previous centuries. In particular, the achievements of Origen had served to establish a tradition of Christian exegesis which, with certain changes of emphasis from time to time, was to become the rule for succeeding generations of interpreters. Augustine, however, did not by any means accept the whole of Origen's conclusions uncritically, but made his own characteristic offering of balanced scholarship. He approached the task of commenting on Biblical history in no mood of light optimism, and took the view that difficulties were inevitable both because of the restricted range of human understanding and because it seemed a part of the divine plan to reveal much with complete clarity but also, by quirks and oddities, to draw men's minds humbly on to profounder contemplation. 'In his care for our spiritual welfare,' Augustine explained, 'God has so arranged the sacred Scriptures as not merely to feed us on straightforward passages but also to stimulate our powers by means of obscurities.'[4] But Augustine adds that, even so, the obscure passages may usually be interpreted with the help of those portions of Scripture which offer plain and direct teaching. For practical purposes the quintessence of truth which the Church has distilled from the simpler passages of Scripture is sufficient, but it is not to be neatly obtained at the cost of all mystery. 'People must be taught', he observes in his advice to Christian catechists, 'the importance of the veiled truth whence the Scriptures obtain their name of "mysteries" and must realize the value of difficulties and obscurities in arousing a love for truth and in dispelling slackness and boredom.'[5]

Elsewhere Augustine supplies something of an answer to the enquiry how inspiration is bestowed: 'The Holy Spirit, assuredly governing and ruling the minds of holy men in their deliberations about what they should write, has left one historian free to construct his narrative in one way and another in a different manner'.[6]

We are thus reminded that revealed truth is not, as it were, trumpeted out mechanically but is mediated through human interpreters. The Holy Spirit may provide the substance of eternal truth, but this has to be adjusted to the capacity of the prophet and his hearers, or to the taste and presuppositions of each particular age. Hence, it might be said, arise the awkward discrepancies between several inspired accounts of the same series of events, and hence the painful task of accommodating the honoured deposit of truth to the forms and language of each succeeding age. If Christ had addressed his followers in terms implying an acquaintance with our present-day assumptions in the fields of, say, physics and chemistry, He would not only have been incomprehensible to his hearers but also, we may be sure, destined to appear woefully archaic a century or two hence. Augustine touches on these difficulties in his work *On the Harmony of the Gospels*. The principle is laid down that the Apostles 'wrote with the pen of the Holy Ghost',[7] yet 'we must avoid the view that truth is protected by a kind of defence made up of consecrated sounds, as if God were in the habit of entrusting to us not merely the matter itself but also the precise words in which it is to be expressed. The matter to be learnt is far more important than the terms in which the teaching is conveyed.'[8] The Holy Spirit, in fact, guides the Gospel-writers in what must always be a delicate task for the historian, in the choice, out of many incidents, of those which are most significant and worthy of record; yet truth is to be gradually discerned rather than forced home, willy-nilly, by bludgeonings of supernatural power. The interpreters of the divine word speak as persons, each belonging to a particular time and place, and each endowed with unique character and perceptions, so that a certain relativity enters in even where the most august matters are concerned. For such reasons, Augustine concludes, the Evangelists write *concordi quadam diversitate*[9]—with unanimity but with differences of expression.

Augustine, in his eagerness to produce a single, coherent narrative from the four Gospels, makes use of a number of ingenious devices that help to reconcile divergences. Basing his observations on certain rules composed by Tichonius the Donatist for the purpose of simplifying the interpretation of the Scriptures, Augustine explained, for instance, that confusion might be caused by the

fact that one Evangelist describes the whole of an incident while
the others mention part of it only.[10] Again, with a certain disregard of the virtues of chronological order, Augustine invokes
the principle of 'recapitulation' whereby, as he puts it, 'some
occurrences are so related in Scripture that the narrative seems to
be following the order of time or the sequence of events, when as
a matter of fact it goes back without explanation to previous occurrences which had been passed over'.[11] Or, to take a third point,
differences between the Synoptists and St. John are justified on the
ground that Matthew, Mark and Luke 'concern themselves principally with the things which Christ wrought in the flesh and with
the precepts concerning the right use of this mortal life which He
handed down to those who bear the burden of the flesh, whereas
John soars like an eagle above the clouds of human infirmity and
looks upon the light of unvarying truth with perfectly keen and
steady gaze'.[12]

But such devices of historical interpretation bear little permanent
importance by comparison with two principles of more general
applicability which Augustine touches on. The first of these
declares, in the spirit of Goethe's

'Wer den Dichter will verstehen
Muss in Dichters Lande gehen,'[13]

that the critic must be in sympathy with the Gospel-writers if he
is to expound them satisfactorily. Mistaken interpretations must
needs be corrected, but, if offered 'in love', may yet be serviceable
up to a point, whereas pride and deceit bar anyone from perceiving
or imparting religious truth.[14]

Then again Augustine works on the principle that 'the Lord is
King, be the earth never so unquiet'.[15] As with Scripture, so with
all history, the main lessons are, in Augustine's opinion, simple and
straightforward, but a strain of paradox bears witness to the impact
of a Power whose activity now comes within the range of human
comprehension, now surpasses it. In such circumstances, symbolic
modes of expression may have to jostle plain narrative, and it
becomes an awkward task to draw the clear-cut line between such

CHRISTIAN INTERPRETATIONS OF HISTORY

events of historical record as must be taken in the strictly literal sense and those which should be regarded symbolically, not least because this distinction has always to be related to the continual advances in, or at any rate changes in the presuppositions of, the general fund of knowledge. Augustine realized all this well enough, but by way of reaction from the exuberant allegories which strongly appealed to him but which seemed to threaten the firm foundation of the Faith, he cautiously laid down the general rule that literal meaning is to be abandoned only when it becomes clear that the author intended the passage to be understood in a symbolic sense or if failure so to interpret it would be manifestly out of harmony with the general tenor of the Biblical record. 'I do not', he says, 'blame those who have succeeded in extracting a spiritual, allegorical meaning from some narrative contained in Scripture, provided that, in the first place, its truth as history remains unimpaired.'[16] When, however, there was any shadow of doubt, Augustine's pastoral instinct no less than his humility bade him uphold the solid truth of Biblical history, at the cost of frank admission there were some things which he was unable to understand: 'I prefer a cautious admission of ignorance to a false profession of knowledge'.[17]

Augustine's confidence that history 'leads somewhere' and has a purpose arises naturally from his acceptance of the Scriptural view that the controlling factor is God, whose 'right hand is full of righteousness',[18] rather than blind or capricious chance. For, when Fortune is held to reign, ideas of eternal and changeless recurrence oust any hopes of progress towards an appointed end. 'The ungodly man', said the Psalmist, 'walks in a circle',[19] or, in the ampler words of a Renaissance humanist, 'by an everlasting decree of nature, all things apparently change by going round and round in a kind of circle, so that vice amounts to the same as virtue and ignorance to the same as knowledge, while shameful deeds follow after honourable ones like darkness after light'.[20] The point had earlier been taken by Justin[21] that belief in unending repetition, such as formed part of the lofty Stoicism of the Roman Empire, was bound to destroy the value of all moral effort with its affirmation that 'the same things shall ever recur, and you and I shall again live in the same manner, having become neither better nor worse'. Similarly Augustine, in his work *On the City of God*, exclaims in horror against this notion that 'time revolves and everything is repaired and renewed in continual rotation',[22] whereby, as he puts it, the soul which has reached a deceptive bliss would return to real misery and that without ceasing. Such speculations he assigns to ignorance and to the vain attempt to measure the divine power by human capacities.

The popular doctrine of the Millennium, or thousand-year reign of Christ, interposed as a sort of preliminary climax before the end of the ages, was also held by Augustine in scant regard, and those who affirmed it on the strength of Daniel's prophecies or of apocalyptic passages in the Gospels were met with the general answer, 'it is not for you to know the times or the seasons which the Father hath put in his own power' and with the advice to continue instant in watchfulness and prayer.[23] On Augustine's view, the course of events from the beginning of the world right through to its end represented a purposeful advance; he therefore had little hesitation in adopting a theory of the six epochs of history, parallel with the six days of Creation, such as had long been current in Christian speculation.

As early as the middle of the second century the Epistle of Barnabas concisely parcels out the ages. God had six working-days in which to carry out the task of Creation, while the author of the Second Epistle of St. Peter had echoed the Psalmist in declaring that 'one day is with the Lord as a thousand years and a thousand years as one day'.[24] The deduction follows that the end of the world will occur after six thousand years. This range of time has to be divided up into the six periods, but apparently they are not by any means equal. 'Barnabas' offers no clear indication of the limits of each, but no doubt he fixed them, as Augustine did later on, in accordance with the genealogical tables given at the beginning of the Gospels of St. Matthew and St. Luke. In their developed form as given by Augustine, the periods run in neat correspondence with the ages of man's life.[25] The stage of the infancy of the human race, running from Adam to Noah, answers to the first day of Creation, and the light then bestowed by the *fiat* of the Almighty is represented by the light bestowed on the fallen parents of the human race by the proclamation that the Redeemer would in due time be manifested. The period of childhood, extending from Noah to Abraham, is symbolized by the Ark with its promise of salvation for the redeemed people by contrast with the remainder of mankind, just as the creation of the firmament parted one lot of waters from the other. Next comes *adolescentia*, the time of youthful vigour, which covers the years from Abraham to David. As the earth was separated from the waters on the third day, so, during this third period, the Chosen People were separated from the mass of the heathen. This Elect Race was to 'worship the one God so that, like a well-watered land, it might bring forth wholesome fruits, even the Scriptures and the Prophets', but the evening of the day was sombre, marked by the sins and faithlessness of Israel and, in particular, of Saul. The period of early manhood started happily with the enthronement of King David like the sun at its rising and his successors appearing in turn like the moon and the stars, until the sins of the royal house led to the overthrow of the empire and an evening of pitiable servitude closed in.

The fifth day of creation, on which the waters brought forth abundantly as did every winged fowl after its kind, found its counterpart in the period of later manhood, when for fourteen generations the Chosen People were scattered 'among the nations as in the wide sea and had no fixed resting-place, like the birds of the air'. The period of old age is marked by the arrival of the long-prophesied Messiah in the fullness of time. From the side of this Second Adam there proceeds, at the Crucifixion, a second Eve, the Church, who, along with Christ, has dominion over the 'beasts of the earth', that is to say, tames and educates Jew and Gentile alike, in accordance with the arrangement made by God on the sixth day of Creation. The perfect number, seven,[26] marks the fullness of achievement, when 'God rested from all his work' and when, in the periods of history, Christ returns in glory and establishes the peace of the sabbath which has no ending.

Such schemes of historical development as this one, which may owe some of its artificial simplicity to the need of clear teaching for Christian initiates, were dear to the early Church and appealed also to the mediaeval instinct for symmetry and feeling for the charm of numbers. Nor were they rejected by the sophistication of later times. Bossuet, for instance, in the seventeenth century, spoke of the Seven Ages of the World, marked by the names of Adam, Noah, Abraham, Moses, Solomon, Cyrus the restorer of the Jews, and Jesus Christ. Into this scheme he grafted three subsidiary epochs, the capture of Troy, the building of Rome and the overthrow of Carthage, and then brought the whole to a somewhat abrupt close with the addition of two more such epochs under the auspices respectively of Constantine, the first Christian emperor, and Charlemagne, 'the great protector of Rome and Italy or rather of the whole Church and the whole of Christianity'.[27] The precise classifications vary from author to author and are not of prime importance, but the claim implied by the pattern of events as set out by Augustine and his followers is that the purposeful governance of God is lucidly displayed operating, as in the whole of creation, so particularly in the education of mankind through history, which was felt to provide a series of variations on the theme 'God resisteth the proud, but giveth grace to the humble'.[28] It is in history that God 'teaches Kings these two fundamental Truths: First, That it is he who forms Kingdoms to give them to whom he pleaseth: And secondly, That he knoweth how to make them serve, in the time and order which he hath decreed, to the Designs he hath on his People'.[29]

Augustine retained his Biblical point of view when considering the events of his own day also, but with such modifications as might serve to bring it into accord with observed facts.

Pagans and Christians alike felt the opening years of the fifth century to be essentially a time of crisis, when the old order was being shattered by the irresistible onrush of Germanic invaders. Jerome, bewailing the fate of the 'Roman world in a state of collapse'[30], painted in sombre colours the plight of his Illyrian homeland and with his cry, 'What is safe if Rome perishes?'[31] gave utterance to the question which was in the hearts of all. Then, when calamity came to pass and Alaric's hordes 'captured the city which had captured the whole world',[32] Jerome broke into a lamentation which echoed not merely Vergil's prophetic words, 'The ancient city that for centuries ruled the whole world comes down in ruin',[33] but also the Psalmist's complaint, 'O God, the heathen are come into thine inheritance; thy holy temple have they defiled, and made Jerusalem an heap of stones'.[34] For, since the days of Eusebius, the rule of the emperors had been honoured as the type and reflection of the eternal monarchy of God, while the Empire, which had providentially furthered the spread of Christianity, seemed also to offer a firm political unity which should sustain the religious unity.

The objections which Augustine found himself called upon to meet came from both friends and critics. Pagans declared the disasters of the times to be the inevitable result of abandoning the old worship in favour of devotion to Christ. The Christians, on the other hand, were puzzled to observe that a city, sanctified by the tombs of Peter and Paul and many another martyr, and centre of all hopes of a lasting kingdom of justice and peace, fell so easily before the hostile onslaught. In face of such questionings, Augustine found himself under the necessity of presenting a double apologetic. On the one hand he was concerned to point out that the misfortunes under which the Roman Empire then laboured were in fact lighter than those which had visited earlier ages. In the second place he had to show that the ordering of events in history was fair and reasonable, regard being paid to the ends for which God created the world.

That Rome had prospered so long as the native gods received their due meed of reverence was the natural plea of Roman patriotism, and had not long before found vigorous expression in an appeal addressed by the prefect Symmachus to Valentinian II. Symmachus begged that the old altar of Victory might be restored to the senate-house, on the general principle that the established rites had 'driven Hannibal from the walls and the Gauls from the Capitol',[35] and it needed all the vigour of which St. Ambrose was capable to set such arguments at nought and ensure that the boy emperor 'did nothing other than what our faith reasonably requires'.[36] Augustine's answer to pleas of this sort was an appeal to history. 'People insist on the worship of the old gods', he noted, 'in the hope of avoiding the calamities that oppress us, and forget that the men who worshipped these same gods in time past suffered far heavier disasters.'[37] He took the violent deaths of the first Roman kings[38] as examples of horrors which gave the lie to any ideas of a state of primitive blessedness when the gods cared for Rome and protected the citizens, while the distresses of the Carthaginian wars and, in particular, the cruel death of the gallant Regulus should 'cause these gods to blush unless indeed they are stony-hearted and have no feelings'.[39] Roman history, in Augustine's opinion, presented a grim picture of bitter warfare and still more grievous civil discord that made a mockery of appeals not to desert the ancient manner of securing divine favour.[40] By contrast he claims that it is 'due to the name of Christ and to Christianity'[41] that, against all the customary practice of victorious warriors, the Goths spared a large number of persons whom they allowed to take sanctuary in Christian churches. 'Those', he adds, 'who are now particularly ready with their attacks on Christianity are just the ones who either fled for refuge to places dedicated to Christ or else were conducted thither by the barbarians in order that they might escape with their lives.'[42]

Arguments of this kind are perhaps not much more than the common coin of disputation, but the attempt whereby Augustine sought to justify belief in the divine ordering of history deserves more careful scrutiny. *Plangenda sunt haec, non miranda*,[43] he observed—the situation may be deplorable but it need not occasion surprise to anyone who recalls the prophetic writings and the Gospels. 'Earthly kingdoms', he reminds his hearers, 'have their ups and downs'[44] and 'if heaven and earth are to pass away, why is it surprising if at some time the State comes to an end?'[45] Nevertheless the difficulties are not left to be settled by an appeal to a few texts of Scripture which announce the end of all things, and the whole matter is carefully argued. Augustine takes as his starting-point the assurance that the omnipotent Creator 'would certainly not have been prepared to leave the kingdoms of men and their dominions and servitudes outside the scope of the laws of his Providence',[46] and two of the common assumptions of Biblical writers are adopted. Just as Judas Maccabaeus confidently declared that 'with heaven it is all one to save by many or by few'[47] and 'as may be the will in heaven, thus shall He do', so Augustine was constrained to allow that God's ordinance could not be resisted. It is, moreover, equitable, since good and evil are measured out according to the deserts of man or empire, on the principle that 'the Lord knoweth the way of the righteous and the way of the ungodly shall perish'.[48] The classic example of this truth, in Augustine's view, was of course provided by the history of the Jewish people. For all their weakness they had escaped from the perils of Egypt, and been securely planted in the land chosen for them, through the guidance of the one true God. 'And if they had not sinned against Him and been drawn aside, by graceless curiosity which almost suggested that they were bewitched, to worship other gods and idols and, finally, slain Christ, they would have continued to live in the same kingdom perhaps with wider territories and certainly with increased happiness.'[49] Similarly the pious conduct of a Constantine or a Theodosius gained its due reward of prosperity and even miraculous assistance against foes. But Augustine was enough in touch with reality to admit that such intimations of the divine nature and purpose are but part of the story. Faithful emperors such as Jovian and Gratian might, by a queer streak of disorderly paradox, perish ingloriously after but a short reign, and sovereign power over the dominions of Rome be assigned through God's ordinance to evil men as well as to the praiseworthy.

St. Ambrose, in face of this apparent inequity, had contented himself by observing, 'What man is there who is ignorant that human affairs do not always lead to the expected result, but are subject to alteration and vicissitude?'[50] But Augustine, though he did not attempt a final answer to all such difficulties, yet offers several lines of argument which serve at any rate to lessen the harshness of events. Strongly opposed to all who would explain

life's irony in sceptical or bitter terms, he followed the prophet
Zephaniah in having no use for 'men that are settled on their lees,
that say in their heart, The Lord will not do good, neither will He
do evil'.[51] Nor could he sympathize with those who would cut
away the foundation of morality by describing the costly strivings
of mankind as

> 'Lost labour; when the circumambient gloom
> But hides, if gods, gods careless of our doom.'[52]

Augustine's *apologia* for divine Providence in history follows a
threefold course. He asserts, in the first place, that the calamities
which beset the Roman Empire would be regarded as rightly
punitive by any who took stock of the 'corruption of manners'
which disfigured its society.[53] Disreputable pleasures and vaulting
ambition had, on Augustine's view, reduced the citizens to a state
where 'they were depraved by prosperity and not even to be
reformed by adversity'.[54] Even so, God had displayed his loving-
kindness by moderating the misery which was their due: 'You owe
your lives to the mercy of God who, by sparing you, calls you to
repentance. He it was who, for all your ingratitude, allowed you
to escape the assaults of your enemies.'[55] Adopting the principle
'sweet are the uses of adversity',[56] Isaiah had prophesied, 'The
Lord shall smite Egypt, smiting and healing, and they shall return
unto the Lord',[57] since disasters may have a beneficial effect on the
commonwealth by repressing luxury and teaching wholesome
lessons; and in like manner Augustine, unhopeful though he may
be about the Romans, yet realizes that 'the violence of afflic-
tion proves and purifies the good'.[58] But he devotes more care
to the argument that temporal disaster leads men to concentrate their desires on things eternal and to 'rejoice in that they
have their treasure in a place where no enemy has power to
approach'.[59]

Augustine, in fact, touches on a theory that the difficulties and
paradoxes of history are providential helps calculated to direct
man's gaze from the contemplation of himself and the achievements of his reason upwards to the majesty of God. George

Herbert was later to make the same kind of point, though with graceful moderation and characteristic gentleness, in his lyric 'The Pulley'.

> 'When God at first made man,
> Having a glass of blessings standing by
> "Let us," said He, "pour on him all we can."'

So strength, wisdom, honour and other such graces were bestowed till

> 'When almost all was out, God made a stay,
> Perceiving that, alone of all his treasure,
> Rest in the bottom lay.'

This final blessing was withheld lest man should adore God's gifts and neglect God Himself:

> 'Yet let him keep the rest,
> But keep them with repining restlessness;
> Let him be rich and weary, that at least
> If goodness lead him not, yet weariness
> May toss him to my breast.'

Whether it be a gentle melancholy beside the quiet-flowing Avon or terror and din amidst the crash of a corrupt empire, 'chastisements of love',[60] as the rabbis used to call them, refuse to man an easy self-contentment and remind him of the Master's promise, 'In the world ye shall have tribulation; but be of good cheer, I have overcome the world'.[61]

Nevertheless, it continued to be something of a puzzle for Augustine, as for others, why God, in his power and justice, should allow calamity to fall so indiscriminately upon good and bad alike; and, when all the partial reasons had been given, there still remained an overplus of mystery. Bossuet declared that 'the rules of human justice may help us a little to enter into the depths of the divine justice, whereof they are a shadow, but they cannot reveal to us the full profundity of that abyss'.[62] Similarly Augustine allows a place for that element of reverent agnosticism which must ever accompany man's attempts to map the course of the divine governance. In another connexion he had declared: 'You can say many things about God, but nothing which you say will be truly worthy of Him';[63] so also, in the *De civitate Dei*, he explains that 'God bestows blessedness in heaven to pious men alone, but earthly power to pious and impious alike, in accordance with his good pleasure whom nothing unjust pleases'.[64] He sets up and overthrows men and nations in accordance with principles which defy easy definition by mortals whose powers are inadequate fully 'to investigate the secrets of history and determine with sure judgement the deserts of empires'. Augustine means that the fixed principles of God's laws, good following good, evil following evil, become clear enough from the course of events and, if paradox and complexity work their way in also, that is, after all, true of every sphere in which imperfect human knowledge seeks to plumb the depths of the divine wisdom. In other words, the pattern of history displays what Reinhold Niebuhr calls 'tangents of moral meaning'[65] rather than precise and invariable regularity. The Galileans whose blood Pilate mingled with their sacrifices, and the victims of the collapse of the tower of Siloam, are not necessarily to be accounted sinners above the rest of mankind, yet it is none the less true that wickedness brings its due reward: 'except ye repent, ye shall all in like manner perish'.[66]

There is one other fruitful and reasonable line of thought concerning the decline and fall of the Roman Empire on which Augustine lightly touches. Just as St. Paul saw that the bitter failure of the Jewish people might lead, under the providence of God, to the calling of the Gentiles and the extension of the old Israel to include all the peoples of the world, so Augustine seems to have realized that the deserved collapse of Rome might lead to the conversion of some who would be enabled to press on into the city of God. 'It is right', he says, 'to remember that even amongst the enemies of that city are some concealed who shall become her citizens, and one must not regard it as a fruitless toil to endure their hatred until the time comes to receive their allegiance.'[67] However, this part of the argument that God tolerates evil in order to draw therefrom some greater good is not developed, and it was reserved for Augustine's admirer and devoted pupil, the Spaniard Orosius, to follow up this line of thought.

According to his own account, Orosius had been impelled to wander from his home no less by his zeal for divine learning than by his dread of the Vandal invaders.[68] Driven along, as he records, by 'some secret force', he reached the coast of North Africa where he was hospitably received and at once came under the spell of Augustine's influence. Orosius was employed by Augustine as a messenger to take a letter to St. Jerome at Bethlehem and, while in Palestine, he became involved in the tortuous course of the Pelagian controversy on the subject of grace and freewill. Rejoining Augustine in 416, he was immediately set to work on the composition of a treatise, 'A History in answer to the Pagans', which should fill out the argument of Augustine's On the City of God. The precise nature of the task was made perfectly clear to Orosius. He was instructed to produce another more complete apology which should answer the complaint of those who maintained that the disasters of the times were due solely to the adoption of the Christian faith and the consequent overthrow of the national cults which had flourished in the more prosperous days of the Roman Empire.[69] Orosius was accordingly required to collect from a wide range of historical records a full account of the disasters caused by war, disease, earthquake, flood, fire and all the other irregularities of nature and inhumanities of man and then to demonstrate, from the course of events, that the miseries of past ages were greater than those which vexed the Western world at the beginning of the fifth century. Orosius interpreted his instructions faithfully, though he was well aware of the difficulty of reducing large masses of material to a concise and attractive form in which, moreover, 'truth should be preserved and not just an imaginary picture'.[70] But, though viewing his own capabilities with modest realism, he completed the work speedily and submitted it, for acceptance or rejection, to Augustine's judgement, protesting that the assurance of having obeyed his master's command was his sole and sufficient reward.

The theme, like the style, of Orosius' history is a rhetorical one that leads inevitably to exaggerations and a certain lack of balance. Just as historians at the end of the Victorian era, in their eagerness to show that there was substance behind the 'idea of progress', tended to paint the benefits of a materialist civilization in colours so glowing that the restricted and transient nature of human life was forgotten, so, by a reverse alchemy, Orosius neglected political and social history in order remorselessly to catalogue the tribulations of the world. This task is, however, carried out in no mood of absolute pessimism, for divine guidance is discerned behind all the turmoil and tragedy. Though the passions of sinful man and the punishments inflicted by God together make up a sombre picture, Orosius proclaims his confidence that, with the coming of Christianity, things took a turn for the better which will last until the appearance of Antichrist ushers in the final tribulation.

In his treatment of history, Orosius allows for the fact to which Plato gave classic expression:[71] 'Evils can never pass away, for there must always remain something which is antagonistic to good, having no place among the gods in heaven, hovering of necessity round this mortal nature and this earthly sphere'. But he was concerned less to comment on the problem of evil than to discern the profit which may be derived even from disaster. The purpose of the historical process is, on his view, to draw man back to his Creator,[72] and, in effecting his beneficent aim, God will not hesitate both to reward piety and to make use of 'most kindly chastisements'.[73] 'So as to check our indiscipline,' Orosius notes, 'the earth upon which we live is punished by a dearth of beasts and failure of crops',[74] while the barbarian inroads are to be regarded as part of the same process of painful but necessary education. In furthering his argument, Orosius finds it necessary to narrate the course of events and then to compare past with present. He wrote hurriedly and confined himself to few sources, all easy of access and in Latin.[75] As might be expected in the circumstances, his book is not free from errors alike of fact and of taste, but Orosius marshals his material with very fair skill and provides for himself a serviceable framework of chronology and geography by invoking the idea of four world-empires, the Assyrian in the East, the Roman in the West, the Macedonian in the North, and the Carthaginian in the South, whose rise and fall he traces and comments on.

Orosius found little difficulty in demonstrating the constant disasters which had afflicted earlier ages, whereas the task of minimizing the calamities of his own day required a certain amount of ingenuity. Indeed he seems occasionally to have found it no easy task to accept the truth of his own thesis. 'Often,' he writes in the prologue to his history, 'as I was turning things over in mind, the disasters of the present times seemed to have boiled up beyond bearing.' But he reminds himself of the psychological fact that misfortunes are far more poignant when being actually experienced than when they are softened by memory,[76] and he is able to produce some reasoned arguments in support of the view that the coming of Christianity led to a certain betterment in world conditions. Orosius notes that, apart from any question of the confidence induced by hopes of eternal life, the influence of the Christian faith—even in a defective, Arian version—leads to a certain restraint not found hitherto. It is pointed out that the capture of Rome by Alaric and his Goths was thus rendered less formidable than the sack of the city by the Gauls eight hundred years earlier had been. For Alaric gave orders that those who took refuge in the holy places should be unmolested; indeed the general principle was that, while the soldiers might plunder, they were to refrain from bloodshed.[77] Orosius added an edifying story to the effect that, when the sacred vessels from the basilica of St. Peter were handed over, the barbarians showed such reverence for them that a procession was formed and the plate solemnly carried back to the Apostle's church. Moreover, the visitation lasted only for three days and the damage inflicted during that time was far less than that caused by Nero's fire. These particular examples serve to justify the general principle that, by contrast with the unrestrained ferocity of earlier ages, 'Christian times' had mitigated the impulse to savagery, and by such means had reduced the severity of the punishment which falls deservedly to man's lot.[78]

With carefully worked out arguments of this kind Orosius

strove to convince the men of his own time that their sufferings were in no way exceptional, adding that they were in any event richly deserved: 'and so that no-one could be in any doubt that the barbarian invasion was permitted (by God) as a punishment laid on a proud, luxurious, ungodly city, at precisely the same time the most notable buildings in Rome which the enemy could not burn down were overthrown by thunderbolts'.[79] For all the delight that Orosius took in his Roman citizenship, he was well aware of the Empire's weaknesses and cultivated a wider sympathy for other races than did Augustine. He maintained that Spain had suffered nothing worse from the Vandal invasions than she had done throughout two centuries of Roman rule, and it was his hope that an infiltration of barbarians would render the Empire more robust. In that case, the Providence of God would declare itself for, 'if the barbarians had for this reason only been hurled into Roman territory that throughout East and West the churches are filled with Huns, Suebi, Vandals, and Burgundians . . ., it would seem that the mercy of God is to be praised and extolled in that so many nations are, even at the cost of disaster to ourselves, receiving a knowledge of the truth, to which they would assuredly have never been able to attain but for this opportunity'.[80] The miseries of Rome, in other words, are not merely a punishment for transgression but also a means of salvation to those outside the Empire.

Along such lines as these Orosius vindicates the judgements of God, though he is impelled to admit that they are sometimes 'mysterious'.[81] In an age of stress and upheaval, many Romans took refuge in the bitter lamentations of self-pity. 'Sword, chains, famine,' one poet cried, 'all the plagues at one time are destroying humanity. . . . Peace has fled from the earth: it is the end of everything.'[82] But Orosius, though for him life was no laughing matter, challenged such complaints by his attitude of hopeful acceptance. Not only had he faith in God's ordering of history, but, for all his patriotic zeal, he had been trained by his researches to view events on a large scale and without that smack of parochialism which may be discerned in the speculations even of Augustine. By accepting, with whatever regrets, the possibility that a new political situation might arise when the ancient Empire should have passed away, Orosius helped to disentangle Christianity from the State, and prepared men to accept the idea of the Church as the true empire, claiming a worldwide, spiritual authority more powerful than any secular allegiance: 'Rome possesses through belief', as Prosper put it,[83] 'what it never conquered through force of arms'.

Orosius' work, for all its defects, is yet the first attempt at a history of the world, and one which accords reasonably well with the demand of the ancient rhetoricians that narrative should be concise, clear and truthful.[84] The conquests of Alexander, together with the universal outlook of Stoicism:

'All are but parts of one stupendous whole,
Whose body nature is, and God the soul'[85]

had long before made apparent the need of such a composition. Orosius had to hand, as a skeleton-framework upon which to build, the chronography of Eusebius, while the inspiration which drove him on to interpret the course of world events in terms of the divine will was the Old Testament assurance that God rules, and rules effectively, amongst the peoples of the earth.

Orosius, then, while echoing and developing Augustine's thesis that the distresses of the times were in no way due to the rejection of paganism, took the line that such difficulties were the common lot of mankind and were, in fact, less acute than the sufferings of most earlier ages. But such valiant optimism as that of Orosius could hardly expect to flourish in the uncongenial climate of continued dissolution and fear. As the Western Empire tottered towards its ignoble close, attended by every circumstance of military and financial collapse, hope vanished from the Roman world. The hand of God might still be discerned controlling the course of history, but it was a hand stretched out to punish rebellious nations. Perhaps the fullest and most frank attempt to persuade thoughtful persons in the fifth century that God's ways are just was made by Salvian, a priest of Marseilles. He had experienced a full share of the bitterness of hostile invasions, since the cities of his birth and of his education, Cologne and Trèves, were both captured and sacked by the Franks during his early years, and the question with which, as he records, he found himself confronted was, 'why, if everything in the world is controlled by the care and governance and judgement of God, the condition of the barbarians is much better than ours, why even among ourselves the fortune of good men is harder than that of the wicked'.[86] Salvian safeguards himself with the prudent observation: 'I suppose that a rational and fairly consistent answer would be, "I do not know", for I am ignorant of the secret counsels of God'. But, having made provision for the element of mystery that must inevitably mark the relations between God and man, Salvian proceeds briskly enough with his argument that the oddities of world history 'do not occur because of the negligence or inattention of God but are permitted by his wise ordinance'.[87]

Salvian points out that the historical events recorded in the Bible have an acknowledged and special value as indicating the providential purposes of God who had, nevertheless, allowed Abel, the 'first of his saints', to be cruelly slain. Just as, throughout the ages, prophets and apostles suffered captivity and torments, so must the elect of God look for no royal road now. With a reference to St. Paul's advice to the Thessalonians,[88] Salvian shows that Christians are to expect afflictions, which their hopeful confidence in God should enable them largely to disregard, whereas the wicked may possibly be improved by misfortunes if these have the effect of jerking them out of their follies. But Salvian devotes most of his attention to his main and often-repeated argument that, generally speaking, there is no tension between the supposed goodness of God and the obvious calamities of the day. It is, in his view, simply the case that faults of character have inevitably led to punishment: 'None of our misfortunes may be imputed to God; we are responsible for our disasters. . . . We, yes, we alone, are torturing ourselves even against God's will.'[89] Salvian claims that the pages of the Bible reveal God as 'a most anxious watcher, a most faithful ruler, and a most fair judge'[90] who is loth to punish wicked men but in the end forced on by his justice to do so, whether in an attempt at reformation or in final anger at man's iniquity. 'It was due to his patience', Salvian notes, 'that the Egyptians in their rebellion were often smitten, it was due to his judgement that for their unyielding stubbornness they were condemned to death.'[91]

Salvian therefore defends the thesis that the wickedness of the Roman Empire was such that God, if He is to be true to his nature, must inevitably display anger, and such is the writer's zeal that, as it would seem, he is impelled to stress the iniquity of his contemporaries to the point of exaggeration in order to match it to the patently grievous and widespread misfortunes of the day. Just as Tacitus had extolled the freedom and honesty of the Teutons over against the tyranny and corruption of Domitian's reign, or just as Rousseau, many years later, praised the virtues of the 'noble savage' by contrast with the decadent sophistication of the court of Louis XV, so Salvian contrasts the mutual charity and simplicity of morals shown by the barbarians with the taste for oppression and voluptuousness which distinguished most citizens of the Empire. According to Salvian, poor men, upon whom the rich attempted to fob off the whole crushing burden of taxation, used to flee for refuge to the Goths: 'they seek for Roman mercy among the barbarians since they cannot endure the merciless barbarity which they find among the Romans'.[92] Again the contempt shown by the barbarians for the theatre and the circus rebukes such feckless conduct as that of the citizens of Trèves, who, when their town had been thrice sacked and stood in ruins, showed no signs of repentance but petitioned the emperor for a new amphitheatre to console them for their losses. 'Can God', asked Salvian, 'watch over people who are revelling in the circuses and wantoning in the theatres?'[93] 'The temple of God is despised and a rush made to the theatre: the church is emptied and the circus filled.'[94]

Salvian does not overlook the faults of the barbarians but he notes that, as heathen or at best but half-Christian, they enjoy less opportunity of perceiving the truth of God than do orthodox churchmen: 'There are two sorts of barbarians in the world, that is, heretics and pagans. I assert that, so far as the divine law is concerned, we are incomparably superior to all these; but, as regards life and conduct, I admit with grief and lamentation that we are worse.'[95] 'By calling ourselves Christians,' declares Salvian, 'we increase our offences against God; in us Christ suffers insult, in us the Christian law is accursed.'[96] 'Let us not be surprised that we are beaten with many stripes, since we sin not through ignorance but through rebellion.'[97]

In the manner of some Hebrew prophet announcing that God will sweep the corrupt nation 'with the besom of destruction',[98] Salvian castigates the Romans of his day. Though he mentions a few persons, such as the patriarch Noah, who were the recipients of God's special bounty amidst a faithless generation, he does not investigate the case of the righteous man involved in the guilt, or at any rate in the punishment, of his contemporaries. Salvian considers the Empire as a whole and finds, in its decline and fall, not a problem or an accident but a proof that God—a God of justice—rules the course of history. 'In this one respect,' he says, 'we can surpass the Apostle (Paul). He says that he suffered shipwreck three times; whereas we have not merely been wrecked three times, but so wicked are men's lives that there is scarcely a Christian who does not seem to be in a state of continual shipwreck.'[99] In face of such a wilful and persistent course of wickedness, the crowning disaster of the barbarian invasions could no longer be delayed unless God were to degrade men by refusing to take their deeds seriously, and thus to deprive history of its proper meaning and virtue.

CHAPTER VI

THE TREATMENT OF HISTORY IN EARLY
CHRISTIAN ART

Who shall be filled with beholding his glory ? Ecclus. xlii. 25

It is a commonplace that the records of a nation's life are to be
drawn not merely from written sources but also from the monuments which, incidentally rather than of set purpose, declare the
beliefs and recount something of the history of the age in which
they were constructed. This rule may not apply with much force
to times such as our own which are characterized by a multiplicity
of styles and self-conscious revolts against particular styles; but, by
contrast, the uniformity which underlies the richly varied types
of mediaeval art provides a common ground from which may
readily be deduced the characteristic temper of the Middle Ages,
that is to say, a faith that existence, alike in its beauty and squalor,
is touched with divinity. On this reckoning, the course of events
is seen to display both meaning and purpose, in that God declares
therein the mighty works which reflect his glory, while the
tumultuous strivings of mankind are privileged, by his decree, to
colour for good or ill a pattern of history that is not merely
transient but lies, in solemn dignity, under the sentence of judgement. Such an approach to reality as this may, however, bear along
with it a grave risk of romantic imaginings and ingenuous credulity on the part of those who would maintain that it is not given
to men nicely to define the limits to be observed by the Almighty,
and that He may, indeed, be expected to show his power not
merely in regularity and order but also in miraculous paradox.
On the other hand, to maintain the primacy of God in human
affairs is to discern a unity and richness in history which must go
unperceived by those who content themselves with piecemeal
portions of scientific observation.

The learned Guibert de Nogent, who had little use for popular
miracle-mongering and, in the twelfth century, anticipated the

cool scepticism of the Renaissance, yet entitled his history of the First Crusade *Gesta Dei per Francos*—the achievements that God, the supreme Ruler of the universe, had carried through at a particular time and place, by means of his instruments, the French. About the same time Otto of Freising felt himself bound to write with scrupulous accuracy since, apart from any other considerations, it is the mosaic of facts that manifests the vast and glorious pattern ordained and controlled by God. Otto could therefore never content himself with any partial chronicling but was impelled to wrestle with his abundant material in the attempt to compose a universal history, through which often tragic record there yet runs a strain of lyricism and joy. The note of grateful wonder sounds, indeed, throughout the Middle Ages and beyond them. For instance, it echoes still in the tart polemic of the Reformer Mathias Flacius who scorned the contention of the humanists that 'world movements proceed from human sources', declaring that, since God is the prime mover in history, history is best described as the record of God's will.[1] Along such lines scholars sought to expound the truth, which the mediaeval artists, whether consciously or not, assumed, that the course of events is transfigured and made significant because God is working in them and they declare his power; and with this view, in its simplest forms of expression, the primitive monuments of the early Church are in complete accord.

The paintings in the Roman catacombs, of which the earliest examples may, with fair certainty, now be assigned to the beginning of the third century,[2] declare precisely this theme of the wondrous intervention of God in human affairs, for the subjects which recur with almost tedious iteration are those which most clearly proclaim the power of God to intervene in the course of history and, against all the odds, to deliver the people that put their trust in Him. The favourite Old Testament scenes[3] depicted in these mural paintings are Noah floating on the waters in his ark, Abraham being checked from sacrificing his son by divine command given in the nick of time, Moses striking the rock in the wilderness and thus causing a stream of water to gush forth and relieve the distress of the thirsty Israelites, Jonah delivered from the belly of the whale, Shadrach, Meshach and Abednego standing unscathed in the burning fiery furnace, and Daniel, safe and confident even in the lions' den. Then, from the Apocrypha, comes Susanna, protected by the benevolence of God from the malicious accusations of the Elders; while the New Testament provides the paralytic man, healed and bearing away the bed on which he has previously lain helpless, and, along with other such examples of miraculous deliverance, the curious, mummified form of Lazarus emerging, at the Lord's command, even from the recesses of the tomb. Such events of Christ's life as his Passion, Resurrection and Ascension, are entirely neglected, and all the stress is laid on God's mighty works of charity to favoured individuals. A contemporary author drives the point home: 'He who raised Lazarus after four days—he who delivered Jonah on the third day alive and unharmed from the belly of the whale, who delivered the three children from the furnace of Babylon and Daniel from the lion's mouth, will not lack power to raise us up also'.[4] Where this lesson is not immediately obvious, as perhaps in the illustrations of Moses striking the rock, the feeding of the five thousand, or the Samaritan woman at the well, the teaching is emphasized that the important 'medicines of immortality'[5] which provide a guarantee of salvation are the Christian sacraments, baptism and the eucharist.

At the beginning of the fourth century, when the emperor Constantine bestowed peace and a certain patronage on the Church, many new subjects were introduced into Christian art, but there was no neglect of the earliest theme of divine deliverance which had been peculiarly appropriate for times of stress and persecution and had given to those who entered the subterranean, grave-lined galleries a message of hope and assurance.

'Now that other lads than I
Strip to bathe on Severn shore'

wrote an English poet who enjoyed no such certainty and who was almost too vividly aware of the fleeting, fugitive nature of the pride and joy of life,

'They, no help, for all they try,
Tread the mill I trod before'.[6]

But the simple churchmen, as they gazed at the figures which
bedecked the funeral chamber, were reminded that man's life is no
such helpless, grievous pilgrimage, and that the Psalmist's confident
cry would assuredly be fulfilled that 'The Lord delivereth the
souls of his servants: and all they that put their trust in Him shall
not be destitute'.[7]

Nor were such subjects confined to the Roman catacombs. At
Dura, on the river Orontes, the earliest known Christian house-
church was discovered as the result of some chance trench-digging
by British troops, engaged in a demonstration against the Arabs
shortly after the first World War. The date of this house-church
appears, from an inscription, to be A.D. 232 and in any event it is
earlier than 260, when the Roman frontier-post was captured by
the Persians and abandoned as a prey to the sands of the desert. In
the baptistery chapel which forms part of the building a series of
wall-paintings is preserved, and these reveal much the same char-
acteristics as distinguish the art of the catacombs. On the south
wall the Samaritan woman at the well occurs once more, and,
near by, a representation of David and Goliath. This is an uncom-
mon subject, but the names added beneath the figures remove the
possibility of mistake, and here, too, the same lesson, that God is
powerful to intervene in the course of history against all the prob-
abilities, is pressed home upon those who remember David's words:
'The Lord that delivered me out of the paw of the lion, and out
of the paw of the bear, He will deliver me out of the hand of this
Philistine'.[8] On the opposite wall appear three women standing
beside what has been described as 'a large sarcophagus with gabled
lid'. This may indicate the women at Christ's sepulchre, but other
interpretations have been suggested, such as that favourite mediaeval theme, the parable of the wise and foolish virgins. However
that may be, the other two scenes depicted on the same wall are
clear enough. One reveals St. Peter's attempt to walk on the waters
of the Sea of Galilee. He is beginning to sink, but Christ stretches

out his hand for the Apostle to grasp and thus save himself from the consequences of his presumption. Next comes the familiar incident of the healing of the paralytic at Capernaum, but this time it occurs in two scenes. In the first one Jesus, clad in tunic and mantle, is shown stretching out his right hand in a gesture of compassionate power over the sick man lying on the couch, while, in the second picture, the paralytic, now cured, is seen walking away and clasping his bed upside down on his back. Then on the west wall, behind the baptismal font—or, as some would have it, the tomb of an unknown martyr—two other significant subjects appear. Adam and Eve are there, standing one on each side of the fatal tree, between pilasters which indicate the walls of the earthly Paradise, and then, higher up and on a larger scale, the Good Shepherd, carrying a ram on his shoulders, in the midst of his flock. For 'as in Adam all die, even so in Christ shall all be made alive'.[9]

Teaching such as this, thrust insistently on the beholder by the crude, plebeian but often vigorous wall-paintings of the catacombs and primitive churches, is repeated with greater elegance and *finesse* in the plastic art of the Christian sarcophagi. Here, as in so many other fields, the Church took over contemporary practice and 'brought it in subjection unto Christ' by imparting to it new vitality and unmistakable character. The Roman custom of burying the dead in ornamented stone coffins was already of long continuance when the first Christian examples appeared, shortly after the middle of the third century. It so happened that, about this time, alterations in style, reflecting a changed mood, favoured Christian ideas. For, as emperor succeeded emperor with bewildering rapidity, each to enjoy a short and harassed spell of unstable dominion before meeting death by violence, the old triumphant theme of victory over the barbarians, as shown in the vast battle-sarcophagi with which successful generals had been honoured, lost its appeal. The faces carved on the tombs now begin to display anguish rather than pride, and heroic scenes acquire a tinge of bitterness and depression. The valiant lion-hunt,[10] for instance, comes to be associated more and more with the sudden and pitiable deaths of individual huntsmen till, in the failure of style which marks the distressful reign of the emperor Decius, nothing is left of the brave spectacle except a formalized lion's head, resembling a pitiless, grinning death-mask that mocks the uncertainties of mankind in torment. Popular interest and hope came to be centred on immortality, and the old mythology earned its final rejuvenation as a symbol of life and death; as when the tumultuous richness of Dionysiac revelry was used to portend the full and happy life in store for the initiate.[11]

It may be claimed that no mood could have more providentially smoothed the way for the proclamation of the Gospel than this third-century feeling of human insufficiency, together with the eager search for an assurance that 'the best was yet to be'. With this temper the Christian conviction chimed in readily enough that man in his own right is but 'the flower of the grass'[12] whereas God rules among the nations of the world and leads history onwards beyond transitoriness to the unchanging abode of eternal values. Moreover, Christians were spared the sting of resentment or distress at contemporary disasters because they tended to see in these tribulations the 'Woes of the Messiah' which were expected as a prelude to the end of the world.

The attitude described by St. Cyprian as relying on God who 'is well aware of what is going to happen and has a care for his own to ensure their true salvation'[13] is compactly summarized on one of the oldest of the extant Christian sarcophagi, a large tub-shaped example found at Rome but now preserved in the Louvre.[14] For here the threatening lions appear but also, standing in their midst, the Good Shepherd as a guarantee of redemption, amid the direst perils, even 'from the mouth of the lion'.[15] Indeed what may be described as the first and most characteristic theme of Christian art is the representation of the Good Shepherd, typifying the activity of God in seeking and saving, placed over against the *Orans*, a woman standing with arms raised in prayer and representing fallen humanity, begging for admission into Paradise.[16] Not only are these two figures to be seen in the earliest catacomb-paintings, as, for instance, in those of the crypt of Lucina, but they also form a favourite subject on the sarcophagi carved during the thirty-five years from the reign of Decius to the accession of Diocletian in A.D. 284.

In the course of this period the vogue of the lion-hunt or the lion-mask yielded to that of the 'contemplative philosopher', and, once again, the Christians adapted current practice to their needs. For the figure of the philosopher, aspiring to teach the truth about the destiny of mankind, seems to have been originally due to the influence of the Neoplatonists, whose most notable representative, Plotinus, taught at Rome from 244 to 270; though in Christian hands the philosopher is, of course, he who finds the answer to all mysteries in the scroll of the Gospels.[17]

Nowhere is the combined *motif* of Good Shepherd, *Orans* and philosopher better displayed than on a sarcophagus, found near the via Salaria at Rome and now preserved in the Lateran Museum.[18] Within a frame composed of two vast rams' heads, the figures are arranged with classic grace and balance. To the left sits the grave and bearded philosopher. He holds the Gospel, with its answer to the riddle of existence, while on each side of him stands a companion in an attitude of eager expectancy. At the other end of the frieze there is again a group of three persons, for the philosopher's wife is seated there between her attendant maidens. In her left hand she clasps a scroll, as though she herself were not destitute of sacred learning, while her right hand is raised in a gesture of prayerfulness. The maidens are not looking at her; indeed one is turning away with hands outstretched in the typical posture of the *Orans*, and all three have their gaze fixed upon the central figure in the composition, a youthful curly-haired shepherd, standing between two rams and holding a third on his back, as he turns to face the suppliant women. By the emphasis of the grouping the sculptor has made it quite clear that the Divine Redeemer is the answer of Christian philosophy to an anxious world as well as the gracious Guardian to whom alone prayer is properly addressed.

From about the year 280, however, the character of the Good Shepherd and the *Orans* was transformed so that they came to symbolize the *pax christiana* in Paradise, and their popularity waned rapidly in favour of a fashion which, to some extent sacrificing beauty of form and style, sought to crowd as many Biblical scenes as possible on to the panels of the sarcophagus. The events chosen were, at first, usually the stock examples of God's benevolent intervention, with the story of Jonah as the prime favourite. This spirited narrative receives varying treatment; but the theme of re-demption from danger and death is seldom far from the sculptor's mind. It is, for instance, vividly indicated on a notable sarcophagus now at the Lateran Museum,[19] which displays a composition crowded indeed, yet vigorous and rhythmical. The middle point of the scene is occupied by two vast whales, of almost identical shape and size. Their heads are turned in opposite directions, and into the mouth of the creature on the left Jonah is being flung by the crew of a ship under full sail, while on the right he is vomited out on to a shore that is agreeably diversified by reeds and bushes as well as by a heron, a crab, two snails and a lizard. An angler, with a basket on his arm and a small boy to help him, is seen in the act of dragging a fish out of the water, while, above, a shepherd is tending his beasts in front of a sheepfold of elaborate workman-ship. To complete the story of Jonah, he is shown, for the third time, recumbent under his gourd tree; but here the artist abandons the Biblical narrative. For there is no sign of any questionings over the fate of Nineveh, and Jonah lies at his ease, still naked, in an attitude modelled on pagan representations of Endymion. He typifies, in fact, the soul that has passed through the gate of death into Paradise. As though to enforce this lesson, an upper layer of carving, on a reduced scale, shows the familiar scenes of the raising of Lazarus and Moses striking the rock, together with another group which may be intended to represent Lot and his friends fleeing, at God's command, from the wrath which over-threw the cities of the plain;[20] while advantage is taken of an unoccupied corner of the sea behind one of the whales' heads to show a diminutive Noah in his ark. For the sculptor of this Lateran sarcophagus, as for the early Church in general, the course of past history no less than the run of contemporary events was valued chiefly as the means whereby God was enabled to display his works of power.

However, the fact that God had made free use of history as an instrument whereby to declare something of his nature and purpose was perhaps easier to proclaim as a generally accepted truth than to illustrate in detail. The artist, like the historian, found himself required to steer a careful course between photographic realism and unchastened forms of impressionism, and compelled to present his record in a symbolic or partially symbolic manner. For 'symbolism is the law of all the arts in so far as they are concerned not so much with the circumstance which they represent as with the feelings and thoughts evoked by the particular circumstance';[21] and the true artist, like Balaam of old, is he 'whose eye is opened'[22] and who is thus able to draw out from behind the blank surface of things the truth and beauty which a dull and untutored gaze must fail to detect. The primrose by the river's brim continues to be a yellow primrose, but it is something more in that it displays a charm which may be perceived but hardly analysed and which bids the contemplative soul to trace therein some reflection of the mind of the Maker.[23]

There is one form of ecclesiastical symbolism, a kind of mnemonic shorthand, which presents no greater difficulties than does the flying of a national flag as a reminder of corporate greatness. This is the use of devices or badges designed to recall incidents in Scripture or truths of the Faith, and, to judge from observations made by Clement of Alexandria in his work 'The Tutor', such was already a common practice by the end of the second century. For Clement writes: 'Now let the device on your signet-ring be a dove or a fish or a ship running before the breeze or a tuneful harp, such as Polycrates used, or a ship's anchor, which Seleucus regularly engraved as his device, or, if there should be a fisherman, he will call to your remembrance an apostle and the children drawn up out of the water. For you must not engrave your rings with the countenance of idols, you who have been forbidden to have any dealings with them at all, nor indeed is a sword or a bow appropriate to those who seek after peace nor wine-cups to those who live a life of sobriety.'[24]

To take but one of the examples mentioned by Clement, the

fish, or fish and loaves, which appears in some of the oldest paintings of the Roman catacombs,[25] at once concisely suggests the miraculous feeding of the five thousand, which finds its counterpart, in the continuing life of the Church, through the no less wonderful provision of the eucharist by the Lord who comes to be known himself as 'true Bread and Fish of the living water'.[26] It was realized very early that the five letters of the Greek word for fish, $i\chi\theta\acute{v}s$, make up the initials of the phrase 'Jesus Christ, Son of God, the Saviour',[27] so that the fish was appropriately used not only in connexion with the eucharist but also to recall the sacrament of baptism, whereby, as Tertullian put it, 'we little fishes, following the example of our Fish, Jesus Christ, are born in water'.[28] The fisherman, who is shown on the Jonah-sarcophagus in the Lateran Museum, stands as a summary reminder of the same sacrament, whereby, as it were, the fish are caught for the aquarium of Christ and there rendered immune from the assaults of man and the wiles of the devil. Whether the fish-symbol alluded to baptism or to the eucharist in a particular case is not always to be determined with ease. Nor, perhaps, is the distinction a very important one; for when it appears in a catacomb or on a sarcophagus the fish is, on either interpretation, the valued token of immortality.[29]

The assertion is often made that this sort of symbolism, concise to the point of obscurity, is due to the *disciplina arcani*, or system of secrecy imposed on the faithful by fear of arrest and execution. But while it is certainly true that, from time to time, the Fathers of the Church[30] sound a warning note to the effect that the greatest care must be taken to preserve the sacred mysteries from profanation, the Christian attitude towards pagan hostility was by no means entirely one of self-effacement. In so early a document as the eye-witness account of the martyrdom of St. Polycarp, the rule is laid down that no one need court a martyr's death by attracting attention to himself through provocative behaviour or heroics.[31] On the other hand Polycarp himself is an example of those who boldly and without equivocation obeyed the New Testament injunction to be 'ready always to give answer to every man . . . concerning the hope that is in you'.[32] The shorthand symbolism of anchor, fish and so on is, in fact, designed rather to instruct than to conceal, and in this way it resembles the emblems of the saints —the axe or spear which were the instruments of a martyr death, or else some object connected with a famous miracle—which, in the Middle Ages, became the standard means of identifying a particular figure.

But the principle of symbolism in Christian art reaches much deeper than the provision of a series of convenient hieroglyphics. For it is bound up with any attempt, whether in art or in historical writing, to express religious ideas, if only because supernatural truth, indeed any truth where interpretation is called in to supplement bald narrative, tends to defy the neat summaries of logical analysis. The books of the Old Testament, with their primitive speech and deep sense of religion, are symbolic through and through. That is to say, the marvels of nature are valued not so much for their own sake as because 'the Lord hath his way in the whirlwind and in the storm, and the clouds are the dust of his feet',[33] while the course of history gains importance less from its own intrinsic interest than as manifesting the truth that 'as for the transgressors, they shall perish together . . . but the salvation of the righteous cometh of the Lord'.[34]

Similarly, in the Gospel parables, Christ draws out from quite ordinary words and scenes the power to communicate supernatural truth, thus investing his earthly stories, as Sunday-school teachers used very reasonably to put it, with heavenly meaning. Moreover, the treatment by Christ of incidents drawn from Old Testament history as symbols of his own Person and work helped, no doubt, to establish that idea of the accord between the Old Testament and the New which had so deep an influence on Christian art, both in its earliest expressions and throughout the Middle Ages. Apart from the references to specifically 'Messianic' passages, Christ (or, if it be preferred, the writer of the Gospel) explained that the lifting up of the brazen serpent by Moses in the wilderness was a forecast of the Crucifixion,[35] while Jonah's 'three days and three nights in the whale's belly'[36] was prophetic of the death and resurrection of the Son of Man. St. Paul treated the

Scriptures in the same kind of way, employing, for instance, the story of Isaac and Ishmael to typify the relationship between 'the Jerusalem that now is' and 'the Jerusalem that is above';[37] and, in the close parallelism drawn by the author of the Epistle to the Hebrews between the sacrificial systems of the Old and New Testaments, Aaron and Melchizedek develop their full importance only when they and their actions are recognized as prefiguring the Christ.

The view gradually gained acceptance that, in the providential ordering of affairs by God, the events of the Old Testament were carefully designed to foreshadow and prepare the way for those redemptive actions which were to mark the decisive turning-point in the history of the world. St. Augustine expressed this belief by the formula, 'In the Old Testament the New lies hid; in the New Testament the meaning of the Old becomes clear',[38] while Paulinus of Nola put the matter thus in his poetic jingle: 'The Old Law establishes the New, the New Law completes the Old. In the Old you find Hope, in the New Faith. But the grace of Christ links Old and New together.'[39] Yet this proleptic honour enjoyed by the events of the Old Testament in no way deprived them of straight-forward historical reality; indeed it is their historicity that bestows upon them an evidential value denied to imaginative speculations. The matter is summed up thus by St. Augustine: 'Abraham our father was a faithful man who lived in those far-off days. He trusted in God and was justified by his faith. His wife Sarah bore him a son. . . . God had a care for such persons and made them at that time to be heralds of his Son who was to come; so that not merely in what they said, but in what they did or in what happened to them, Christ should be sought and discovered. Whatever Scripture says about Abraham is both literal fact and prophecy, as the Apostle says somewhere: "it is written that Abraham had two sons, the one by the handmaid, the other by the freewoman; and these things have an allegorical meaning". Now these two women represent the two Testaments.'[40]

The primitive symbolism of the catacombs and early sarcophagi, with its emphasis on deliverance from danger as indicated by the

conventional figures of Noah in the Ark or Daniel in the lions'
den, soon yielded, at any rate in the West, to a full and free use of
characters and scenes drawn from the historical books of the Old
Testament. Thus, when Paulinus of Nola restored the church of
St. Felix between A.D. 400 and 403, he bedecked it with a series of
mosaics, arranged in chronological order to display incidents
drawn from the Pentateuch and the books of Joshua, Judges,
Samuel and Kings. These mosaics have perished, though Paulinus
has left a detailed record of them,[41] but part of a comparable set of
pictures in mosaic still distinguishes the church of S. Maria
Maggiore at Rome.[42] The twenty-seven panels which remain, and
which probably date from the time of the rebuilding of the basilica
by Pope Xystus III about A.D. 435, illustrate a varied selection of
the events chronicled in Scripture from the meeting of Abraham
with Melchizedek to the judgement and execution by Joshua of
the five kings caught in the cave at Makeddah.[43] While some of
the subjects, such as the representation of Abraham entertaining
the three angels at the oaks of Mamre,[44] possess clear theological
importance, many of them have no special lesson to inculcate but
owe their place in a scheme of church decoration to the belief that
all facts in the Bible are part of God's revelation and deserve a
careful and reverent scrutiny. They are put forward as objectively
true happenings, but, when interpreted aright, are seen to be something more, in that, as Émile Mâle said of the patriarchs and
prophets carved in the stonework of Chartres cathedral,[45] they
form a kind of *via sacra* which leads up to Christ.

Except for the adoption of some conventional and purely decor-
ative *motifs*—birds, flowers, hovering *genii* and so on—from the
pagan art of the day, the early Christian painters and sculptors
confined themselves to religious themes and to a choice of subjects
drawn from the Bible. It may therefore be convenient to glance
at their methods of recording acknowledged fact by noting the
way in which representations of Christ, and in particular the
Crucifixion, are put forward during the first five or six centuries.[46]

It is remarkable that no attempt at a description of the personal
appearance of Christ is to be found either in the Scriptures of the

New Testament or in the writings of the first generations of Church Fathers. Towards the end of the second century references occur to a relief 'executed by order of Pilate'[47] and held in high regard by the followers of Carpocrates. But these men were Gnostic sectaries, remote from the main stream of Christian tradition, and, in any case, nothing is known of the nature either of the portrait thus alluded to or of the image which the emperor Alexander Severus is said to have set up in the shrine which he built about the year A.D. 230 to contain figures of Christ, Abraham, Orpheus and 'others of the same character' as well as his own ancestors.[48] No account need be taken of the group of about forty cloths and winding-sheets which are venerated as displaying more or less clear traces of the Saviour's face or body. The most famous of these are the Holy Shroud of Turin,[49] St. Veronica's handkerchief, and the various figures which compete for the honour of being the portrait sent by Jesus Himself to King Abgar of Edessa;[50] but all may be assigned with fair certainty to artists from the East or from Gaul who worked in the Carolingian period or rather later.[51] Nor is it necessary to pause over the attractive tradition, popularized in the eighth century by Andrew of Crete, that St. Luke painted a number of pictures of Jesus and the Virgin Mary wherein Jesus is shown with 'eyebrows joining in the middle, noble eyes, a long face, head slightly inclined and well-proportioned body'.[52]

Two answers have been given to the question why the earliest Christians shrank from exactly describing or portraying their Master. On the one hand it has been held that, in true Johannine spirit, they were less interested in the earthly Jesus than in the Incarnate Lord, the Way, the Truth and the Life. But what probably weighed more strongly with the artists who painted the frescoes in the catacombs and first house-churches was that abhorrence of any attempt to depict God which the Church received as a legacy from Judaism, and which testifies to an instinctive feeling that the Divine eludes the normal modes of artistic and historical presentation. Tertullian[53] and Clement of Alexandria[54] had stern comments to offer on the making and painting of images, which was conceived of as a deplorable practice smacking of paganism or, at least, heresy. Similarly, the bishops assembled at the Council of Elvira in A.D. 306 resolved that 'there should not be paintings in a church, or you may get an object of reverence and worship depicted on the walls'. Even Eusebius of Caesarea, who had no particular passion for doctrinal orthodoxy, felt impelled to rebuke Constantia, sister of his royal patron Constantine, for desiring to see and to copy a picture of Christ, which Eusebius had purchased in order to prevent it from being hawked about in the streets,[55] while, half a century later, Epiphanius, bishop of Salamis, was constrained to tear down from the doors of a church in Palestine a cloth on which was painted the picture 'of Jesus Christ or of some saint'.[56]

In default of authentic records, Isaiah's text: 'He hath no form nor comeliness, and when we shall see Him there is no beauty that we should desire Him'[57] led to some surprising speculations about Christ's physical appearance. Clement of Alexandria, with this passage in mind, notes that 'the Holy Spirit attests by Isaiah that the Lord Himself was ugly'.[58] Origen, again, accepts the statement of his pagan opponent Celsus that the appearance of Jesus was mean but refuses to allow that it was 'ignoble' or 'puny',[59] though elsewhere he makes the interesting, perhaps profound, suggestion that Jesus seems beautiful to some observers but to others ugly in accordance with their character.[60] With a side-glance at the Gnostics, who refused to allow to Jesus the lineaments of mortality, orthodox churchmen strove to press home the doctrine that He 'assumed the form of a servant', by pointing out that, whatever qualities He might possess of rare magnetism and vitality, his outward aspect was 'homely, commonplace, and insignificant'.[61] Not unnaturally there were others, such as Ambrose in the West and Chrysostom in the East, who took a very different view. Jerome thought that Christ must have had 'a bright and flashing look about his face and in his eyes, for otherwise the apostles would not have immediately followed Him';[62] and by the end of the sixth century it had become usual to speak of Christ in some such terms as 'of moderate height, with a fair face, lightly curled hair and attractive hands'.[63]

The earlier Christian artists, however, usually approached the task of depicting Christ in a different manner. As if in harmony with St. Paul's declaration 'though we have known Christ after the flesh, yet now henceforth we know Him no more',[64] they strove to proclaim the Gospel truth by means of a compact and unaffected symbolism based upon texts of Scripture. The aim is not so much to represent Jesus in his concrete, external aspect as to express the idea of the Word's saving work and its bearing upon the destinies of mankind. On the ceiling of some of the oldest Roman catacombs, such as the crypt of Lucina, is shown a shepherd boy, bearing a sheep upon his shoulders. The style and posture may owe something to earlier representations of Hermes, bringing a ram for sacrifice, but the rich significance of the figure is Christian through and through. Ezekiel had recorded the divine message: 'I will set up one shepherd over them, and he shall feed them, even my servant David, he shall feed them and he shall be their shepherd',[65] or, in the words of the second Isaiah: 'He shall feed his flock like a shepherd; he shall gather the lambs with his arm'.[66] To such language the New Testament presented an answering echo in the parable of the Shepherd searching for the lost sheep and in the Johannine discourse concerning the 'good Shepherd who layeth down his life for the sheep'.[67] Jesus was therefore presented to the gaze of worshippers in the catacombs not merely as a Galilean peasant who lived when Pontius Pilate was procurator of Judaea but as the Shepherd who bears the sheep that look to Him for help even through the valley of the shadow of death. Outward reality here yields to eternal truth.

When Christ is shown as a participant in scenes drawn from the Gospel, He is, at first, often depicted as youthful, beardless and with short hair. He appears as such in that wall-painting in the house-church at Dura which records the healing of the palsied man at Capernaum. This kind of portrait is in close agreement with the type found in some of the Roman catacombs, as, for instance, in two illustrations of the raising of Lazarus, one in the catacomb of Priscilla and one in the catacomb of Peter and Marcellinus, which exhibit Christ in a fairly naturalistic manner but, at the same time as playing a part in events recorded with the curt impressionism then in vogue.[68] The figure of Lazarus, tightly bound in the grave-clothes and standing between two pillars at the entrance of his tomb, is confronted by Christ, who raises a magician's wand as if to proclaim that to Him alone has been entrusted 'all power in heaven and earth'. That is the whole of the picture, and it is enough, not indeed exactly and fully to represent the occurrence, but to draw forth the substance of its meaning, at the sacrifice, it may be, of some comparatively irrelevant detail. Just as legendary incidents can be illustrated in a realistic and historical manner, so, by a converse process, what is accepted as 'pure fact' admits of symbolic treatment designed to express the inmost, essential truth.

The question has often been put why many of the oldest portraits of Christ should show Him thus, as a curly-haired youth, or even as a boy.[69] It has naturally been supposed that, for this type of portrait, the Christians were indebted to the Hellenistic love of representing the immortals in terms of the most arresting human beauty, and indeed there clearly are affinities between the Christian and the Hellenistic styles. But it seems that when Christ is shown, in historic scenes, as a youth, the influence that has been decisive with the artist is not so much any desire to equate Christ with the perfections of Apollo or to bestow upon Him the ideal charm which is sometimes assigned to the emperor Augustus as to continue the tradition of the Good Shepherd of David's line, shown, like the son of Jesse himself, as a 'youth' 'of a beautiful countenance and goodly to look upon'.[70] The force of such attempts to interpret Christ in Biblical terms is illustrated, rather oddly, by the vision vouchsafed to St. Perpetua and her companions shortly before their execution in the year A.D. 203. For, according to a contemporary account, the martyrs were confronted by the sight of the Lord who, in the image of the prophet Daniel, was 'like unto a man white-haired, having hair as white as snow' but whose face was, nevertheless, 'the face of a youth'.[71] Representations of Christ as a young man generally prevailed up to the end of the fourth century, and occasional examples occurred thereafter, but they soon yielded to the other, almost equally primitive, fashion of portraying the Saviour as an august, bearded figure, the calm embodiment of sovereign authority.[72] Artists, moreover, began to prefer a straightforward and realistic portrayal of scenes drawn from the Gospel story, and the masterpieces of compressed symbolism which suggested and interpreted incidents gave place to a more realistic, and even photographic, treatment which set out these incidents as the artist pictured them in his own mind.

The contrast between the two styles is displayed in the twenty-six mosaic pictures of events from the life of Christ which, since the sixth century, have looked down from the walls of the noble church of S. Apollinare Nuovo at Ravenna.[73] In the miracle scenes Christ is shown as beardless and graced with an undying youthfulness as He accomplishes his marvels with an easy gesture of effortless command. The number of other persons shown in each panel is very small, usually two or four, and the whole composition with its touch of simplicity and *naïveté* is designed to suggest the truth of acknowledged, historical facts rather than exactly to delineate them. On the other hand the Passion scenes display a notable realism. Here the story is told in less compressed fashion, so that there is no need of that tabloid form of presentation which conveys essential truth at the cost of omitting detail. The figure of Christ still dominates the picture, but He is shown as a mature, bearded man, distinguished from those around Him by the serene majesty of his demeanour. The artist still allows himself the liberty to interpret what he chronicles, as may be seen in the large halo[74] that encircles Christ's head; but, for the most part, the pictures were intended to represent 'just what actually happened'. The Apostles at Gethsemane sleep naturally enough in the garden with its long perspective, and the people who throng about Pilate's judgement-seat make up a real crowd that exhibits characteristic feelings of hatred or indecision.

The mosaics of S. Apollinare Nuovo illustrate the story of the Passion in considerable detail, but the artist, unlike the writers of the Gospels, shrank from recording the Crucifixion. The discovery of anagrams scratched on the walls of Pompeii make it clear that the shape of the Cross was valued as a charm at least as early as

A.D. 79, in which year the fatal dust poured down from Vesuvius;[75] while Tertullian[76] bears witness that, by the end of the second century, the pious folk of North Africa were accustomed to mark their foreheads with the sign of the cross at mealtimes, before retiring to bed, and frequently throughout the day. Yet, while the Cross is no doubt alluded to in such emblematical forms as the anchor, and a few small crosses occur, both in East and West, as the accompaniment of epitaphs,[77] no picture of the Crucifixion is to be found in the wealth of mural painting in the Roman catacombs or, indeed, anywhere else for some considerable time. The reasons for this striking omission by the artists of the primitive Church of any record of what might well be described as the central fact of Christian history are not easily given with assurance. It is true that the paintings of the catacombs are funerary, and intended to display scenes of God's power to deliver from danger, which might stimulate the hope of immortality; but, according to St. Paul, Christ 'made peace by the blood of his cross',[78] so that a reminder of this achievement could hardly be out of place in a cemetery. The faithful, however, may well have shrunk from incurring the mockery of the heathen, in whose eyes the Crucifixion was a sign merely of disgrace. Still more, they would often have seen with their own eyes the hideous spectacle of a crucified man, and have recoiled from representing the Saviour in such terms, just as churchmen of our own day, though ready enough to allow a formalized crucifix, find the tortured realism of certain Spanish and Italian examples unedifying and indeed repellent.

Even after the triumph of Constantine had made the cross a popular and victorious emblem, the death of Jesus was customarily hinted at in pictures of the sacrifice of Isaac or the Lamb bearing a cross rather than openly displayed. Indeed the first clear portrayal of the Crucifixion—apart, perhaps, from a few engraved gems the precise date of which is uncertain[79]—occurs as a panel on the wooden doors of the church of S. Sabina at Rome, that was built about A.D. 430. Here Christ is shown, between two smaller representations of the robbers, with hands extended in the conventional posture of the *Orans*,[80] the figure often used to typify earnest prayer to God. Familiarity with the *Orans* would take away something of the horror implicit in a crucifixion scene, and, at first glance, the cross can hardly be perceived. The ends of the beam are, indeed, just visible beyond the fingers of the two hands, which are pierced by large nails, but the attitude of the body, naked save for a loincloth, is upright and free from any suggestion of suffering, while the feet are unbound and firmly planted on the ground.[81] Such early approaches towards depicting the Crucifixion are but occasional and tentative; within a century or two, however, the scene comes to be set forth often enough, in a manner that fittingly and gracefully combines realism with interpretation. As crucifixion ceased to be a normal mode of capital punishment, and as heathen mockery became less strident, some of the older objections to showing Christ on the cross disappeared; and, when the custom of illustrating Biblical manuscripts approved itself, artists no longer shrank from the task of including the climax of the Passion story. The earliest of these pictures now extant is contained in a copy of the Gospels, of Syrian workmanship, bearing the date A.D. 586 and known as the codex of Rabula.[82] It is probable that the monkish artist copied rather than invented the scheme of his illustrations. Be that as it may, the Crucifixion scene, as shown in the codex of Rabula, is of the type that, with but slight variations, predominated for many years in the West as well as in the East.

A particularly graceful and harmonious example is to be seen among the wall-paintings of the eighth-century church of S. Maria Antiqua at Rome.[83] Here Christ is shown as an almost life-size figure. He gives the impression of standing against the cross rather than hanging from it, but his feet, though close to the ground, are securely nailed. His arms are stretched out to their full extent along the beam of the cross, and his head, framed in a circle of dark hair, is gently inclined to one side as He looks towards the figure of the Virgin standing by. St. John occupies his regular place opposite Mary, while Longinus, with his spear, and the man holding up a sponge maintain the balance of the picture, being placed one on each side of the cross and close to it. The somewhat crowded composition of the codex of Rabula is here simplified by the omission of the two robbers. Christ is clad in a long robe reaching to his ankles, and He maintains an air of calm dignity even though Longinus is driving his spear home and the blood flows. The halo behind Christ's head, obscuring the top end of the cross, completes the solemn, hieratic air which is as characteristic of the whole picture as it is, for instance, of the Gospel according to St. John. In both records, the artistic as well as the literary, there is no shrinking from the brutality of the occasion, but the promise of the Resurrection cannot be forgotten, and the tragic sense is, inevitably, shot through with confidence and triumph. Christ reigns from the tree; and those who have eyes to see may perceive the purposes of God, at their highest and fullest, worked out in the rough and tumble of the historical process.

CHAPTER VII

APOCRYPHAL STORIES

He that uttereth truth sheweth forth righteousness. Prov. xii. 17

The tradition of careful scholarship, coupled with the conviction that history is best explained in terms of the will and governance of God, which had distinguished the work of Eusebius was continued by a succession of conscientious but less gifted followers. Three of them in particular, Socrates, Sozomen and Theodoret, exercised a widespread and enduring influence by means of the so-called *Tripartite History*, composed from their works, which, along with the Latin translation of Eusebius, was the main source-book from which the Middle Ages learnt about the early development of the Christian Church. But more to the mediaeval taste than these sober and straightforward chronicles were the apocryphal stories which, making little or no pretence at being constricted by the austere requirements of scientific truth, flowered exuberantly in a climate that favoured pious and romantic imaginings.

Wordsworth, it is true, maintained that the spiritual love of God and his creation

> 'Acts not nor can exist
> Without Imagination, which, in truth,
> Is but another name for absolute power
> And clearest insight, amplitude of mind,
> And reason in her most exalted mood.'[1]

In writing thus, the poet seeks to praise not so much naïve story-telling as that intuition which may, on occasion, range more deeply through the unknown than does logical thought, with its settled rules of orderly procedure. Nevertheless, Wordsworth's 'imagination' is, in some sort, a myth-making faculty, and myth may perhaps be claimed as the tribute that man pays to mystery.

'*Épaississez-moi un peu la religion*', exclaimed Mme de Sévigné—
'thicken my religion a bit: it evaporates entirely when you start
refining it'.[2] And the activities of God, as also of the notable
creative figures of human history, are fringed about with myth,
if only because the richness of personality has a way of rising above
commonplace definition and of attracting stories designed to illustrate and to interpret its elusive character. It is in that spirit that the
Jewish scholars worked when they revised their Scriptures from
time to time in the light of what seemed to be fuller discovery
about the ways of God or when they composed the supplementary
works of Haggadah to safeguard the precious truths of orthodoxy.
'If', wrote a Rabbinic commentator,[3] 'you would learn to know
Him at whose word the world came into being, learn Haggadah;
for by this means you will come to know the Holy One and cleave
to his ways.'

The author of the Book of Jubilees, a pious Pharisee who lived
in the second century B.C., is concerned to rewrite Genesis in such
a manner as to show that much of the sacred Law was reverently
observed by the patriarchs of old even before the days of Moses.
Moreover, the patriarchs are deserving of all praise and reverence,
and any incidents which give a contrary impression are explained
away or else, when it was found hard to provide an adequate
excuse for questionable conduct, omitted altogether. But along
with this doctrinal interest may be noted a desire to supplement
the often meagre records of Scripture by adding colourful detail
that makes the well-loved figures stand forth clear and in character
before the mind's eye. Terah, for instance, the father of Abraham,
appears in Genesis as a name and no more, but, in the Book of
Jubilees, he springs vividly to life. The times in which he lived
were troublous, since the Prince of Wickedness sent 'ravens and
birds to devour the seed which was sown in the land, in order to
destroy the land and rob the children of men of their labours'.
Terah joined, apparently with some reluctance, in the idolatrous
worship then favoured by his countrymen, thus providing a notable contrast to the enlightened virtue of his son. 'Father,' said
Abraham, 'what help and profit have we from those idols which

thou dost worship, and before which thou dost bow thyself? . . . They are a great cause of shame to those who make them and a misleading of heart to those who worship them. Reverence them not.' To this exhortation Terah replied, 'I also know it, my son, but what shall I do with a people who have made me to serve before idols? If I tell them the truth, they will slay me; for their soul cleaves to the idols to worship them and honour them; keep silent, my son, lest they slay thee.' Abraham, after suffering a rebuff from his two brothers, waited in silence for a number of years and then, as a prelude to his departure from Ur to Haran, 'arose by night and burned the house of the idols'. Many people 'sought to save their gods from the midst of the fire' and one of the wicked brothers lost his life while doing so.

The book of Jubilees has much more to tell of Abraham, and its author displays the customary eagerness of apocryphal writers to tear away the veil of reticence drawn in the canonical books over the exploits of heroes in their childhood and over scenes of death and burial. An example of the former class of stories is provided by the description of how, when Abraham was fourteen years old, he separated himself from Terah 'that he might not worship idols with him' and the divine favour was displayed in that Abraham was enabled to drive away the malevolent ravens which were destroying the corn-crop; 'and of all the ravens throughout all the land where Abraham was there settled in that land not so much as one'.[4]

'History', declared Carlyle,[5] 'is the essence of innumerable biographies', and the Church took over from the Jews, along with their belief in the importance of history, a keen interest in the life and fortunes of its significant figures and a pious desire to keep them close at hand by telling stories about them. Hence arose the copious literature connected with the deeds of the saints and martyrs. It is a strangely varied collection of material. Certain of the so-called Acts of the Martyrs, based upon records made by Roman officials and presented in unadorned simplicity, offer historical truth in the severe and objective form of a legal *précis*. Other narratives again, which may without doubt be classed as the eye-witness accounts of contemporaries, are rightly described as historical documents of high value. But, all too often for our taste, sympathy and imagination, together with less creditable impulses towards the fanciful and the bizarre, press in and envelop the human lineaments in an aura of romance.

There is nothing very surprising in this process, nor is it by any means confined to circles where religious interests predominate. The historians of Greece and Rome, for instance, also tend to idealize their portraits. A Cambridge scholar recently observed that 'Cato was hardly dead before his party began to canonize him'[6] while the biographer Plutarch, in the judgement of another critic, 'writes as a moralist not as an historian'. 'It was natural', we are told, 'that a Greek of feeling should look back upon the past through the transfiguring mists of time and see things in an idealized way.'[7] But if such a romantic tendency is natural in the balanced philosophizings of Plutarch, it is to be expected also in the pious record of saintly lives and exploits which, standing over against doctrinal subtleties and careful chronicling, represents the spirit of the Church in its uncritical and popular form. It would be a mistake to dismiss all such literature as historically worthless, but Cranmer was right to describe its narratives as 'uncertain stories'[8] because the authors were frequently making no attempt at all to present an accurate report of unvarnished fact. Though they may so far bow to established convention as to protest that they are basing their accounts on impeccable sources, they are yet concerned primarily to emphasize a particular truth of religion or extol some notable virtue or, more often, to minister to those needs which, in our own day, are usually served by the journalist or the writer of fiction.

The simple Christian had access to the Scriptures, and to traditions, varying somewhat from church to church, which acted as a kind of supplement to the canonical writings. There was not much else in his background of culture, so that it was within a limited field of interest that he had to satisfy not only his deep striving after God but also his instinct for excitement and the picturesque. It has been said of the pagan Philostratus, who wrote a life of Apollonius the Wonder-worker as well as a set of *Lives of the Sophists*, that in his biographies 'the line between natural phenomena and miracle, between magic and reality, is a vanishing one',[9] and the same judgement applies to a large part of Christian hagiology—Acts of the various Apostles, lives of the saints, and so on—with its mixture of reverential awe and desire for such entertainment as can be provided by a racy and perhaps amusing story that drives home an appropriate moral.

The temper of the times in which the Christian Church grew up was as favourable to miracles as our own age is suspicious of them. One of the recognized sidelines of the profession of letters was to relate marvels in honour of a particular deity, and simple folk enjoyed accepting such stories. Nor were churchmen so barren of invention or impervious to the spirit of the age as to fail in the task of entertaining their simpler brethren with an edifying counterpart to the jaunty fables of paganism. Even the Four Gospels themselves had not been wholly exempt from what might be described as apocryphal touches, which are most readily discerned in St. Matthew's narrative. The story that, when the half-shekel temple-tax was demanded, a fish with the appropriate coin in its mouth was conveniently hooked,[10] or the attractive incident of Pilate's wife's dream,[11] bear the characteristic stamp of the legendary style, and the same may be said of another Matthaean addition—the account of the opening graves and reanimated corpses on the first Good Friday.[12] This last episode may, however, be regarded as a genuine, if perhaps hazardous and exaggerated, attempt at interpreting events. The Biblical writers both lacked the modern apparatus of footnotes and appendices and also had, as a rule, too keen a sense of style to burden their narrative with pedantic exposition. The story had to tell its own tale and point its own moral. While, therefore, apart from more general considerations, the silence of the other three canonical Gospels makes it unlikely that any inhabitant of Jerusalem actually witnessed so dramatic a resurrection as the literal sense of St. Matthew's words would indicate, yet the truth was thereby pressed home that the sacrifice of Christ upon the Cross was not merely earth-shaking in its significance but made its victorious power felt in the silent abodes of the dead.

It must be accounted a sign of critical acumen, or providential guidance, in the scholars and leaders of the early Church that they adopted into the canon of Scripture four Gospels and no more. There were many other competitors for favour in the second and third centuries, but, whereas the omission of any one of the canonical four would have gravely curtailed knowledge of the mystery of Christ, to have imported any of the others would have meant that the Church could no longer make a serious claim to base its revealed doctrines on recorded fact. The, often fragmentary, texts of the apocryphal Gospels and Acts, while they may well contain genuine sayings of the Lord and valuable traditions, yet present themselves even to the casual reader as historical novels at best and sometimes as insubstantial fantasies. They possess the fairy-story quality of mingling everyday affairs with portents, but the subjects to be contemplated with affection are not some mythical Lob-lie-by-the-fire or Puck of Pook's Hill but rather the pillars of the Christian Church. The characters are real enough, and it was the author's delight to imagine them as taking part in strange and dramatic scenes. He may have failed even to ask himself the question whether it was right to allow fancy to dictate his theme.

The marvels in which the apocryphal literature of early Christianity abounds have about them something of the 'shimmering and ambiguous' nature of miracle in which a robust symbolism is mingled with accounts that represent, or are put forward as representing, straightforward reality. To take a crude and comparatively late example, a fifth-century document known as the Acts of Peter and Andrew[13] recounts the conversion of a certain rich man named Onesiphorus. 'If I believe in your God', he asked, 'shall I be able to perform miracles just as you do?' Andrew explained that renunciation of all his possessions was necessary, and Peter added the comment that it is easier for a camel to go through a needle's eye than for a rich man to enter the Kingdom of God. Onesiphorus, who had been growing more and more angry as the conversation proceeded, then challenged Peter with the words: 'If you show me this sign, then I shall believe in your God, and not only I but the whole city also. But if you fail, you will be severely punished.' 'Peter was exceedingly troubled', the story goes on to relate, 'and stood with hands outstretched to Heaven, praying: "O Lord our Master and God, hearken unto me at this hour. For thou hast entrapped us by thy words." ' Immediately the Saviour appeared in the form of a twelve-year-old boy wearing a linen garment smooth within and without. And He said to them: 'Keep up your courage and fear not. . . . Let the needle and the camel be brought.' And so saying He departed into Heaven. But a certain huckster in the city, who was one of Philip's converts, heard this and ran to look for a needle with a large eye, so as to do the Apostles a service. But when Peter found out about this he said to the huckster: 'My son, do not look for a needle with a large eye, for with our God nothing is impossible. Bring us instead a needle with a small eye.' The needle was brought and the whole population of the city came along to watch. Peter looked up and saw a camel approaching, and he asked that it should be brought to him. Then he fixed the needle into the ground and cried with a loud voice: 'In the name of Jesus Christ who was crucified under Pontius Pilate I command you, O camel, to pass through the needle's eye'. Then the eye of the needle opened like a gate and the camel passed through it, and the whole crowd was amazed. Peter said to the camel once more: 'Pass through the needle again'. And the camel passed through a second time. Onesiphorus despairingly insisted that the camel should go through with a woman riding on its back, and, when that feat had been success-fully accomplished, Onesiphorus was convinced and cried out: 'I have farms, vineyards and lands . . . and many slaves. I will bestow my goods upon the poor and free my slaves if I may but perform one miracle just as you do.' Peter said to him: 'If you desire, you also shall perform a miracle in the name of our Lord Jesus Christ'.. Peter was afraid that Onesiphorus might fail, since he was unbap-tized, but a voice came: 'Bid him do as he likes, for I will fulfil his wish'. So Onesiphorus stood before the needle and commanded the camel to go through. It went through as far as its neck and then stuck. Onesiphorus asked why. 'Because you are not baptized in the name of the Lord.' There is no need to add that the same evening Onesiphorus and a thousand others received baptism at the Apostles' hands.

It is hardly to be supposed that the narrator intended the details of his artless legend to be taken very seriously. One may, however, surmise that he was eager to force the lesson home that ability to work miracles or to surmount any crisis resides not in human nature but in the boundless power of God, which He will offer to those who, in union with the Church, yield themselves willingly to his service. But the writer prefers to point this truth allusively, in a memorable tale, rather than by means of a homily. Again and again the apocryphal Acts present truth in the allegorical form of a somewhat extravagant fable. The Acts of Philip,[14] for example, tell how Philip, his sister Mariamne and Bartholomew journeyed through a wilderness. One morning 'a wind suddenly arose, strong and dark, and out of the darkness there rushed against those servants of God a vast, dusky dragon. Its back was black, its belly was like coals of brass sparkling with fire and its body extended for more than a hundred cubits. And it was followed by a multitude of snakes and their young. And the whole desert shook, far and wide. When Philip saw the dragon he said to Bartholomew and Mariamne: "Now we have need of the Saviour's help. Let us remember the word of Christ who sent us forth and said: Fear nothing, neither persecution, nor the serpents of that land nor the dusky dragon. Let us stand then like pillars firm fixed before God, and all the power of the enemy shall be brought to nothing and his threatening shall cease. Therefore let us pray and sprinkle the air with water from our cup, and the fog will be dispersed and the smoke will settle." So they took their cup and prayed: "Thou who sheddest dew on all fires and endest darkness, and puttest the bit into the dragon's mouth, bringing to naught his anger and turning backward the wickedness of the adversary . . . come and be with us in this desert". Then Philip turned and said to Bartholomew and Mariamne: "Now stand and raise your hands, clutching the cup, and sprinkle the air in the form of a cross, and see the glory of the Mighty One". And straightway there was a flash of lightning, which blinded the dragon and her brood. And immediately the dragon and the snakes were withered up, and rays of light entered the holes and smashed the eggs of the snakes. But the apostles kept their eyes shut, and were unable to look at the marvellous flash of lightning. And so they escaped unharmed and went on their way, praising our Lord Jesus Christ.'

This all looks like an arresting fable and no more, but when it is interpreted with the help of a sermon[15] attributed to Macarius, a hermit of the Egyptian desert, the rich, allegorical purport becomes clear. According to Macarius, the desolation, the gloom, wind and smoke represent man's journey through the present age. 'His path lies through frightening places, where dragons dwell and lions and poisonous beasts.' The dragon, of course, is the Prince of Darkness whose overthrow is connected with the raising of the hands in prayer, since, as Macarius explains, 'mighty demons . . . are burnt up by prayer, just as wax melts in the flame'. The lightning-flash stands for 'the divine brilliance of the Spirit' which speedily withers the crawling brood of evil passions, and, entering the recesses of the heart, destroys the 'impulses of sin' which the snakes' eggs serve to typify.

It has been widely held that the facts of history often need careful selection and interpretation if their full significance is to be realized, and that those who attempt this task run the risk of going beyond the due mean. But in most of the apocryphal literature the exaggerations are not a matter of the skilful artist who, for all his ability, may yet make a false line or two, or use a harsh colour. Rather they are the products of a fertile imagination that seeks to convey spiritual truth, or merely to give pleasure, by making use of historical forms which are empty of historical content.

An example of the manner of apocryphal composition and the motives which underlay its practice is provided by a Coptic papyrus fragment[16] in which the Scriptural narratives of the Resurrection are expanded and embellished. Mary, Martha and Mary Magdalene go to the tomb, in order to anoint Jesus' body. When they find the tomb empty, they are grieved and weep. The Lord appears to them and says 'Why do you weep? Cease weeping, for I am He whom ye seek. But let one of you go to your brethren and say "Come, the Master is risen from the dead".' 'Martha came and told us of this. We said to her "What hast thou to do with us, woman? He who died is buried, and it is not possible that He lives." We did not believe her when she said that the Redeemer was risen from the dead. Then she went to the Lord and said to Him: "No-one amongst them has believed my tidings that thou livest". He said, "Let another of you go to them and tell it to them again". Mary came and told us again and we did not believe her. She returned to the Lord, and she also told Him what had happened. Then the Lord said to Mary and her sisters, "Let us go to them". And He came and found us within and called us outside. But we thought that it was a ghost, and did not believe that it was the Lord. Then He said to us: "Come and [see]. Thou, Peter, who didst deny Me thrice, dost thou deny Me now as well?" We approached Him, though we felt in our hearts that perhaps it was not He. Then He said to us: "Why do ye still doubt and remain unbelieving? I am He who told you about my death and my resurrection, that ye might realize that I am He. Peter, place your fingers in the marks which the nails have made in my hands, and you, Thomas, place your finger in the hole pierced by the lance in my side; and you, Andrew, touch my feet and see that they are those with which I walked upon earth. For it is found written in the Prophets: Visions seen in dreams have no firm place on earth." We assured Him: "We have realized in truth that thou hast returned to earth in the flesh". And we fell on our face and confessed our sins, because we had been faithless.'

The author has used the various Gospels as material for a mosaic, selecting and combining such incidents as might serve his purpose, and that purpose is to emphasize the unbelief of the Apostles so that their final acceptance of the bodily presence of Jesus may also be stressed. Clearly some people in the community had refused to admit the truth of the bodily Resurrection; and the Apostles are therefore shown as exhibiting the hardness of heart characteristic of human nature but also as overwhelmed by the weight of evidence. The Gnostic heretics[17] are being attacked, those who feed on the 'strange food, which is heresy'[18] and fail to realize that 'He was in the flesh even after the Resurrection',[19] and, as this second-century writing shows, the Gnostic claim to rely on secret traditions is answered by the production of orthodox apocrypha designed rather to give vivid instruction in true doctrine than to trifle with any details of scientific investigation.

In this respect the Christian writers were following precedents laid down for them by those who composed Jewish Haggadah. The Book of Jubilees, for instance, gains its authority as being a revelation made to Moses on Mount Sinai, where, at God's command, the 'angel of the presence, who went before the hosts of Israel' dictates to Moses such details, supplementing Holy Writ, as were known and remembered only in the courts of Heaven. Similarly, the convention observed in apocryphal Gospels is that Jesus communicates secret doctrines to privileged hearers. The Gospel of Bartholomew, for instance, opens in this fashion: 'After the resurrection from the dead of our Lord Jesus Christ, Bartholomew came unto the Lord and questioned Him, saying, "Lord reveal unto me the mysteries of the heavens". Jesus answered and said unto him, "If I put not off the body of the flesh, I shall not be able to tell them unto thee". Bartholomew therefore drew near unto the Lord and said, "I have a word to speak unto thee, Lord". And Jesus said to him, "I know what thou art about to say; say then what thou wilt and I will answer thee". And Bartholomew said, "Lord, when thou wentest to be hanged upon the cross, I followed thee afar off and saw thee hung upon the cross, and the angels coming down from heaven and worshipping thee. And when there came darkness, I beheld and I saw thee that thou wast vanished away from the cross, and I heard only a voice in the parts under the earth, and great wailing and gnashing of teeth on a sudden. Tell me, Lord, whither wentest thou from the cross?" And Jesus answered and said, "Blessed art thou, Bartholomew, my beloved, because thou sawest this mystery; and now will I tell thee all things whatsoever thou askest me".' Thereafter follows a description

of Jesus' descent into Hell, and other mysterious topics, the august
source of the information guaranteeing its truth.[20]

The relationship between the Acts of the Apostles and the
apocryphal Acts is comparable with that which exists between
the canonical and the apocryphal Gospels. In a recent study of
the question,[21] the 'straightforward narrative' of the Acts of the
Apostles is set over against the apocryphal Acts whose affinities
may be said to lie with the ancient romance-literature. Adventur-
ous wanderings and miracles which attest the supernatural power
bestowed upon those who practise them characterize both canonical and apocryphal Acts, but, in the former, the wanderings are
connected rather with the proclamation of the Gospel than with
travel for adventure's sake, while the miracles are related with a
sobriety and restraint which the writers of the apocryphal Acts
have not the slightest intention of copying.

The Acts of the Apostles aims at being an historical work,
whereas the apocryphal writers attempt to spread propaganda,
often heretical, in an attractive dress. Alain de Lille, in his advice
on the composition of sermons,[22] was later to give it as his opinion
that 'the preacher should use stories to drive home his meaning,
because people are more accustomed to learn through concrete
instances', or, as Jacques de Vitry put it,[23] 'Many are spurred on by
example who are unmoved by precept'. Recognizing this truth,
the writers of legend, whether in the early or in the mediaeval
Church, honeyed their exhortations with arresting incidents in
which saintly persons find their principles vindicated by a clear
and miraculous intervention of the power of God.

The form of pagan Hellenistic romances, with its mixture of
amazing miracles and romantic detail, was taken over and served
to create a Christian literary *genre*. Intended for simple folk who
liked a good story rather than for sophisticated persons, it was to
find its most exuberant flowering in the mediaeval legends of the
saints.

The writer of the prologue to the Passion of St. Fortunata notes
that: 'The Martyrdoms of the Saints possess less authority for the
reason that in some of them falsehoods are found mixed up with

truth';[24] and thus he sums up very moderately a judgement about most legends of saints, which can be more forcibly expressed. The imagination, stirred by the thirst for marvel and by the zeal to surpass amazing stories by others still more amazing, has all too often overpassed all bounds in a sphere where limitless horizons open before creative power. Hagiologists write as advocates or poets rather than as historians, and indeed as poets who make free use of stock characters. The various saints or apostles display few signs of individuality. In place of the strange variety of living history, apocryphal writing tends to make its heroes merely personifications of the appropriate virtues. And the miracles which these idealized figures carry out are no less stereotyped. Just as today successful *bons mots* are attributed to more than one public character, so, in an earlier age, more than one apostle or saint is allowed to perform marvels that repeat or 'improve on' the classic types of the miracles of Christ.

Five elements may be distinguished in apocryphal Acts. First, there is the interest in journeys, whether through real or through imaginary lands, in the style which the influence of the *Odyssey* imposed upon a copious pagan literature of exciting travelogue. The journeys of St. Andrew round Greece and St. Thomas' adventures in India link their Acts with this class of writing. More important is the element of aretalogy, that is, the account of marvels carried out by men endowed with especial gifts of God. The Apostles proclaim the virtues (ἀρεταί) of their Master, and the miraculous actions which they are empowered to perform attest their divine commission. The Acts of Peter is largely taken up with the competitive wonder-working of Peter and Simon, and, in a manner which contrasts sharply with the usual form of the miracles of the canonical writings, the bystanders are forced to believe by displays of supernatural power frequently exercised in trivial matters. For instance: Peter turned and saw a sardine hung in a window, and took it and said to the people: 'If ye now see this swimming in the water as a fish swims, will ye be able to believe in Him whom I preach?' And they said with one voice: 'Verily we will believe thee'. Now there was a bath for swimming near at hand, so Peter said, 'In thy name, O Jesus Christ, forasmuch as hitherto it is not believed in, in the sight of all these live and swim like a fish'. And he cast the sardine into the bath, and it lived and began to swim. And all the people saw the fish swimming, and it did not so at that hour only, lest it should be said that this was a delusion, but he made it to swim for a long time, so that he attracted many people from all quarters and showed them the sardine that was made a living fish, so that certain of the people even cast bread to it; and they saw that it was whole. And seeing this many followed Peter and believed in the Lord.[25]

Other features common to pagan romances and apocryphal Acts are power over demons, authority over wild beasts and the ability to make detailed prophecies. Nor are these the most remarkable manifestations. The story of Icarus made the idea of men flying through the air familiar even to such critical spirits as Lucian,[26] and the Apostles fly also in that they are borne from place to place on clouds.[27] Again, the marvels do not necessarily cease with an Apostle's death. When St. Paul was beheaded, milk rather than blood spurted out over the executioner's clothes,[28] while even more remarkable portents accompanied the martyrdom of St. Matthew. For, according to a late version of his Acts,[29] when the Apostle had been burned to death the body and robes were intact, 'and sometimes he was seen on the bier, sometimes following or preceding it'. When the procession reached the king's palace, Matthew was seen to rise from the bier and ascend to heaven, led by a beautiful child, and twelve men in crowns, 'and we saw the child crown him'. The coffin was weighted with lead and sank in the sea, but next morning 'a cross came up out of the deep, and at the lower end of it the coffin in which the body of Matthew lay, and in a moment the child set the coffin on land'.

It has been observed that 'the swarm of bees which descended on the cradle of St. Ambrose, and which visited St. Isidore also, had already deposited its honey in the mouth of Pindar and of Plato',[30] and in other matters also the Christian saint resembles the heroes of paganism. Those who overcame fierce dragons or remained unhurt after drinking poison and performed many another marvel were held worthy of divine rank, or something very near it, whether they were wonder-working seers, such as Alexander of Abonuteichos, or Christian Apostles.

Thus the philosopher Empedocles is made to say,[31] 'It is as an immortal God and no longer a man that I have my converse with you all, being held in honour, as is fitting, and crowned with fillets and garlands of foliage. Whenever I visit flourishing cities, I am worshipped by men and women. They follow in their thousands, enquiring which is the path that leads to their profit. Some of them desire an oracle, while others long to hear an inspired word powerful to heal all manner of disease.' So with the Apostles. The multitude worship St. Thomas as God,[32] and the portrait-painter represents St. John as an 'old man crowned with garlands', and sets 'lamps and altars' before the picture. 'My only God', the artist Lycomedes explains, 'is He who raised me up from death; but if, next to that God, it be right that the men who have benefited us should be called gods, it is thou, father, whom I crown and love and reverence as having become my good guide.'[33]

Closely connected with the element of aretalogy is the delight taken in freaks and portentous marvels. The one-eyed giant, Polyphemus, lends uncanny charm to the *Odyssey*, while, in a romance of Alexander,[34] still more remarkable persons appear. For Alexander meets a man, hairy as a pig, who seizes and eats a woman. The creature cannot speak, but bellows like a dog, and lives with his companions in a swamp. The Apostles also inhabit a world where strange people dwell and marvellous plants grow, where a dog speaks aloud to Peter and, at his command, lifts up his forefeet and rebukes Simon the magician,[35] or a wild ass preaches a sermon to Thomas and then to the assembled multitude.[36] It is, indeed, a world similar to that of mediaeval imagination, wherein St. John Schorne, rector of North Marston, can conjure the devil into a boot,[37] or sciapods, who dwell, no doubt, in distant parts of Africa, lie on their backs and screen the sun from their faces by raising their vast feet as a covering.[38]

But apocryphal writings were expected to teach as well as to amuse, and long, hortatory addresses are freely tacked on to the miraculous narratives. Belief may be urged or ethical instruction given, while the Gnostic influences which lie behind many such works impart to them a strain of extreme asceticism: 'Blessed are they that have renounced this world, for they shall be well-pleasing unto God. Blessed are they that possess their wives as though they had them not, for they shall inherit God.'[39] As the athlete had been the ideal of ancient Greece, so the ascete became the figure most admired in the Christian Church.

Finally there is the element of rather stilted and formal romance. The figures of Mygdonia, Thecla, Maximilla and the rest who play their part in the apocryphal Acts lack individuality, and present themselves as the stock heroines of the Greek romances, with, however, the difference that the theme of true love overcoming all obstacles is modified into the theme of men and maidens who find themselves so strongly attracted by the teaching of the Apostles that they feel impelled to renounce love in favour of asceticism. This rigorism can be carried to extreme and violent lengths. Thus, a youth who had been baptized by St. Thomas murdered his former paramour, who declined to become his 'consort in chastity and pure conversation',[40] lest she should commit adultery with another. The story of Petronilla,[41] St. Peter's daughter, displays something of the same spirit. Having been freed from a chronic paralysis, which her father suspected was for her good, she proved to be so beautiful and attractive that a certain Count Flaccus came, supported by an armed band, in a determined attempt to persuade or compel her into marriage with him. Petronilla begged for a delay of three days, during which she gave herself up to prayer and fasting, and when Flaccus arrived to claim his bride he found that, in fulfilment of her dearest wish, she had died.

The writers of apocryphal Acts thus had certain rules laid down for their observance. The prime requirement was that they should tell a good story, but, as throughout the Ages of Faith, the narrative was shot through with religion, and the Apostles and their companions are called upon to provide classic examples of the triumph of good in its truceless struggle with the forces of evil. In the modern novelette, as in the Greek romance, true love prevails:

the writers of apocryphal Acts, for all their extravagant and tedious miracle-mongering, were concerned to demonstrate the power
of the love of God.

In the early ages of the Church, it may be supposed, the claim
of such legends to historicity was but lightly regarded. For, though
they began to appear in fair abundance as early as the middle of the
second century, they exercised no influence on the wall-paintings
of the catacombs or on any other type of Christian art for several
centuries. The carvings on sarcophagi,[42] together with the early
mosaics, continue to proclaim the Gospel in strictly Biblical terms,
and to find in the Scriptures sufficient instances of the power of
God to render it unnecessary to search for less certain examples in
apocryphal legend. In mediaeval times, however, all is changed.
The artists, again faithfully following the popular taste, tend with
ever-increasing freedom to borrow their themes not so much
from the canonical books as from apocrypha, and many a storied
window can be interpreted only by reference to such works,
which were gradually exalted from the status of imaginary essays
to that of accepted, historical truth by generations impatient of the
silences and the restraint of the Scriptures.

Such reserve was felt to be particularly irksome in the case of
the Virgin Mary, whose appearances in the Gospel story, after the
Nativity, are scanty and unspectacular. She is mentioned once,
right at the beginning of the Acts of the Apostles, as companying
with the faithful at Jerusalem, and then the curtain of silence falls.
Gaps in the narrative of scripture were. therefore filled in from
two groups of apocryphal documents. The former derives from
the Book of James, usually known since the Renaissance under the
cumbrous title of *Protevangelium*, a work which is mentioned by
Origen and may be assigned to the end of the second century or
beginning of the third.[43] It records how, in response to the distressful prayers of the pious Joachim and Anna, a female child was
vouchsafed to them and consecrated to the service of the Lord.
When she was a year old, 'Joachim made a great feast and invited
the priests and the scribes and the assembly of the elders and the
whole people of Israel. And Joachim brought the child to the

priests, and they blessed her, saying, "O God of our fathers, bless this child and give her a name renowned for ever among all generations", and the people said: "So be it, so be it, Amen." And he brought her to the high priests and they blessed her, saying, "O God of Heaven, look upon this child, and bless her with the last blessing which hath no successor".' Two years later Mary in the company of Hebrew maidens bearing lamps proceeded to the Temple where 'the priest received her and kissed her and blessed her and said: "The Lord hath magnified thy name among all generations; in thee in the fullness of time shall the Lord make manifest his redemption unto the children of Israel". And he made her sit upon the third step of the altar. And the Lord God put grace upon her, and she danced with her feet and all the house of Israel loved her.' Then follows the account of Mary's betrothal to Joseph, who was distinguished among a number of widowers assembled in the Temple by the fact that a dove flew out of a rod which he was holding and settled on his head. Hereafter the New Testament narrative is followed with the addition of certain miraculous happenings. In a somewhat amplified form, falsely attributed to St. Jerome and known as the Gospel of the Birth of Mary, the substance of the Book of James was incorporated in the so-called *Golden Legend*, a compilation of lives of the saints made from a wide variety of sources by Jacobus de Voragine, a thirteenth-century archbishop of Genoa. This work, frequently copied and, later, rapidly reprinted in Latin and in almost every European language, soon became the standard source-book for such stories throughout the West.

But more attractive to the mediaeval world even than the accounts of Mary's infancy was the record of her death, resurrection and bodily assumption into heaven. The artists may once again be taken as representatives of popular feeling. From the twelfth century onwards their works in stone or stained glass distinguish seven stages in the glorifying of the Queen of Heaven, and with that arrangement the narrative of the *Golden Legend* is in accord. First of all, when the Virgin had reached the age of seventy-two years and was 'greatly esprised and embraced with desire to be with her son Jesus Christ',⁴⁴ she was visited by the archangel Gabriel and told that 'her soul would be taken from the body' in three days' time. She was presented with a palm-branch, culled in Paradise, to be borne before her bier.

The next scene shows the circumstances of the Virgin's death. All the Apostles were snatched up 'from the places where they preached' and brought upon clouds to the door of Mary's house, where St. John explained to them the reason for the concourse. 'And when the blessed Virgin Mary saw all the Apostles assembled, she blessed our Lord, and sat in the midst of them where the lamps, tapers and lights burned. And about the third hour of the night Jesus Christ came with sweet melody and song, with the orders of the angels, the companies of the patriarchs, the assembly of martyrs, the convents of confessors, the carols of virgins. And tofore the bed of our blessed Lady the companies of all these saints were set in order and made sweet song and melody.' Then, in response to Christ's invitation, 'Come from Lebanon, my spouse, come from Lebanon, come, thou shalt be crowned', Mary gives her willing acceptance: 'I come, for in the beginning of the book it is written of me that I should do thy will', and 'thus in the morning the soul issued out of the body and fled up in the arms of her Son'.

The two following scenes are closely combined in the written narrative. The Apostles, as commanded by the Lord, bear the Virgin's body to the valley of Jehoshaphat, alongside the Mount of Olives. The journey is distinguished by miraculous occurrences: in particular, when a malevolent Jew approached the bier and clutched at it with the hostile intent of overturning it, 'suddenly both his hands waxed dry and cleaved to the bier, so that he hung by the hands on the bier, and was sore tormented and wept and brayed'. Nor was he restored to health until he had made profession of the true faith in abject humility. The entombment follows, and the Apostles keep watch for three days in accordance with a commandment of the Lord. Next occurred the resurrection of the Virgin, when 'Michael the angel came and presented the soul of Mary to our Lord' and, in response to the divine command, 'the soul came again to the body of Mary, which issued gloriously out of the tomb'.

Closely connected with this event is the Assumption, or passing of both soul and body from earth to heaven in the midst of 'a great company of angels'. Mediaeval artists showed the Virgin ascending in an aureole of brilliant light, which is reverently upheld by the angels who may not touch the body itself. Often linked with the Assumption, and a favourite theme with mediaeval artists, occurs the incident of doubting Thomas, who is made to play the same ignoble role on this occasion as he did in the Biblical account of the appearances of the Risen Lord: 'And St. Thomas was not there, and when he came he would not believe this. And anon the girdle with which the body was girt came to him from the air, which he received, and thereby he understood that she was assumpt into Heaven.' The episode of the crowning of the Virgin by Christ, in accordance with the words of the Psalmist: 'The Queen stood at my right hand in a vesture of gold', gained great popularity during the thirteenth century, but, in the *Golden Legend*, is merely alluded to in the promise, 'Thou shalt be crowned', and is nowhere found in the earlier accounts from which Jacobus de Voragine drew his material.[45]

Jacobus de Voragine can hardly be described as of sceptical temper, yet he notes, concerning the story of the Assumption, 'all this heretofore is said and called apocryphum', while his learned and influential contemporary Vincent of Beauvais, whose *Mirror of History* traced the course of events from the lifetime of Abel to the year 1253, declares: 'Though this story should be assigned a place amongst the apocryphal writings, yet it seems a pious action to believe it'.[46] These words, in the expert judgement of Dr. Emile Mâle, 'sum up the feeling of the mediaeval church'. Mâle goes on to say: 'The history of the death, ascension and coronation of the Virgin is entirely apocryphal, but these tales were so beloved that there is perhaps not a single one of the great French cathedrals which does not show at least one episode drawn from them. The glow of popular piety needed certainties, and the Church had no desire to take away from the faithful the joy of believing.'[47] A

similar opinion was stated by Henri Leclercq, a Roman Catholic
scholar who may with little hesitation be described as the greatest of
modern experts in the field of Christian antiquities. He writes: 'The
inspired Scriptures, Gospels, Acts and Epistles give us no information about the mother of Jesus after the day of Pentecost, but the
apocryphal works do not copy this discretion: as for the commentators, exegetes and story-tellers whom the absence of all detail,
indeed of any assured fact, stimulates rather than deters, they rival
the authors of the apocryphal tales and produce precisely the same
result. In my opinion, one must not supply a missing account—
even though one may be surprised and regretful at its absence—on
pain of running the risk that one will be spreading abroad imaginary facts, which some readers may find edifying while others are
scandalized. Truth in history is so fair a thing that one could not
possibly show it too much respect, and a confession of ignorance
serves this truth better than the most ingenious conjectures can do.
The silence observed by the apostolic writings is continued in the
most ancient monuments of the Christian tradition.'[48]

It is indeed the case that, for more than five centuries, no father
of the Church, not even one of those who, like St. Ambrose, were
most concerned to maintain the importance of the Virgin in the
economy of salvation, gives the slightest indication, either by
approval or by disapproval, that a doctrine of the Virgin's bodily assumption into Heaven had been so much as considered by thinkers
of repute. Some were even doubtful whether she had died at all,
and inclined to the view that, like such heroes of the Old Testament as Enoch and Elijah, she had been 'translated that she should
not see death'.[49] The first reference in the East to the Assumption
is found in a turgid, rhetorical sermon attributed, falsely as it
would seem, to Modestus, a bishop of Jerusalem who died in the
year 634. Here it is proclaimed that, after her burial at Gethsemane,
St. Mary was 'made alive by Christ, being embodied in incorruptibility for ever, since He raised her from the tomb and took
her to Himself, in a manner known only to Himself'.[50] Bishop
Andrew of Crete, who had been a monk at Jerusalem, referred to
the Assumption, in the course of a sermon preached about A.D. 715,

as 'newly proclaimed',[51] while fifty years later John Damascene confirmed what had hitherto been a very uncertain doctrine with the prestige of his revered name.[52]

In the West, belief in the Assumption gained acceptance slightly earlier, and first in Gaul. Writing about the year 590, Gregory of Tours concludes an account of the Virgin's death with the words, 'Lo the Lord stood at hand, and commanded that the sacred body should be lifted up in a cloud and taken off to Paradise, where now, joined once again to its soul, it enjoys the blessings of eternity',[53] and the so-called Gothic Missal bears witness that the doctrine was recognized in the liturgy of Gaul during the seventh century, some time before it was officially approved at Rome.

It may now be asked whence arose this tradition of the Virgin's Assumption which, gradually accepted by churchmen of East and West, hardened into the clear-cut narrative of the *Golden Legend*. The answer is that it came from a group of documents, extant in several languages, which are to be classed as typically apocryphal legends. The most widely influential of these is a Latin version, attributed in an entirely spurious manner to Melito, bishop of Sardis, and known as the 'Passing Away of the Virgin Mary'.[54] Although this work was condemned at Rome by a decree attributed to Pope Gelasius, it forms the basis of the story of the Assumption as given by Gregory of Tours, and is thus the sole begetter of a doctrine which, in spite of some determined protests by individuals, was eagerly incorporated into the mediaeval system of belief.

The Latin text is derived from slightly earlier Coptic versions, and the story of the death and exaltation of the Virgin is thus to be attributed to the pious and fertile imagination of fourth-century Egyptian Christians. The present Catholic Coptic bishop of Assiut, in the course of an article which he wrote on 'The Assumption in the Liturgy of the Church of Alexandria',[55] depicts the character of these Egyptian people when he observes that they 'retain a strong and simple faith. One must remark that the oriental, this child of the sun and the exuberance of light, is always attracted and charmed by the marvellous. His mentality hardly loves metaphysic, rationalism can have no power over him.' The bishop comments on the 'noticeable differences' that are to be found in the legends of the Egyptian tradition, and concludes that 'imagination plays a great role, and the marvellous causes confusion'. No such hesitancy appears in the bull *Munificentissimus Deus* whereby, in the year 1950, Pope Pius XII proclaimed that 'the moment has come, in accordance with the designs of Providence, to pronounce solemnly on the signal privilege which the Blessed Virgin enjoys, namely that the immaculate ever-virgin Mother of God, her earthly life ended, was taken up body and soul into the glory of Heaven'. This formal addition of the doctrine of the Assumption to the essential truths of the Faith represents a notable triumph for the popular piety of Spain, Italy and Latin America, from which countries, in particular, there have flowed to Rome throughout the last century frequent petitions signed by millions whose enthusiastic zeal to pay honour to the Virgin was seldom clouded by any awareness of the critical questions involved. A notable feature of the bull is that, whereas the Pope refers to the doctrine as 'grounded upon Scripture, deeply implanted in the minds of the faithful, attested by the immemorial practice of the Church, fully in harmony with other revealed truths, and lucidly set forth by the zeal and learning of theologians', he refrains from commenting on the historical sources which gave rise to the belief. That is because, as one Roman Catholic apologist recently put it, 'the story is not a legendary amplification of authentic reminiscences: the narratives grew up by spontaneous generation'.[56]

There is, of course, no means of disproving the doctrine of the Assumption, for, in the absence of historical data, it is not given to mankind lightly to confine the power of a God 'whose judgements are unsearchable and whose ways past finding out'.[57] It may, indeed, be argued that the exceptional privilege accorded to the Virgin of being the willing instrument of the Incarnation is the guarantee of especial favours bestowed upon her after death. So, on the other side, apprehension may reasonably be felt lest the resolve to match the incidents and achievements of the life of Christ with similar events in the life of the Virgin—the Immaculate Conception parallel with the Virgin Birth, the Assumption parallel with the Ascension, and so on—may in the end be destructive of Christian monotheism. Such arguments may be variously estimated. But the grave difficulty concerning the doctrine of the Assumption that remains when all has been said about it and about is that, according to the recent papal definition, something has been solemnly stated as assured historical fact that has no other strictly historical basis even pretended than a Coptic romance. The matter is clearly put in the systematic treatises on dogmatic theology. For instance, Monsignor Joseph Pohle writes concerning the death and burial of the Virgin: 'Scripture is silent on all these points and the oldest extant accounts are based entirely on apocryphal sources . . . there is no historical argument to prove the fact'. 'The bodily resurrection and assumption of our Lady can no more be established by historic proofs than her death and burial. . . . The first five centuries present an empty void, and no historic bridge connects us with the eyewitnesses of the event.' 'The doctrine has to be based on more or less aprioristic reasons.'[58]

The intuitions of spiritually-minded men, who claim to be able to deduce what God must be expected to do if He is to remain true to his unchanging nature, may not lightly be dismissed, but spiritual insight is not necessarily accompanied by keen respect for historical fact; and historians, however devout, can never afford to neglect the advice which Gautama the Buddha is said to have delivered to mankind: 'Accept not what you hear by report, accept not tradition, do not hastily conclude that "it must be so" . . . . Hold fast to the truth as to a refuge.'[59]

Those who substitute 'Ought-ness' for 'Is-ness' are acting in something like the fashion of abbot Agnellus who wrote laudatory lives of the bishops of Ravenna even when he admittedly knew nothing about them, in the assurance that, as he put it, he could be telling no lie since men who filled so exalted a position must of necessity have been eloquent, temperate, charitable and filled with pious zeal.[60] It is, moreover, a perilous thing to dictate to God what He ought to do—as the people of the Hebrews seem to have shown when they refused to accept the Messiah as sent by God unless He exhibited all the qualifications which they deemed appropriate.

While no teaching can be despised which chimes in with affectionate brooding over the mystery of the Incarnation, to elevate the doctrine of the Assumption to equality with the fundamental truths of the Christian creeds is to abandon the ancient claim of the Church to declare, as its Gospel, the mighty works of God manifested in history.

CHAPTER VIII

FACT AND SYMBOL

Your God is the God of gods, and the Lord of kings, and a
revealer of secrets. Dan. ii. 47

'In history', a French scholar observed, 'everything is a matter
of commonsense and proportion',[1] and if it be asked what the
proportion is which must thus scrupulously be respected, the
answer may be given that it is the relationship between the accurate collection of facts and the further task, more delicate and controversial, of selecting some things for record to the neglect of
others and of perceiving in history traces of pattern and purpose.
There will always be some who, following Carlyle, take their
delight in the bare record of events and refuse the claim of 'a
mere earthly historian' to discern 'their inscrutable purport'. For,
as Augustine Birrell protested, 'the fields of history should be
kept for ever unenclosed, and be a free breathing-place for a
pallid population well nigh stifled with the fumes of philosophy'.[2]
Others, however, will exhibit a certain scorn for historians who
are 'mere copiers of nature', and will declare, with the present
Dean of St. Paul's, that 'there are no events which have any existence for us in which interpretation of some kind is not inextricably
mingled'.[3] Historical truth, indeed, appears to be uneasily balanced
between the poles of fact and interpretation, and tension between
the two extremes can never be wholly resolved unless either the
blank surface of annalistic reporting is to be taken as the whole
duty of the historian or, on the other hand, imagination is to be
allowed to rove unchecked by any scruple.

The writers of the early Church, no less than the secular historians, make their approach to reality by varied paths. Sober
chronicle, based on a carefully constructed scheme of dating, could
never be neglected by generations which attributed something of
canonical authority to the work of Eusebius. But this staid and
cautious method of immortalizing the past is, as Eusebius himself

showed, by no means incompatible with the discovery of a Guiding Principle which alone gives significance to the course of events or with the recognition of history as a divinely appointed means of education. Cassiodorus, writing in the sixth century, put the matter thus: 'In addition to the various writers of treatises, Christian studies also possess narrators of history who, calm in their ecclesiastical gravity, relate the shifting stir of events and the unstable history of kingdoms with eloquent but cautious splendour. . . . They strive to assign nothing to chance, nothing to the weak power of the gods, as pagans have done, but to attribute all things truly to the will of the Creator.'[4] The rhythm in most history-writing, and not least in that which is concerned with the affairs of religion, thus appears as a twofold one—long and patient analysis varied, as the course of events is unrolled, by moments of comprehension and synthesis.[5] In other words, the collection of facts demands as its complement the skill which arranges and interprets them. There are, moreover, the popular undertones of history, which, since they help to make up 'the spirit of the age', the sensitive historian may hardly disregard.

In the early Church, these undertones ring clear enough. First there is hope, the strong hope that is discerned most readily in the catacomb paintings or carved sarcophagi. With their avoidance of novelty and their backward look at the well-known Biblical stories of deliverance in the past as the pledge of future confidence in a God who always acts in character and true to type, these works display, in homespun fashion, what Spinoza thought to be the 'very essence of religion; belief in a Supreme Being who delights in Justice and Mercy'.[6] Growing up alongside, but distinct from, this artless hope of salvation, appeared the exuberant crop of wonder-tales, composed, it may well be, in a spirit of half-serious fantasy but accepted with eager literalness by later generations intoxicated with the joy of believing. Such miraculous stories may link earth more closely to heaven, but they also serve, at least in the judgement of J. A. Froude, to 'swathe authentic figures in an envelope of legend through which usually no trace of the genuine lineaments is allowed to penetrate'.[7]

The succession of straightforward, sensible writers who, ac-knowledging the inspiration of Eusebius, sought to continue his methodical work, mingle these varied strands in that they exhibit, along with much competent chronicling, a determination to draw out the meaning and purpose of history from behind its blank mask of everyday affairs. Nor were they always above yielding to the charm of miraculous accounts which had sometimes little to commend them, save, perhaps, an awareness that Heaven lies about the deeds of man. Foremost among these fifth-century disciples of Eusebius comes Socrates Scholasticus, of Constantin-ople, who carried the story of the early Church on from the Council of Nicaea to the year A.D. 439, in the reign of Theodosius II. A lawyer with an interest in theology, Socrates made careful use of good sources both written and oral. Having no taste for party strife, he was enabled to take a cool and dispassionate interest in the affairs of the day, and concerned himself with political and even military matters no less than with questions of doctrine, on the ground that secular and religious affairs are bound together 'by a kind of sympathy'.[8] The personality of emperors rather than of bishops attracted his attention, since, though he deplored flattery and extravagant panegyric,[9] he realized that 'from the time when the emperors began to adopt the Christian faith, the fortunes of the Church have been dependent on them, and councils of very great importance have been held, and are held, at their command'.[10] The dominant theme of Socrates' work is the dis-turbance caused by heretics in Church and State, and, as a prudent, law-abiding citizen, he deplores the way in which the good order of the Empire is threatened by bickering over ecclesiastical subtle-ties. Yet he preserves his somewhat detached attitude even with regard to heretics, and is prepared to judge them more soberly than Eusebius did. For instance, though he viewed Nestorius with neither affection nor respect, he examined the heresiarch's works with care and avowedly refused to depreciate him in order to gratify the orthodox, thinking that Nestorius, though misled by ignorance and a *penchant* for rhetorical display, was innocent of the Unitarian learnings that had been alleged against him.[11] Indeed, his dislike of the polemical temper and of episcopal pretensions caused him to show marked lack of sympathy with such vigorous prelates as John Chrysostom and Cyril of Alexandria.[12] Though his work is not without its faults, Socrates achieves considerable success in his aim to present ecclesiastical history in clear and simple words, 'not bothering about majestic style but noting down what I found in the written records or heard from reliable informants'.[13]

Sozomen, another lawyer of Constantinople, also wrote a Church history, designed to cover more or less the same period as that treated by Socrates, from whose work he borrows freely but without acknowledgement. Sozomen's background differs from that of Socrates in that, whereas the latter was a townsman and received his early education from pagan grammarians, Sozomen was brought up in the village of Bethalia, near Gaza, in an atmosphere of pious credulity. His grandfather had been converted by Hilarion, the disciple of Antony of Egypt, and Sozomen not unnaturally interests himself in the ascetes of the desert. His history therefore abounds in digressions concerning the lives and miraculous achievements of monks, whom he regards as representing Christianity at its highest and best. Nevertheless he lays it down as his guiding principle that 'a historian must regard everything as secondary to Truth', and declares that, in order to maintain strict accuracy, he had paid close attention to the means of eliciting the facts, and had examined the documents that set forward heretical opinions as well as those which favoured orthodoxy.[14] Sozomen, like Socrates, arranges his material in accordance with the reigns of the emperors and matches this annalistic method with his sober, impersonal style. He tries to be fair to opponents as well as to friends, guarding, however, against any possible misconceptions by stating that such praise as he may bestow on the heretics refers to their eloquence rather than to their teachings. Sozomen appears to have striven towards his ideal of veracity by attempting to check and revise what Socrates had written and by undertaking a fuller examination of the appropriate sources.[15] But his own *Ecclesiastical History* shows some signs of hasty composition, and there is a streak of *naïveté* in it which allows such creatures as dragons to make an occasional appearance. Closely linked with these two successors of Eusebius comes Theodoret, bishop of Cyrus. In the composition of his Church history, which covers the years from 323 to 428, Theodoret makes full and free use of the slightly earlier work of Socrates and Sozomen and, while he adds little of substance to their record, his quotations from original documents, even though sometimes marred by inaccuracy, are of much value.[16] He concerned himself principally with the Arian controversies, which he reviews in a partisan spirit, tending to blacken or whitewash the leading figures as they appear, in strict accordance with their ecclesiastical allegiances.

In spite of certain characteristic differences, Socrates, Sozomen and Theodoret form a 'synoptic' group of authors, whose points of view, like the range of their enquiries, reveal close similarity. In the first place, they take up and emphasize Eusebius' dualistic presentation of facts whereby God and the Devil are shown forth as the protagonists on the stage of history; and they look back to a primitive purity of Christian doctrine and manners which had been marred by the machinations of the heretics. Socrates, indeed, implies that it is precisely the disturbance caused by heretical activities that spurs the Church historian to his task. 'I thought it right,' he says, 'since vain and crafty disputations have confused the true faith, to record what the churches used to stand for.'[17] Theodoret, in particular, is very clear in his belief that the heretics provide manifest examples of the mischievous plots which the Devil lays against the Church.[18]

The three historians propound a second doctrine, by no means peculiar to them, that the fortune or misfortune of a reign depends on the piety of the emperor. In this respect they are at one with the Old Testament writers, whose aim it was to establish the principle of God's justice. 'Never have I yet seen the righteous man forsaken nor his seed begging their bread',[19] declares the Psalmist in defiance of what must sometimes have been his personal observation, and Socrates, Sozomen and Theodoret pursue the same line of thought with a consistency which can become disingenuous. The

fate of Julian, for instance, is put forward as a classic example of
the misfortune which must be expected by an apostate, but the
circumstance that his successor Jovian suddenly died after a reign
of only eight months is either glossed over in silence or used to
illustrate the principle that God in his mercy supplies blessings and
then withdraws them as a sign of man's iniquity. The inclination
of these three historians to press facts in support of a theory is to
be referred not to craftiness or perversity but to the desire to edify
and instruct which is one of the justifications for history-writing.
With the same object, records of miracles which, in the mediaeval
manner, closely interweave things human and divine, are allowed
to find their way into sober chronicling.

Socrates, Sozomen and Theodoret resemble Eusebius in that
they state facts without developing any further enquiry into causation than to refer it to the will of God. Their style of narrative
smacks of colourless reporting rather than of any joy in artistic
creation, while the characters have a stiffness and lack of individuality that make them resemble a row of Byzantine portraits
painted by men who knew nothing of perspective.[20] Their work,
however, is by no means to be despised. They make no attempt
to supersede the *Ecclesiastical History* of Eusebius, which soon came
to be regarded with unquestioning respect. Indeed, Theodoret
explicitly states: 'I will make the conclusion of Eusebius' work the
starting-point of my exposition'.[21] But they collected and arranged
a great deal of material, and, for all the limitations imposed upon
them by their lack of genius, they were driven on by their majestic
theme to invest history with high value and dignity.

Whereas Herodotus of old had directed his attention primarily
to the laws and customs of the peoples which interested him, while
Thucydides almost restricted his field to military history in accordance with the maxim of Heraclitus that 'war is the father of all
things',[22] early Church history had what Croce calls 'a spiritual
value as its subject, by means of which it illuminates and judges
facts'. We may invite Croce to continue his exposition. 'Ecclesiastical history', he says, 'now appears, no longer that of Athens
or of Rome, but of religion and of the Church which represented

it in its strifes and in its triumphs—that is to say, the strifes and triumphs of the truth. . . . And since history becomes history of the truth with Christianity, it abandons at the same time the fortuitous and chance, to which the ancients had often subjected it, and recognizes its own proper law, which is no longer a natural law, blind fate, or even the influences of the stars, but rationality, intelligence, providence. This conception was not unknown to ancient philosophy, but is now set free from the frost of intellectualism and abstractionism and becomes warm and fruitful. Providence guides and disposes the course of events, directing them to an end, permitting evils as punishments and as instruments of education, determining the greatness and the catastrophes of empires, in order to prepare the Kingdom of God. This means that for the first time is really broken the circle of the perpetual return of human affairs to their starting-point; history for the first time is here understood as progress, a progress that the ancient historians did not succeed in discovering save in rare glimpses, thus falling into inconsolable pessimism, whereas Christian pessimism is irradiated by hope.'[23]

A contemporary of these Eastern historians and, like two of them, trained up to the practice of the law, Sulpicius Severus[24] stands out amongst those who continued the tradition of Christian history-writing in the western half of the Empire. The untimely death of his wife caused him, in the words of his friend Paulinus of Nola, 'with a sudden impulse to throw off the yoke of servitude to earthly things, even though he bore away the palm for eloquence'[25] and, under the influence of St. Martin of Tours, to adopt the monastic life. He at first played some part in the Pelagian controversy, but, having been guilty of what he came to regard as indiscreet loquacity, he imposed upon himself the penance of life-long silence and settled down to the task of historical composition. As the result, so he informs us, of many requests, he undertook to supply a concise outline of events from the beginning of the world down to his own times, thus testifying to the unity and interdependence of mankind and to the universal providence of the one God who interests himself in the destiny of every nation.[26] The task, he explains, is a heavy one, since the contents of many volumes had to be compressed into two short books, and 'with all my zeal for brevity I yet strove to omit nothing that happened'.[27] After the warning that his abbreviation of the Biblical stories could not be regarded as exempting his readers from consulting the originals, he starts off, briskly enough, in his careful, annalistic fashion, though the events of the New Testament are left out, 'lest the concise nature of the narrative should detract from the dignity of the subject-matter'.

The notes on the history of the early Church, though extremely compact, give evidence not merely of critical ability but also of a command of Tacitean prose-style, and, even if the work is slight, it yet displays that feeling for accurate presentation of material which Eusebius bequeathed to his successors. Fifth-century churchmen, however, tended to disregard this painstaking *Chronicle* by comparison with a less scholarly work of Sulpicius, the biography of his hero St. Martin. The author makes his purpose clear: 'I think that I shall perform a worth-while duty if I describe the life of so holy a man, knowing that it will prove an example to others in the future'.[28] He protests the reliability of his account: 'Now I beg my readers to believe my story. They must realise that I have not written down anything without careful investigation; indeed I should have chosen to remain silent rather than tell untruths.' Yet Sulpicius, though accepted by later critics as the 'cautious guardian of truth and accurate narrator'[29] which his *Chronicle* shows him to be, felt obliged to express the sympathy and reverence which he felt for St. Martin by relating a colourful series of wonder-stories about him. Martin restores to life a slave who had hanged himself; he climbs on to the roof of a burning house and bids the flames retreat; he outwits the Devil who, appearing in a variety of human forms, plays tricks of fiendish ingenuity. The author's appreciation of his hero is shown not by abstract comments but, in the fashion of the times, by concrete examples of remarkable deeds which could be carried out only by a wise and saintly man. The exaggerations found in this work of an otherwise accurate historian, though perhaps in some respects blameworthy, yet testify to the depth of the impression which St. Martin made on his contemporaries. Habits of sober and systematic narrative yield to the romance of holiness.

Socrates and Sozomen in the East, and Sulpicius Severus in the West, represent that dominant tradition in early Church history which, though claiming no divine exemption from error, yet aimed at observing the 'faithful sincerity'[30] which the pagan Ammianus held to be the sure foundation of historical writing.

The Victorian scholar who noted that 'ecclesiastical history is a solemn and melancholy lesson that the best, even the most sacred, cause will eventually suffer by the least departure from truth'[31] did but echo the warnings of a far-off age. St. Augustine, at any rate, displayed his vigilant zeal for the truth by the rebuff which he administered to Jerome in anger at his explanation of the passage in the Epistle to the Galatians where St. Paul accuses St. Peter of inconstant timidity. Jerome had avoided the scandal of a fracas between two leading apostles by suggesting that the whole affair was an '*officiosum mendacium*', a piece of trumped-up play-acting carried through with the object of conveying instruction. But Augustine saw quite clearly that once falsehood of any kind is admitted into Scriptural history, however praiseworthy the end may be which is served by such questionable means, the authority of the Biblical record is undermined. 'We must make the effort', he says, 'to bring a man to the knowledge of Holy Scripture in such a fashion that he would take so reverent and honest a view of the sacred books as to refuse to be gratified by well-meant falsehoods anywhere in them, and would rather pass over what he fails to understand than prefer his own interpretation to their truth.'[32] Augustine realized that there might be 'well-meant falsehoods even about the praise of God, designed to inflame love for Him in men comparatively hard of heart' but he knew also that once such fictitious matter had been admitted into 'holy books', or indeed any other kind of literature, 'nowhere therein could the authority of truth stand unchallenged'.

Such championship of honesty in historical record is one of the established principles which own no boundary of age or clime. The satirist Lucian recurs again and again to the plea that 'History has this and this only for its own; if a man will start upon it he must sacrifice to no god but Truth; he must neglect all else; his sole and unerring guide is this—to think not of those who are listening to him now, but of the yet unborn who shall seek his converse'.[33] Yet this task, for all its ring of simplicity, demands rare qualities of tact and insight. A certain scorn is reserved for persons sometimes known as 'undertakers who lay out the corpse of history',[34] men who carefully record facts but fail to draw out their coherence and import. For Plato's famous doctrine of 'ideas' is a reminder that reality is not just a matter of bare, outward seeming, but is found only in that sphere where everyday appearances are interpreted and shown forth in their full and final significance. Whatever other pitfalls may have confronted them, Christian historians were at least spared from that rationalistic temper which dehumanizes history and, in the manner of Voltaire, reduces the complex causes of events to some such lowest common factors as 'climate' and blind chance.

'Chance', said Bossuet, 'is but a name wherewith we conceal our ignorance',[35] and the reluctance of even the most sophisticated historians to rest content with impersonal fortune as the controlling factor in events may be illustrated by the example of Polybius. Starting off in the strictest mood of scientific detachment, Polybius at times appeared able even to do without 'chance' and to solve all the historian's problems in terms of mechanical law. 'Of what use to the sick', he wrote, 'is the physician who is ignorant of the causes of bodily conditions, and of what use is the statesman who cannot divine how, why and whence each event has originated?'[36] On this reckoning it is no difficult task to forecast the future: 'A regular course is appointed by nature in which constitutions change, are transformed and finally return to their original state. Anyone who clearly perceives this may perhaps be wrong in his estimate of the time the process will take, but, so long as he lays animosity and envy aside when he makes his calculations, he will seldom be mistaken as regards the stage of growth or decline at which a particular constitution has arrived, or the point at which it will undergo some decisive change.'[37]

But, as he contemplated the destiny of men and nations, Polybius found certain intractable elements which eluded clear-cut rules and precise definition. Fortune has therefore to be invoked after all, and that not so much in the Thucydidean sense of 'accident' as in a form scarcely to be distinguished from Providence. In a speech put into the mouth of the famous orator Demetrius of Phalerum, Polybius maintains that 'Fortune always defeats our expectations by some novel stroke, and displays her power by the surprises which she gives us. She now makes it clear to mankind that, by raising the Macedonians into the prosperous position which the Persians once enjoyed, she has merely lent them these blessings until she decides on some other manner of treating them.'[38] Fifty-three years later the monarchy of Macedon fell, 'so that', the speaker concludes, 'anybody who wished to comment on these events might well describe what happened as a heaven-sent visitation and say that the wrath of God fell upon the Macedonians'.[39] At this point, Polybius the detached man of the world seems almost to merge in Polybius the prophet who, impatient of history explained in terms of utility or pleasure, might even echo, as did the Christian historians: 'The Lord hath prepared his seat in heaven, and his kingdom ruleth over all'.[40]

Something like the same experience befell von Ranke, greatest of German historians and widely acclaimed in the nineteenth century for his skill in applying to historical studies the scientific technique which had gained such notable success in other fields. 'So long as history was regarded as an art,' proclaimed J. B. Bury, 'the sanctions of truth and accuracy could not be severe. Not till the scientific period began did laxity in representing facts come to be branded as criminal.'[41] And Ranke was an historian after Bury's heart. Consumed by a passion for documents and aspiring to banish all traces of enthusiasm and partisanship from his mind, he took critical, colourless statement as his aim, and adopted an austere objective for his world-history: 'it will simply show how things actually happened'.[42] So, when a literary bishop who had composed a brochure on the Reformation eagerly hailed him as a comrade, Ranke retorted: 'You are in the first place a Christian. I am a historian. There is a gulf between us.' Ranke condemned inaccuracy even in the pages of a novel. 'I was offended', he wrote, 'by Scott's treatment of Charles the Bold and Louis XI in his *Quentin Durward* which was in complete contradiction to the historical sources. I studied Commines and convinced myself that a Charles the Bold and a Louis XI, as portrayed by Scott, never existed. This the estimable and learned author knew himself, but I could not forgive him that in his story he presented outlines which were thoroughly unhistorical and which he gave in such a way as if he believed them. . . . I conceived the idea that in my works I would avoid all fabrication and fiction, and stick severely to facts.'[43] However, for all Ranke's claim to approach his task in a mood of dispassionate accuracy, he yet professed the solemn purpose that 'all my attempts should be devoted to the perception of the living God, the God of our nations and of the world'. And, when history is seen to draw within its orbit majestic workings of the divine power, then zeal for the neat patterns of truth has to walk side by side with awareness of mystery.

It would seem that historians of the future—those who accept careful honesty as their unquestioned aim—may yet have to struggle with the answers to three questions. They may perhaps ask whether, and on what principles, selection of facts for record, with the implication that much is purposely left untold, leads to clear understanding; they may enquire how far historical truth is relative to the capacities of those who report and receive it, and they may even toy with the idea that exaggeration is sometimes allowable in order to balance what has been left out. The early Christian historians, for the most part, refrained from such academic speculations, but their work testifies to an awareness, no doubt instinctive rather than carefully reasoned, that such problems exist. The strain of exaggeration that accompanied attempts to throw into clear relief such revered figures as St. Martin, though hazardous and opening a way for ridicule, yet finds some defence in unexpected quarters. Ranke, for instance, to take him again as an example, deals with the subject of biographies in a manner that might seem at variance with the strictly scientific method for which he is famed. 'It is striking', he writes, 'how history, when resting on the memory of men, always touches the bounds of mythology. The delineations of character become more sharp and vigorous; they approach in some respects to an ideal which the imagination can lay hold of; events are painted in a more marked and distinct manner; accessory circumstances or causes are forgotten or neglected.'44

In much the same spirit Macaulay, in his essay on Macchiavelli, explains the classical tradition of history-writing. 'The relation is, no doubt, in all its principal points, strictly true. But the numerous little incidents which heighten the interest, the words, the gestures, the looks, are evidently furnished by the imagination of the author. The fashion of later times is different. A more exact narrative is given by the writer. It may be doubted whether more exact notions are conveyed to the reader. The best portraits are perhaps those in which there is a slight mixture of *caricature*, and we are not certain that the best histories are not those in which a little of the exaggeration of fictitious narrative is judiciously employed. Something is lost in accuracy, but much is gained in effect. The fainter lines are neglected, but the great characteristic features are imprinted on the mind for ever.'45

The group of problems connected with the impact of the infinite God upon a finite world and with the necessity to compress events, however marvellous, into manageable compass, was to some extent met, by early Christian writers, with the device of symbolism. 'Unspeakable mysteries', noted an English physician turned philosopher, 'are delivered in a vulgar and illustrative way; being written unto man, they are delivered not as they truly are but as they may be understood';46 and what Sir Thomas Browne means is that symbolism is bound up with any attempt to express religious truth, in historical writing as in art, if only because 'while we are veiled in with mortality, truth must veil itself too, that it may the more fully converse with us'.47

St. Augustine, who well realized the snares and uncertainties of symbolism, explained that much of Biblical history is simply narrative 'with no further significance'. This, however, serves as a kind of framework for the richly significant events, which are to be treated both as literal fact and as symbolic, that is, capable of conveying fuller truth than appears on the surface. Augustine differs notably from his predecessor Origen in the value which he lays upon the literal, as contrasted with the symbolic, value of Biblical history. Whereas for Origen it is the underlying suggested truth, drawn out from its ignoble mantle of brute fact, that is to be revered, Augustine tended to regard symbolic interpretations as helpful additions which, in one form or another, will probably be suggested by the story to the receptive mind of the thoughtful reader. He shrinks from any unrestrained symbolism which may serve to dissipate factual truth into a vain aura of imagination and from the risks of arbitrary pronouncements that God did not wish this, that or the other statement to be taken in a literal sense, realizing that, once the obvious meaning of words begins to be whittled away, no cry of 'How long?' will stay the critic's onslaught and no firm vantage-point may be attained at which the expositor can dig in his heels and say, 'Thus far and no farther'. Therefore, though Augustine declares: 'It is a wretched slavery that takes figurative expressions literally',[48] he yet lays down this rule: 'When you hear a symbolic exposition given of a passage in Scripture which records events, you should first of all get it clear in your mind that the event recorded took place as it is recorded; otherwise, if you take away the basis of fact, you may find yourselves attempting to build on air'.[49]

Augustine's approach to the matter may be closely likened to the principle laid down by Dr. Edwyn Bevan in his Gifford Lectures on '*Symbolism and Belief*'. Bevan divides symbols into two classes, those behind which we can see and those behind which we cannot see. By the former he means, to take an obvious example, the idea of the Virgin Birth as symbolizing Christ's 'luminous superiority that impressed simple hearts'. For those who take the completely 'symbolic' view, however, this truth could be more accurately stated by the use of some such phrase as 'the pre-eminence of this particular union of divine with human nature' than by talking about a Virgin Birth. Similarly, those who declare the Resurrection of Christ to be 'purely symbolic' are, in fact, ready to put another imagined sequence of events in place of the Gospel narrative. On the other hand, descriptions of the beginning or end of the world, or the use of such expressions as the 'Love of God' or the 'Will of God' are inevitably and always symbolical, simply because of the limits of human language and imagination. In such cases it is not possible to 'see behind' the symbol, which provides the truest statement of reality that can be reached in the present state of human enlightenment. 'A man's goings are of the Lord', said the author of the book of Proverbs, 'how then can man understand his way?'[50] and the early Christian historians were inevitably driven on to make some use of symbolism in so far as they admitted a divine and therefore mysterious impact on events.

It must be allowed that, however serviceable symbolic expression may be, the hazards which attend its use are obvious enough. 'The tragedy of symbol,' it has been remarked, 'is that, like all material things, it is subject to the immutable laws of life and death, and that which was originally charged with vivid spiritual experience becomes, in the course of the ages, first dulled, then liable to misrepresentation and ultimately devoid of meaning or, perhaps worse, charged with false values by blind superstition.'[51] Failure to allow for the natural tendency to interpret symbolic modes of expression as though they were concrete and literal has led, for instance, to curious ideas concerning Heaven and Hell which have emerged in the course of history. For the fiery apocalyptic of the tormented Jewish nation was never intended to become a schematic picture of the state of the departed.

Nevertheless the value of symbolism more than offsets the perils of its misuse. It may be desirable, for instance, to employ symbolism in order neatly to express complicated forms of truth. 'Discursive speech', we are told, 'is a relatively poor instrument for representing complex relationships. Degrees of kinship which could hardly be explained in words can be read off a family tree at a glance.'[52] And, just as 'in the visual symbol we contemplate the whole of a proposition in a flash', so, in literature, symbolism can minister to truth by assisting in the task of compression. 'I am the true Vine'[53] takes the place of much lengthy explanation.

Symbolism serves also to secure timelessness for the object represented. When such artists as Tissot tried to achieve vivid realism by depicting Christ's face as characterized by the distinctive traits of a first-century Palestinian, one kind of truth was gained at the expense of another. For Christ, shown in this photographic manner, ceases to be our 'eternal contemporary'.[54] The perils of 'popular realism' are thus exposed by Bishop Westcott:[55] 'There is a charm, no doubt, in being enabled to see some scene far removed from us in time or place as it would have presented itself to an ordinary observer; but exactly in proportion to the grandeur of the subject such a superficial portraiture is likely to be misleading. The spectator is tempted to rest in that which he understands at once; and the loftier though vague impression which he had before is lost and not assisted by the external details which profess to give the literal truth. Or, to put the truth in another light: the divine act was fitted to convey the divine meaning at the time of its occurrence, in relation to those who witnessed it, but a realistic representation could not give the same impression to a different age. This is signally the case with scenes in the Gospel History.'

Moreover, symbolism may conveniently be used to express the mood of the moment by drawing nature in 'to rejoice with them that do rejoice, and weep with them that weep'.[56] Scenes do not present a standard appearance; they are, to a certain extent, coloured by the mind of the beholders. Sometimes it may be a case of 'nothing but blue skies from now on'; sometimes 'the lights have gone out all over Europe'; sometimes, in the poet's words,

> 'All these were sad in nature, or they took
> Sadness from him, the likeness of his look.'[57]

An instance of this power of feeling to colour fact is to be found in a painting called 'The Shout', by the Norwegian artist Edvard Munch.[58] The picture shows a quiet sea-coast, with two fishing boats in the middle distance. A simple wooden pier juts out near by. At its farther end two small figures, clothed in black, stand motionless, while the foreground is occupied by someone who raises her hands to cup her face, as the cheeks draw in and the mouth is rounded in an agonized shout. Something terrible has happened, and the lines of earth and sea and sky have been so drawn as to suggest that all nature is shuddering in sympathetic horror.

And, as with the artists, so with the historians, 'some kinds of selection and stress lead to clearer understanding'.[59] When a momentous battle is to be fought that will decide whether or no the Israelites are to fulfil their destiny in the Promised Land, the heavens are bidden to watch in silent expectancy: 'Sun, stand thou still upon Gibeon; and thou, moon, in the valley of Aijalon.'[60] The apocryphal Gospels, with their tendency to carry interpretation to excess, furnish elaborate examples of this sympathy between nature and decisive events. The Gospel of James, for instance, records how at the birth of Christ 'I looked up to the air and saw the air in amazement. And I looked up unto the pole of heaven and saw it standing still, and the fowls of the heaven without motion. And I looked upon the earth and saw a dish set, and workmen lying by it, and their hands were in the dish—but they put not the food to their mouths, and the faces of them all were looking upwards. And behold there were sheep being driven, and they went not forward, but stood still; and the shepherd lifted his hand to smite them with his staff, and his hand remained up. And then, of a sudden, all things moved onwards in their course.'[61] This astonished joy of the created order was to find its sad counterpart at the time of the Crucifixion, when 'from the sixth hour there was darkness over all the land until the ninth hour'.[62]

It is fatally easy to import too much symbolism into historical, as into artistic, interpretation, with the result that the outlines of the subject become blurred and indistinguishable, but without that sympathetic intuition, which often amounts to what earlier generations knew as 'faith', much of the rich purport of things will inevitably be missed. 'We need new eyes in history', wrote G. G.

Coulton, 'even more than new documents'[63] and Dr. Edwyn
Bevan may again be called on to supply a commentary. 'I remember once', he wrote, 'at Oxford, at the Ashmolean, looking
through, not very carefully, a series of water-colours by Turner of
Oxford, and when I went out again from the museum into the
streets, it all looked different; there were new lights on trees and
houses; it all looked like a picture painted by Turner.'[64] Westcott
elaborates the same theme: 'The understanding of Nature is
deepened and enlarged with the progress of life. Every discovery as
to the history of creation, sooner or later, places new forces in the
artist's hands. It may be some detail as to the formation of rocks,
some law as to the arrangement of leaves and branches, some
phenomenon of light and vapour, which has been more firmly
seized, and shortly the painter's interpretation of the landscape
will offer a fuller truth. The instructed eye will discern the importance of some minute effect and the artistic instinct will know how
to convey it to the ordinary spectator.'[65] For the early Christian
historians, everyday scenes, as also the notable events of past history, were bathed in the light of the purposes of God. Whether
these historians were correct in all their views is a matter which
does not admit of any neatly scientific demonstration, since in history, as in most other things which concern us nearly, the bound-
aries of what can be weighed, measured or mathematically proven
are soon overstepped, and the region is entered where, as Pascal
put it, *il faut parier*,[66] a bet has to be made, in faith, that the opened
eye is seeing aright and its vision profoundly true.

'History-writing', declared Thomas Madox, court-chronicler
to Queen Anne, 'is in some sort a religious act; it imports solemnity
and sacredness, and ought to be undertaken with purity and rectitude of mind';[67] and it is as witnessing to this mood that the early
Christian historians stand before us. It must at times be confessed
that 'we have their treasure in earthen vessels',[68] since as stylists
and craftsmen they are, for the most part, but moderate per-
formers. Nevertheless they deserve credit for an honest attempt
to record 'what happened' yet without loss of a keen awareness of
the mystery and pattern shown forth in events. Incidentally they

declare the honourable part played by those who are fellow-workers with God, if indeed, as the Oxford poet has it:

> 'in the light of light
> man's little deeds, strewn on the sands of time, sparkle
> like cut jewels in the beatitude of God's countenance.'[69]

According to the Ionian philosopher, 'Mind came and set all things in order';[70] and so it is the historian's mind that imposes order on the chaotic disarray of facts and interprets the blurred form of things. 'Angels alone', we are reminded,

> 'Perceive
> With undistempered and unclouded spirit
> The object as it is; but for ourselves
> The speculative height we may not reach.'[71]

In our world of becoming, some strain of imperfection may well creep into history-writing, as into everything else, and the gratification of complete certainty no doubt eludes us. Yet, in the words of one of the first Christian scholars, 'as the eye seeks the light, as our body craves for food, so our mind is impressed with the natural desire of finding out the truth of God and the causes of what we observe'.[72] Such is the historian's honourable quest and such his delight until, in his true *patria*, he knows even as also he is known, and the veiled clarity of insight gives place to the fullness of vision.

APPENDIX

THE HISTORICAL BACKGROUND OF THE DOCTRINE
OF THE ASSUMPTION

The Biblical record concerning the life of the Virgin is fragmentary and abrupt. It is stated in the Acts of the Apostles (i. 14) that, after the Ascension, 'Mary, the mother of Jesus', together with the women, his brethren and the Twelve, 'continued stedfastly in prayer' at Jerusalem, but at that point historical sources fail, and the natural curiosity of the devout is thereafter appeased by a rich outpouring of apocryphal narrative. Orthodox churchmen appear to have maintained the reserve, or ignorance, of the writers of Scripture. For when, in the latter part of the fourth century, a notable increase in respect and veneration was accorded to Mary, no allusion is made to any exceptional occurrences connected with her death. St. Ambrose, for instance, describes her as the ideal virgin, *imago virginitatis*,[1] who 'gave birth to the Author of salvation',[2] and, reversing the achievements of Eve, 'rains down upon earth the grace of Christ',[3] securing the 'redemption of all';[4] but no reference to any doctrine of an Assumption crowns his panegyric. He has, indeed, nothing at all to say on the subject of her death beyond noting, in his commentary on St Luke's Gospel,[5] that it is a mistake to interpret the text (ii. 35) 'a sword shall pierce through thine own soul' as a reference to martyrdom: 'neither Scripture nor history teaches that Mary departed this life by suffering a martyr's death' (*corporalis necis passione*).

Uncertainty about the manner of Mary's death is displayed even more notably by Epiphanius, bishop of Salamis (*c*. A.D. 315–403). Epiphanius, a zealous champion of orthodox faith, was for over thirty years head of a monastic community at Eleutheropolis, near Jerusalem, and would thus have been well acquainted with any local traditions on the subject of the Assumption if these had been current in his day. But, though keenly interested in the Virgin and her privileges, his ignorance of the facts makes him refuse to commit himself even on the question whether the Virgin died or was translated to Heaven without experiencing death.

Two passages in Epiphanius' work *Against the Heresies*[6] bear on the matter. He writes as follows: 'Now if any persons think that I am mistaken, let them search through the Scriptures, and they will find there no mention of Mary's death and no indication whether she died or did

[1] *De virginibus*, ii. 15. [2] *De instit. virginis*, 88. [3] *Ibid.* 81.
[4] *Ep.* xlix. 2. [5] ed. C. Schenkl in C.S.E.L. xxxii, p. 74. [6] lxxviii. 11.

not die, whether she was buried or not buried. Moreover, though John accomplished his journey to Asia, yet he nowhere states that he took the holy Virgin along with him, but Scripture is completely silent on this subject because of its marvellous nature so as not to confuse the mind of man. For my part, I venture on no pronouncement, but keep my own counsel and remain silent.' Epiphanius goes on to say that some people have discovered hints about what finally happened to the Virgin in the Lucan reference to a 'sword piercing through thine own soul', and in the picture which the book of Revelation[1] offers of the woman to whom were given 'the two wings of the great eagle, that she might fly into the wilderness . . . from the face of the serpent'. 'But,' continues Epiphanius, 'I make no precise definition as regards this subject. I do not affirm that she remained immortal, neither do I assert that she died. For Scripture surpasses the mind of man and has left the matter an open question, for the sake of that precious and most noble vessel so that no one should connect her with earthly things. The fact is that we do not know whether she died or not.' A little later on in his book Epiphanius again discusses the matter in a mood of reverent agnosticism:[2] 'If indeed the holy Virgin died and was buried, yet her falling asleep was honourable, her death was unsullied and her crown a virgin's crown. If she was slain in accordance with the prophecy that a "sword should pierce through her own heart", she enjoys a martyr's fame and her holy body, by means of which she brought Light into the world, is held in honour. Perhaps indeed she remained alive. For it is quite possible for God to do exactly as he wishes, and nobody knows anything about what happened to her in the end.' Language such as this makes it extremely difficult to imagine that there was any reputable tradition of the Virgin's Assumption current in Palestine towards the end of the fourth century, and it remains to consider how the story arose.

It must be premised that the word Assumption, in its normal present-day usage, signifies the ascent of the Virgin, in body as well as in soul, to the blessedness of Heaven. But, in writings of the patristic age, this is certainly not always the meaning of the word *assumere*, or *assumptio*. Augustine calls the death of the Apostles their *assumptio*,[3] and Gregory of Tours can, in similar fashion, speak of the 'assumption of St. Martin'[4] when he means the entry of a holy person into heaven without any suggestion that his body was exalted along with the soul. To take a later example, Usuard, in the ninth century, notes that August 15th is the day on which the 'Falling-asleep of Mary, the holy mother of God'[5] is

[1] xii. 14.   [2] lxxviii. 24. P.G. xlii. 737.   [3] C. Faustum, xxxiii. 3.
[4] De miraculis S. Martini, i. 32.   [5] P.L. cxxiv.

celebrated and he then goes on to say that the resting-place of the Virgin's body is unknown, and that a reverent admission of ignorance on such a subject is preferable to apocryphal fancies. He is therefore in no way committed to a doctrine of the Assumption as this is taught today, yet he can without any feeling of inconsistency describe August 14th as *Vigilia Assumptionis sanctae Mariae*.

But while there may be considerable ambiguity about the use of the term *assumptio*, the manner in which the doctrine of the corporeal departure of the Virgin from earth to heaven developed is fairly clear. During the fifth century, the *cultus* of the Virgin came to be quickened by doctrinal controversy. In their zeal to attribute to the Saviour human experiences and a real victory which was not merely a sham fight, the Nestorians found themselves drawn on to emphasize the manhood rather than the Godhead of Jesus. They tended to interpret the mystery of the Incarnation as an indwelling of God within the human personality, unique in degree but logically comparable with the indwelling of God in the saints, and they recoiled in particular from the use of the word Theotokos to describe the Virgin. 'Has God a mother?' enquires Nestorius. 'In that case we may excuse paganism for giving mothers to its divinities; and in that case Paul was a liar when he testified concerning Christ that he was "without father, without mother, without genealogy". No, my friend, Mary was not the mother of God, for "that which is born of the flesh is flesh, and that which is born of the spirit is spirit".'[1] Remarks of this nature stimulated such replies as the panegyric preached in 429 by Proclus, bishop of Cyzicus and later patriarch of Constantinople, on the 'Virgin Mother of God in whose womb He dwelt whom Heaven could not contain'.[2] The Council of Ephesus, in 431, enthusiastically approved this high estimate of the part played by Mary in the scheme of redemption[3] and, even though the threat of Nestorian speculations was soon removed, devotion to the Virgin continued to grow.

Popular piety was therefore well attuned to accept colourful, if imaginary, stories designed to proclaim her dignity and privileges, and prominent amongst such apocryphal narratives may be ranged the series of texts which tell of Mary's death and assumption into Heaven. This legend is found with many variations in Greek, Latin, Coptic, Syriac, Arabic, Armenian and other languages, and, in its original form, cannot be later than the fifth century, by which time there was a clear need of

[1] Loofs, *Nestoriana*, p. 252.   [2] *P.G.* lxv. 681.
[3] However, the *Encomium in S. Mariam Deiparam*, attributed to Cyril of Alexandria (*P.G.* lxxvii. 1029), is probably not genuine.

dramatic narrative concerning the Virgin's death to match the *passiones* customarily read in Church on the days set apart for the commemoration of martyrs. The significant silences of the writers of Syria and Palestine, and of pilgrims to the holy places, make it unlikely that the story of the Assumption arose in any such part of the world as that, and Egypt is the probable place of origin. At any rate Egypt provides several versions of the story, written both in the Sahidic and in the Bohairic dialect.

The Sahidic narrative which claims to have been composed by 'Cyril, archbishop of Jerusalem,' excludes a corporeal assumption, and treats rather of the Virgin's body as concealed until the Day of Judgement. According to this account, the Jews displayed great animosity and fear: 'And they passed a decree unanimously, saying, "We must not let her be buried in the city, lest mighty deeds be worked at her tomb similar to those which her Son performed, and lest the people believe in her and change our Law". And the high priests and scribes said "Let us go and burn her body with fire, so that no man will ever be able to find it". And the Jews lighted a fire, and they pursued the Apostles with the bier whereon was the body of the Virgin. And when the Apostles had arrived at the valley of Jehoshaphat they looked behind them, and they saw the Jews pursuing them, and they dropped the bier upon the ground, for they were afraid that the godless Jews would kill them. And whilst the Jews were rushing on to overtake them the Apostles betook themselves to flight and escaped. Now the body of the holy Virgin they could not find, and all that they found was the wooden bier, and they lighted a fire and threw the bier into it. And they went into every place, saying "Perhaps her body hath been carried away secretly", but they could not find it. And a very strong sweet smell emanated from the place whereon the body of the Virgin had been laid, and a mighty voice came from heaven, saying unto them, "Let no man give himself the trouble of seeking after the body of the Virgin until the great day of the appearing of the Saviour". And the Jews fled, greatly alarmed.'[1]

However, in the other versions of the story, to which 'Cyril's' narrative is closely akin, the Assumption is included as an integral part. The Bohairic text, which pretends to be an eye-witness account compiled by 'Evodius, the archbishop of the great city Rome, who was second after Peter the Apostle', explains that the Apostles, together with a number of 'ministers' including Evodius, and the Virgin attended by her maidens, were gathered together in a house, hiding from the hostility

[1] E. A. Wallis Budge, *Miscellaneous Coptic Texts* (1915), p. 648.

of the Jews. Christ appears in the sight of all and, after announcing that He 'must needs take a great offering' from their midst the next day, departs, leaving them in a state of joyful but questioning expectancy.

With much fulsome repetition the narrative proceeds, in language which again and again echoes passages from Scripture: 'Now it came to pass at the hour of the light on the twenty-first of the month Tobi, which was the morrow, that Christ the true Word came unto us riding on a chariot of cherubim, thousand thousands of angels following Him, the powers of light surrounding Him and singing before Him, and David the holy singer riding on a chariot of light, having his spiritual harp, crying out and saying, "Let us sing unto the Lord, for with glory hath He been glorified". And our Saviour stood in our midst, the doors being shut, and stretched forth his hand towards us all, the multitude of the disciples being gathered together, and said unto us, "Peace be unto you all".'[1]

Christ then informs the Apostles that the time has come to 'receive my virgin mother, who has been to Me a dwelling-place on the earth for nine months, and take her up with Me to the heavenly places of the heavens, and give her as a gift to my good Father'. Both the Apostles and the women in attendance on the Virgin express grief and distress, and Mary herself weeps at the thought of the terrors of death until reassured by Christ's promise of his unfailing succour. The account of her death runs as follows: 'In a moment and in the twinkling of an eye, he appeared whose name is bitter with all men, even Death. It came to pass when she saw him with her eyes, her soul leaped from her body into the bosom of her beloved Son in the place where He was sitting; for God the Word was sitting with us in the place where we were and He fills heaven and earth. And it came to pass, when He had hold of the soul of his virgin mother—for it was white as snow—He saluted it, and wrapped it in garments of fine linen, and gave it to Michael the holy archangel, who bare it on his wings of light, until He appointed the place for her holy body. All the women that were gathered to her, when they saw that she was dead, wept and groaned.'

Christ then pronounces an elaborate blessing on his mother's body, and the burial is described in these words: 'Now when our good Saviour had said these things over the body of his mother He wept, and we also were all weeping with Him. He arose and took hold of the heavenly garments and shrouded her holy body. And our Saviour spake with the Apostles, saying, "Arise, take up the body of my beloved mother, which was to Me a holy temple, and bear it on your shoulders.

[1] Forbes Robinson, *Coptic Apocryphal Gospels*, p. 52.

... Do thou, my chosen Peter, bear her head on thy shoulder, and let John also carry her feet; for ye are my brethren and my holy members. Let the rest of the Apostles sing before her. Go ye all forth with her from the least to the greatest to the east of Jerusalem, in the field of Jehoshaphat. Ye shall find a new tomb, wherein no man has yet been laid. Lay her holy body there, and keep watching it three and a half days. Be not afraid. I am with you." '

Reference is then made to Psalm xlv. 15 and Psalm cxxxii. 8, and the narrative continues: 'Straightway our Saviour rode upon his chariot of cherubim, all the orders of the heavens following Him and singing his praise, so that the air was filled with the abundance of the sweet savour. Thus did He receive the soul of his mother into his bosom, wrapped in napkins of fine linen, sending forth flashes of light; and went up into the heavens whilst we all looked at Him. Straightway they took up the body of the Virgin. My father Peter was carrying her head, my father John was carrying her feet, and the rest of the Apostles, with censers of incense in their hands, went before us singing, and all the virgins went behind her.' The Jews expressed wonder and penitence: 'But the Apostles bore the body of the Virgin, and put it into the tomb according to the word of our Saviour, and they remained watching it three and a half days'.

The story concludes with the corporeal assumption: 'Now when they had reached mid-day on the fourth day, the Apostles being gathered together with one another, and with virgins also by the tomb wherein was the body of the Virgin singing and making melody, behold! a great voice came from heaven like the sound of a trumpet, saying, "Go ye everyone to his place until the seventh month" ... And it came to pass in the seventh month from the time that the Virgin, the holy God-bearer, Mary, went forth from the body, which is the month Mesore, we arose on the fifteenth of this month, and gathered together to the tomb wherein was the body of the Virgin, the virgins also being with us. We spent all night watching and singing, offering up incense, the virgins having their lamps burning. Now at the hour of the light on this same night, there came unto us in the place where we were dwelling our Lord Jesus Christ in great glory, and said unto us, "Peace be unto you all, my holy Apostles. . . . The body of my beloved mother, behold! it is with you, and my angels watch it according to the command of my Father, because it was a temple of his Son, even of Me; but her soul is in the heavenly places of heaven, and the powers of the height sing her praise. And now I have sent for her to be brought, that she may come and manifest to you the honours wherein she dwells, which

I promised you in return for those things which you left behind you here." Whilst our Saviour was yet speaking with us, we heard hymns in the height. Straightway we looked, and saw a great chariot of light. It came and stayed in our midst, cherubim drawing it, the holy Virgin Mary sitting upon it, and shining ten thousand times more than the sun and the moon. And we were in fear, and fell on our face, and worshipped her, and she stretched her hand towards us all, and blessed us, and gave us the salutation of peace. . . . And the Lord called into the tomb and raised the body of his virgin mother, and put her soul into her body again; and we saw it living in the body even as it was with us formerly, wearing the flesh. And our Saviour stretched out his hand and set her on the chariot with Him. And our Saviour answered and said to us in his gentle voice, "Behold my beloved mother. This is she whose virgin womb carried Me nine months, and I was three years also receiving suck from her breasts which were sweeter than honey. Behold! you see her face to face, raised by me from the dead, and she has blessed you all." . . . And when our Saviour had said these things, He spent all that day with us and with his virgin mother. Afterwards He gave us the salutation of peace; and went up to the heavens in glory, the angels singing before Him.'

The Greek narrative, which claims John the Evangelist as its author, is similar in general outline. It includes the story of the impious Jew who snatched at the bed, as the Apostles were bearing the body of the Virgin off for burial, and ends up in this way: 'At the departure of her spotless soul, the place was filled with fragrance and a marvellous light, and behold! a voice from heaven was heard saying "Blessed art thou amongst women". And Peter ran and I, John, and Paul and Thomas and we embraced her precious feet so as to be sanctified. And the twelve Apostles placed her precious, holy body on a bed and carried it forth. And behold! as they were carrying it, a certain Hebrew named Jephonias, mighty of body, rushed up and grabbed at the bed, which the Apostles were carrying, and behold! an angel of the Lord with invisible might severed his two hands from his shoulders with a sword of fire, and left them hanging right up in the air near the bed. At this miracle, the whole people of the Jews who saw it cried out: "He who was born of thee, Mary, ever-virgin mother of God, is indeed the true God". And Jephonias himself, at Peter's command, so that the marvellous works of God might be made manifest, stood up behind the bed and cried out, "Holy Mary who didst bear the Divine Christ, have mercy on me". And Peter turned and said to him, "In the name of Him who was born of her, the hands of which you were deprived shall be restored". And straightway at Peter's word, the hands that were hanging near the bed of our lady went back and were restored to Jephonias. And he, moreover, believed and glorified the Divine Christ who had been born of her.

'After this miracle, the Apostles carried the bed on, and laid her precious and holy body in a new tomb at Gethsemane. And behold! a sweet-smelling perfume came out of the holy sepulchre of our Lady the mother of God. And for three days there were heard the voices of invisible angels glorifying Christ our God who was born of her. And when the third day was fulfilled the voices were heard no longer, and thereafter everyone perceived that her spotless, precious body had been translated and was in Paradise.

'And after it was translated, lo! we beheld Elizabeth, mother of the holy John the Baptist, and Anne the mother of our Lady, and Abraham and Isaac and Jacob and David, playing harps and singing Alleluia, and all the choirs of the saints worshipping the precious body of the Lord's mother, and we saw a place filled with a light which nothing can surpass in radiance, and we perceived the great fragrance of that place where her holy and precious body lay, after its translation, in Paradise, and we heard a melody of them that praised Him who had been born of her, a sweet melody which it is granted only to virgins to hear and of which no-one can have a surfeit. So we the Apostles, having all of a sudden witnessed the translation of her holy body, glorified God who had shown us his marvels at the departure of the mother of our Lord Jesus Christ.'

This is the version printed by Tischendorf (1866) from the twelfth-century *codex Monacensis* 276. Other manuscripts, however, record that, along with the Virgin, the Apostles were translated, on twelve clouds of light, into Paradise; and one manuscript[1] ends abruptly without giving any details of the vision of Heaven.

The Latin narrative *de Transitu beatae Mariae* purports to have been composed by Melito, bishop of Sardis, from information furnished by St. John. At the beginning, strictures are passed on 'a certain Leucius' who is alleged to have corrupted the traditions concerning the adventures of the Apostles and death of the Virgin by rewriting the stories in the dualist, or Manichee, interest. 'Melito's' narrative certainly reflects an interest in St. John, and it starts off with a note of his care for the Virgin who had been entrusted to him with the words 'Behold thy mother'. The story then continues with a remodelled Annunciation, in the course of which Mary receives from the angel a palm branch

[1] Ven. Marc. cl. ii, cod. xlii.

culled in heaven, and with stress laid on the miraculous calling together
of the Apostles:[1] 'And behold, suddenly, while St. John was preaching
at Ephesus, on the Lord's day, at the third hour of the day, a great
earthquake occurred and a cloud raised him up and took him away
from the sight of all and brought him before the door of the house
where Mary was. And, knocking at the door, he immediately entered.
But when Mary saw him she rejoiced exultantly and said, "I ask thee,
my son John, be mindful of the words of my Lord Jesus Christ, in
which He commended me to thee. For lo! I am about to depart from
my body in three days' time, and I have heard the counsels of the Jews
who say, "Let us wait for the day when she shall die who bore that
deceiver, and let us burn her body with fire". So she called St. John
and brought him into the secret part of the house, and she showed him
her grave-clothes and that palm of light which she had received from
the angel, charging him that he should cause it to be carried before her
bier when she was on the way to her tomb. And St. John said to her
"How shall I alone prepare thy burial unless my brethren, fellow-
apostles of my lord Jesus Christ, come to pay honour to thy body?"
And lo! suddenly, at the command of God, all the Apostles were lifted
up from the places in which they were preaching God's word and swept
away in a cloud and put down before the door of the house where
Mary dwelt. And they greeted each other and marvelled, saying
"What is the reason for which the Lord has gathered us together here?"'
St. John comes out of the house and answers their question, and all
enter to greet the Virgin and watch with her. 'And they took their
places round about her and comforted her. And when they had passed
three days in praising God, lo! on the third day round about the third
hour of the day, sleep fell upon all who were in that house and nobody
at all could keep awake save only the Apostles and three virgins who
were there. And lo! the Lord Jesus Christ appeared suddenly with a
great host of angels, and a great light came down upon that place, and
the angels were singing a hymn and extolling the Lord. Then the
Saviour spoke, saying, "Come, most precious pearl, enter the treasury
of eternal life".'

The Virgin then prays to Jesus, and receives the assurance of his protection: 'And as the Lord spake these words, Mary rose from the ground
and lay down upon her bed, and rendering thanks to God she gave up
the ghost. But the Apostles saw her soul, that it was of such whiteness

[1] *Transitus* B text. Tischendorf, *Apocalypses Apocryphae.* M. R. James, *The Apocryphal New Testament,* pp. 194-227, gives translations, summaries and short notes on the Assumption legends.

as cannot be worthily described by the tongue of mortal men; for it
surpassed the whiteness of snow and all metal and silver that shines with
great brilliance of light. Then the Saviour spoke, saying "Arise, Peter,
and take up the body of Mary and bear it to the right hand quarter of
the city eastwards, and you shall find a new tomb in which ye shall lay
her: there wait until I come to you". And, saying this, the Lord handed
over the soul of St. Mary to Michael who was set in charge of Paradise
and the prince of the people of the Jews; and Gabriel went together
with them. And straightway the Saviour was received up into Heaven
accompanied by the angels.' The virgins then prepared Mary's body
for burial, and found that it shone with bright radiance and gave forth
a sweet fragrance. The Apostles, chanting solemnly, bore the body
away as they had been instructed. Angelic voices were heard, so that
the onlookers were amazed; but a malevolent Jewish priest stirred the
people to hostility. He tried to overthrow the body to the earth, whereat
his hands withered and clave to the bier, while angels struck the people
blind. However, the afflicted Jewish priest, after confessing Jesus to be
Son of God, is restored to wholeness; and the people who had been
smitten with blindness are cured also, with the exception of those who
remain obdurate and refuse to believe, when St. John 'lays the palm
upon their eyes': 'But the Apostles carrying Mary came to the place of
the valley of Josaphat, which the Lord had shown them, and they placed
her in the new tomb, and closed the sepulchre. Now they sat down at
the door of the tomb, just as the Lord had bidden them; and lo!
suddenly the Lord Jesus Christ appeared with a great host of angels and
a flashing radiance of great brightness, and said to the Apostles "Peace
be with you". But they replied and said "Let thy mercy, O Lord, be
upon us, like as we have hoped in thee".' The Lord asks the Apostles
what treatment they would regard as appropriate for the Virgin, and
Peter declares that her body should be raised up and taken to the blessedness of Heaven. 'Then said the Saviour "Be it done according to your
wish". And He commanded Michael the archangel to bring the soul
of the holy Mary. And lo! Michael the archangel rolled back the stone
from the door of the tomb, and the Lord said "Rise up, my beloved
and my kinswoman: thou who didst not suffer corruption by union of
the flesh mayest not suffer destruction of the body in the sepulchre".
And straightway Mary arose from the tomb and blessed the Lord and
fell at the Lord's feet and worshipped Him. . . . And the Lord kissed
her and departed, and entrusted her soul[1] to angels to bear it into

[1] *Tradidit animam eius angelis ut deferrent eam in paradisum.* But no doubt the body is meant
along with the soul, as is made perfectly clear in the *Transitus* A text, a later production.

Paradise. And He said to the apostles "Come unto me". And when they had come near, He kissed them and said "Peace be with you. As I was even with you, so shall I be even unto the end of the world." And straightway when the Lord had said this He was lifted up in a cloud and received into heaven, and the angels accompanied Him, bearing the blessed Mary into the Paradise of God.'

It is notable that in the Decretal[1] attributed to Pope Gelasius I (A.D. 492–496) the 'book which is called the Passing, that is to say the Assumption, of the Holy Mary' is condemned as being apocryphal and unsuitable for reading by churchmen. Whether this work was precisely the same as the *de Transitu Mariae* of 'Melito' can hardly be determined, but, in any case, the cautious protestations at the beginning of the Latin Transitus-text seem designed to remove the tincture of heresy which stained the story of the Assumption. For the earliest Coptic Christianity was Gnostic rather than orthodox, and the Coptic versions of the Assumption legend bear marks of the dualism which characterizes the treatise *Pistis Sophia* or the *Apocryphon of John*[2] contained in the Berlin papyrus, P. 8502. The general picture displayed in such works points towards a sharp contrast between the Supreme God and the God of the Old Testament who created this beggarly universe, and emphasizes the struggle between the Powers of Light and the Powers of Darkness in which man plays his important part. So, in the version of 'Evodius' (xi), Mary prays 'O my beloved Son, let the tyrannies of death and the powers of darkness flee from me. Let the angels of light draw nigh unto me. Let the accusers of Amenti shut their mouths before me.' The fact that the legend had a Gnostic smack to it may well account in part for its hesitant and comparatively late acceptance in orthodox circles.[3]

The unsubstantial, indeed fanciful, nature of all forms of the Assumption legend is obvious enough to any reader of the texts, yet it is clearly on the basis of such narratives that the doctrine of the Virgin's corporeal reception into Heaven found its way into the works of the Church fathers. Gregory of Tours is the first writer in the West precisely to declare the resurrection of the Virgin, followed by her assumption both

[1] It seems probable that the Decretal was, in fact, composed in Gaul or North Italy some few years after Gelasius' death.

[2] Walter C. Till, 'Die Gnosis in Aegypten', *La Parola del Passato*, xii (1949). Cf. H. Idris Bell, *Cults and Creeds in Graeco-Roman Egypt*, 92 ff. A similarly Egyptian and Gnostic tone rings through the prayers and lamentations found in the 'History of Joseph the Carpenter', ed. S. Morenz, *Texte und Untersuchungen*, lvi (Berlin, 1951).

[3] W. H. C. Frend, 'The Gnostic Origins of the Assumption Legend'. *Modern Churchman*, March 1953.

in body and soul. In his treatise *de gloria martyrum*, composed about A.D. 590, he puts the matter thus: 'Then after the blessed Mary had fulfilled the course of this life and was being summoned to depart from the world, all the Apostles assembled from various places to her abode. And when they learned that she was about to be taken from the world, they kept watch together with her. And, behold! the Lord Jesus arrived in the company of his angels, and taking her soul, He entrusted it to Michael the Archangel, and departed. But at daybreak the Apostles lifted up her body, along with the bed, and placed it in a sepulchre, and guarded it, waiting for the coming of the Lord. And, behold! the Lord stood beside them a second time, and commanded that the sacred body should be lifted up in a cloud and taken off to Paradise, where now, reunited to the soul, it rejoices together with his elect and enjoys the blessings of eternity which shall never have an ending.'[1]

In this passage there is no hint of theological arguments designed to prove the inevitability of the Assumption. The death and translation of the Virgin are put forward in terms of history, history that is obviously derived from the *de Transitu Mariae* or from some closely similar document. Gregory speaks, in the same treatise, of the Virgin 'who was translated to Paradise amidst choirs of angels, the Lord going on before',[2] and a little later on reference is made to her *festivitas*, celebrated in January. It is not, however, made clear whether this was a general feast of the maternity of Mary or was particularly connected with the Assumption, as is the case with the festival assigned to January 18th in certain of the Gallican calendars, such as that of Corbie.

Be that as it may, while Rome remained silent it was in Gaul that liturgical observance of the Assumption became well established. The *Missale Gothicum*, composed before the end of the seventh century, bears witness to the doctrine in the *contestatio* appointed for the festival, when it declares, with elaborate parallelism: 'It would perchance have been too light a thing if Christ had hallowed thee merely at thy coming in, and had not glorified a mother such as thee at thy departure. Rightly hast thou been taken up in joyous assumption by Him whom thou didst bear in sanctity . . . so that the sepulchre of rock might not retain thee who hadst no awareness of earthly things.'[3] By contrast, the earliest Roman liturgies contain nothing of the kind, and, even when subjected to Gallican influences, they speak in general terms of the 'holy mother of God who underwent temporal death but could not be held captive

---

[1] *P.L.* lxxi. 708.
[2] *Ibid.* 713.
[3] *Missale Gothicum*, ed. H. M. Bannister, Henry Bradshaw Society, p. 32.

APPENDIX

by the bonds of death'.[1] Indeed the reception accorded to the festival
of the Assumption appears to have been unenthusiastic, at any rate in
official circles, if one may judge from the fact that Charlemagne, at the
beginning of the ninth century, after listing sixteen feasts as worthy of
universal observance adds, 'as regards the assumption of holy Mary we
have left the matter open for further enquiry'.[2]

In the East, the doctrine of the Assumption gained a more tardy
acceptance by orthodox writers. The earliest attestation appears to be
a turgid, rhetorical sermon, an 'Encomium on the Falling-asleep of the
God-bearer',[3] attributed to Modestus, patriarch of Jerusalem A.D. 633–
634. The grammarian Photius took little interest in this work, on the
ground that it differs in many respects from Modestus' customary style,
and the sermon probably belongs to the end rather than the beginning
of the seventh century. 'Modestus' complains of the silence of the
Apostles concerning Mary's death, and then goes on to show knowledge
of the apocryphal narratives. The Apostles are described as hastening
from all over the world, 'guided and assisted by the powerful influence
from above', to be present at the Virgin's deathbed. Christ appeared,
and 'the blessed Virgin looked towards Him and departed from the
holy body, entrusting to his hands her all-blessed, all-holy soul'. The
body was placed upon 'a litter that bore a holy burden', and then taken
by the Apostles to be buried at Gethsemane; but the reference to the
Assumption, though definite, is not very clearly expressed. Certain
details of the legend are dismissed as apocryphal, and 'Modestus'
merely states: 'She is made alive by Christ, being united with Him
bodily (σύσσωμος) in eternal incorruptibility, since He raised her from
the tomb and took her to Himself, in a manner known to Him alone'.
About 680, John, bishop of Thessalonica, introduced the observance of
the Falling Asleep of the Virgin into his diocese. In his oration he adopts
a somewhat apologetic tone and refers to the difficulty caused by heretical falsifications. He transcribed the apocryphal legend but, though he
included the death of the Virgin, he omitted the account of the Assumption and passed on to a concluding peroration.[4]

[1] *Gregorian Sacramentary*, ed. H. A. Wilson, H.B.S. p. 97. Cf. *Gelasian Sacramentary*, ed.
H. A. Wilson, p. 193.
[2] *Capitula de presbyteris*, xix, *P.L.* xcvii. 326. Nevertheless, the festival is included in the
Regula of Chrodegang of Metz (*P.L.* lxxxix. 1090) and in the list approved by the Council
of Mainz (A.D. 813).
[3] *P.G.* lxxxvi. 3277.
[4] *Patrologia Orientalis*, xix. 375 ff. The ending varies in the different manuscripts. The
original form, as shown in *codex Vaticanus* 2072, merely records that the Apostles, when
they opened the tomb three days after the burial, found the grave-clothes and nothing else.
This account is not inconsistent with the story of the Assumption, but perhaps the author

The homilies of Andrew, archbishop of Crete (d. A.D. 720), who had been a monk at Jerusalem, illustrate the tendency to harden and elaborate the stories told about saintly persons. Andrew gives details of the Virgin's childhood, and discusses the life of her parents, Joachim and Anna, just as he delights to recount the miraculous exploits of St. George and St. Nicholas. The Assumption is discussed freely, but in language which implies that its acceptance is something of a novelty. After a reference to Enoch and Elijah, Andrew declares: 'The things accomplished in her of old, but triumphantly proclaimed by us now, might perhaps seem strange and out of accord with the laws of nature, but when considered in relation to the astounding fact of the marvellous Birth would reasonably be held to be suitable in her case. . . . Now it was certainly a novel occurrence and beyond the scope of human reason that a woman who exceeded the nature of the heavens in purity should find her way into the inmost sanctuary of heaven. . . . How did the corpse disappear? How was it that the winding sheets were not in the coffin? Only because the body escaped corruption and the treasure was translated.'[1]

Andrew refers in this connexion to a patristic comment which was to be widely influential. The work *Concerning the Divine Names* was composed, along with other treatises and letters, by an author who identified himself with Dionysius the Areopagite, mentioned in Acts xvii and held to be a companion of Peter and Paul. These documents are now attributed, with practical certainty, to a period about A.D. 500,[2] but in the eighth century they had come to enjoy high repute as writings of the apostolic age. In the treatise *Concerning the Divine Names* it is stated, after a concise reference to the Virgin's death: 'When, as you know, both we and Hierotheus and many of our holy brethren had gathered together to behold the life-giving, God-receiving body, there were also present James, the brother of the Lord, and Peter, the most distinguished and aged prince of theologians. Thereupon it seemed good, after that sight, that all the holy prelates, as each one was able, should hymn and extol the nobility of weakness endued by God with infinite power.'[3] No allusion is made to an assumption of any kind, but later theologians, eager to find support for this doctrine, grasped on to this passage and interpreted it as though 'Dionysius' had been an eyewitness of the Virgin's corporeal departure from earth to Heaven.

had in mind a translation to an earthly Paradise, as suggested by a number of Eastern theologians, *e.g.* the tenth-century John the Geometer.

[1] *Sermo in dormitionem Mariae*, ii, *P.G.* xcvii. 1081.
[2] Bardenhewer, *Geschichte der altkirchlichen Literatur*, iv. 282 ff.   [3] *P.G.* iii. 681.

Germanus, patriarch of Constantinople[1] (d. A.D. 733), wrote in much the same strain as Andrew of Crete; but it is rather the honoured name of John Damascene, the great doctor of the Eastern Church, whose attacks on the Iconoclasts earned him high praise at the second Council of Nicaea, that furthered the rapid spread of the doctrine. Three homilies 'on the Falling-Asleep of the Blessed Virgin Mary' appear amongst his works, the first and third being short and restrained, while the second is a luxuriant composition, in which the preacher imagines himself to be present, along with the Apostles, on that occasion and recounts at length what he would have seen and the thoughts with which he would have been occupied. The Roman Breviary has, since the sixteenth century, drawn on this second homily to provide lections for August 18th, during the octave of the Assumption, but the homily appears, in fact, to be the work of an interpolator rather than of John Damascene himself.[2]

The passage which treats of the Assumption offers several points of difficulty. In the first place it is stated to be a quotation from the 'Euthymian History', a work which is otherwise unknown. In the second place it describes how the emperor Marcian and his wife Pulcheria sent for Juvenal of Jerusalem and other bishops at the time of the Council of Chalcedon (A.D. 451) and declared that they wished to acquire, for the protection of Constantinople, the Virgin's tomb which, as they had heard, was 'in the place which is called Gethsemane'. Juvenal's reply includes a long quotation from the treatise of the pseudo-Dionysius on the '*Divine Names*', which, however, was almost certainly not written until fifty years or more after the Council of Chalcedon. For reasons such as these the historical value of the homily is negligible, a fact which did not prevent it from becoming widely influential.

Juvenal's reply to the emperor and empress runs as follows: 'In the holy and divinely-inspired Scriptures nothing is found that bears on the death of Mary, the holy God-bearer. But we have learnt from an ancient and most true tradition that, at the time of her glorious falling-asleep, all the holy Apostles, who were travelling about the world for the salvation of the nations, were in a moment of time borne aloft and brought to Jerusalem. And when they arrived in the presence of Mary, they had a vision of angels and heard the divine harmony of the heavenly Powers. And thus, amidst divine and heavenly glory, she committed her holy soul into the hands of God in an ineffable manner. But her body which had received God was carried away, to the sound of chanting from

---

[1] *P.G.* xcviii. 340.   [2] Bardenhewer, *op. cit.* v. 61.

angels and Apostles, and given burial, being placed in a tomb at Gethsemane, where for three days the chanting of the angelic choir continued
without ceasing. After the third day, however, the angelic chanting
ceased. The Apostles who were present (one of them, namely Thomas,
who had been absent arrived after the third day and wished to venerate
the body that had borne God) opened the tomb. But they were completely unable to find the body whose praises all men sing, and when
they found only the grave-clothes lying there and had taken their fill
of an ineffable fragrance proceeding therefrom, they closed the tomb.
Then, overcome with wonder at the mystery, they could only conclude
that He who had condescended to become incarnate in his own person
and be made man of her and be born in the flesh though He was God
the Word and Lord of glory, and who had preserved her virginity
unharmed after her child-bearing, had Himself pleased to honour her
pure, undefiled body with incorruptibility even after her departure
from this life by translating her before the general resurrection of all.'[1]
John Damascene then quotes the passage from 'Dionysius', in a form
somewhat different from the text found in the 'Divine Names', and
adds that Marcian and Pulcheria requested that the sarcophagus and
shroud should be handed over to them for safe custody in the church
of St. Mary at Blachernae.

The silence of all the Fathers of the Church, during the first five centuries, on the subject of the Assumption finds its counterpart in the
accounts of pilgrimages made to the holy places of Palestine. It is,
indeed, certain that in the fourth century no tomb of the Virgin was
known at or near Jerusalem.[2] Eusebius, in the Life of Constantine, makes
no mention of it amongst the numerous shrines built in Palestine by the
empress Helen and her son, shrines which appealed to the curiosity, as
well as to the piety, of pilgrims from far and wide. In A.D. 333 these
holy places were visited by a pilgrim from Bordeaux, who left a careful
record of all that he saw, but has nothing to say concerning the Virgin's
tomb. The enterprising and devoted Etheria (Silvia), who gives a full
account of her travels to Jerusalem and other sacred sites about A.D. 400,
is likewise silent on this subject. So also is Jerome who, after conducting
the Roman ladies Paula and Eustochium on a visit to the monks of
Egypt, settled with them at Bethlehem and established, along with mon-
asteries for men and women, a 'hospice for pilgrims by the high way,
remembering that Mary and Joseph had not found a resting-place'.[3]

[1] P.G. xcvi. 748.
[2] The statement of Nicephoros Kallistos (P.G. cxlvi. 113) that Helena set up a church
over the Virgin's grave is late and wholly unreliable.   [3] Ep. cviii. 14.

There was, indeed, a variant tradition, strongly supported by the Turks today, that the resting-place of the Virgin was not Jerusalem at all but Ephesus, whither St. John had led her. The Council of Ephesus (A.D. 431) met in the city ἔνθα ὁ θεολόγος Ἰωάννης καὶ ἡ θεοτόκος παρθένος ἡ ἁγία Μαρία: "where are John the theologian and the God-bearing virgin, holy Mary". The precise meaning of this elliptical phrase is obscure: does it refer to the tomb of the Virgin or merely to her church? There was indeed a famous church of the Virgin at Ephesus, and, at the time of the Council, Cyril of Alexandria preached a vigorously anti-Nestorian sermon in the 'church of Mary, mother of God', into which the holy Trinity 'had gathered us all together';[1] but perhaps the more natural meaning of the words is that the tombs of the Virgin and of John were to be seen at Ephesus, and certainly this was the tradition which came to be fostered locally. The truth may well be that, the Virgin's burial-place being unknown, Jerusalem vied with Ephesus in claiming the distinction of possessing it. This would lead to the construction of rival churches; and August 15th, the date fixed by the emperor Maurice, about A.D. 600, on which the Dormition should be commemorated, was perhaps originally the dedication-day of such a church at or near Jerusalem.[2]

During the sixth century, numerous relics, such as the crown of thorns or the charger on which John the Baptist's head lay, came to be exhibited to the gaze of pilgrims, and, by a similar process, the holy places worthy of a devout visit were notably multiplied. A certain Theodosius, who describes the topography of the Holy Land on the basis of a pilgrimage which he made about A.D. 530, records: 'There is the valley of Josaphat, where Judas betrayed the Lord. There is the church of saint Mary, mother of the Lord',[3] a succinct notice which, though it invited and received embellishment by later hands, gives no hint that the Virgin's tomb was, at that date, regarded as wonderful or even clearly identified.

The pilgrims from Piacenza,[4] when they visited the valley of Gethsemane about A.D. 570, noted that 'in the same valley is a basilica of saint Mary, which they say was her house, where indeed she was taken up out of her body'. This last statement—*in qua et de corpore*

[1] *Homily IV*, P.G. lxxvii. 992.
[2] Doubts concerning the burial-place may be compared with doubts about the birthplace of the Virgin, which gradually came to be settled under the influence of the apocryphal *Protevangelium of James*.
[3] Palestine Pilgrims Text Society, ii, p. 11. C.S.E.L. xxxix. 142.
[4] *Of the Holy Places visited by Antoninus Martyr*, P.P.T.S. ii, p. 14. Geyer, *Itinera Hierosolymitana*, C.S.E.L. xxxix. 170. 203.

sublatam fuisse—becomes slightly suspect by reason of its omission from the St. Gall manuscript (133), one of the two best authorities for the text. But, whatever may be the value of this reading, it is modified in the interests of precision and developed belief and becomes, in an inferior manuscript tradition, *de qua eam dicunt ad caelos fuisse sublatam*, 'from which they say that she was raised up to Heaven'.[1]

Even by the seventh century those who piously visited the Virgin's tomb were in no way committed to belief in the corporeal Assumption. For instance, Arculf, a bishop of Gaul, undertook a pilgrimage to the Holy Places about A.D. 670 and, on his way home, was driven by contrary winds to the western coast of Britain. He was hospitably entertained by Adamnan, abbot of Iona, who made careful notes of the topographical details supplied by his guest. According to this record, Arculf visited the Virgin's church in the valley of Josaphat which contained 'the empty stone tomb of the holy Mary, in which she rested for some time after her burial. But how or when or by what persons her sacred body was removed from that same tomb, or where it awaits the Resurrection, nobody, so it is said, can know for certain.'[2] Arculf and Adamnan seem ignorant of any doctrine of the Assumption, and they take it that, whatever may have happened to the Virgin's body, it follows the normal human destiny and quietly awaits the day of Resurrection. Similarly, Bede, though the festival of the Assumption had by his day come to be observed by the Anglo-Saxons, records of the church in the valley of Jehoshaphat that, adjoining it, there was an 'empty tomb in which saint Mary, the mother of God, is said to have reposed for a time; but by whom or when the body was taken away nobody knows'.[3]

Another Englishman, St. Willibald, explored the Holy Places about A.D. 725 and an account of his travels was written up many years later, when he was an old man. This *Hodoeporicon*, compiled by a nun of Heidenheim Abbey who was a relation of Willibald, shows knowledge of the legendary accounts of the Virgin's death. Mention is made of the impious Jew whose hands were glued to the bier, and it is recorded that when the eleven had carried Mary to Jerusalem 'then the angels came and took her from the hands of the Apostles and carried her up to Paradise',[4]

---

[1] Cf. Sophronius, *Anacreontica*, xx (about A.D. 625).

$$\Gamma\epsilon\theta\sigma\eta\mu\alpha\nu\hat{\eta} \ \tau\acute{\epsilon}\mu\epsilon\nu\sigma\varsigma \ \lambda\alpha\mu\pi\rho\grave{o}\nu \ \mathring{a}\epsilon\acute{\iota}\delta\omega$$
$$\mathring{E}\nu\theta\alpha \ \tau\acute{\epsilon}\tau\upsilon\kappa\tau\sigma \ \tau\acute{a}\phi\sigma\varsigma \ M\eta\tau\rho\grave{\iota} \ \theta\epsilon\sigma\hat{\iota}o.$$

[2] P.P.T.S. iii, p. 17.
[3] *Concerning the Holy Places*, v. P.L. xciv. 1183.   [4] P.P.T.S. iii, p. 21.

apparently before any entombment had taken place. The sepulchre in the valley of Josaphat is described as having been erected 'as a memorial of her'.

However, another version of Willibald's travels, composed, with additional matter, by one of his companions, strikes a more agnostic note: 'They came into the valley of Josaphat where the tomb of saint Mary is shown. But whether the Apostles buried her there when she had been released from her body left here below, or whether, while they were intending to bury her after they had dug out the tomb there, she was assumed with her body, or, if after being buried she was hidden there, whether she was taken thence and transferred elsewhere or, having received true immortality, she has risen again, it is better to be in doubt than to define anything apocryphal.'[1]

This sturdy refusal to accept doctrines based on dubious tradition is echoed by several more or less contemporary writers. It may be noted, for instance, in an eighth-century 'Letter to Paula and Eustochium concerning the assumption of the blessed Virgin Mary',[2] which gained spurious repute on the ground that it had been written by Saint Jerome and found its way into various breviaries, including the Roman Breviary until the revision initiated by the Council of Trent. Though he speaks with enthusiasm about the Virgin's departure into Heaven, and the festival commemorating it, the author can hardly intend to preach a corporeal assumption to judge from the note of reverent caution which he strikes: 'If perchance an apocryphal work called *de Transitu Virginis Mariae* has fallen into your hands, you should not take doubtful matter as assured truth. It is a work which many Latins, with their love of piety and zeal for reading, embrace rather too eagerly, particularly since nothing of these matters can be known for certain except that on this day the Virgin whom we honour departed from the body.' Reference is then made to the tomb in the valley of Jehoshaphat 'where she is said by all, as you know, to have been buried; but now the tomb is shown empty to people who go to look at it. I speak thus for the reason that many of our friends are doubtful whether the Virgin was assumed together with the body or whether she left her body behind at her departure. But how or when or by whom that most holy body was taken away from the tomb or where it has been laid or whether it rose again is unknown; though some like to maintain that it has already been received and is clothed by Christ with blessed immortality in heaven.'

The author goes on to say that similar traditions are current about

[1] P.P.T.S. iii, p. 46.　　　　[2] *P.L.* xxx. 123.

St. John, in whose tomb only manna is found: 'We are indeed in doubt concerning the precise truth of these matters. Yet we find it better to entrust everything to God, with whom nothing is impossible, than to desire to make any rash definitions on our own authority when we lack proof.' The author alludes to St. Matthew's account of the resurrection of the 'bodies of the saints' at the time of the Crucifixion, and to the view held by some that this represented their final resurrection into Heaven. He closes the debate with the words, 'We do not deny that this happened in the case of the blessed Virgin Mary, though for the sake of caution, and to safeguard the faith, it should be regarded as a pious hope and opinion rather than defined unadvisedly. Ignorance on such a matter does us no harm.' The author thus declares that, while God has the power to effect the assumption of Mary, there is no proof that He, in fact, did so since the only source from which the doctrine is drawn is the unreliable *de Transitu Virginis*.

The ninth-century martyrologists Ado[1] and Usuard[2] speak in the same strain. Usuard puts the matter thus: 'Even though the most holy body of saint Mary, mother of God, is not found on earth, yet pious Mother Church keeps the festival of her revered memory, so as not to doubt that, so far as the flesh is concerned, she has been translated. But where that revered temple of the Holy Spirit has been hidden by the will and counsel of God, the Church with its sound sense has preferred not to know rather than to hold and teach some frivolous, apocryphal story about it.' Such hesitations, however, failed to satisfy the minds of churchmen eager to believe, and this in spite of continued protests such as that voiced in a sermon 'on the Assumption' which is attributed, though falsely, to Ildefonsus, bishop of Toledo: 'We must certainly not omit a story which many, through motives of piety, grasp at most eagerly, namely that the Virgin's body was raised up to the heavenly palaces by her Son, our Lord Jesus Christ. Now this may be a pious belief, yet we should not affirm it lest we seem to be taking doubtful stories as true.'[3] Another sermon, attributed to St. Augustine, but, in fact, a later work and perhaps composed by Ambrosius Aupertus, is expressed more strongly:[4] 'No catholic history records the manner of the Virgin's passing from earth to heaven. And the Church is said not merely to reject apocryphal stories of this sort, but even to remain in ignorance of them.' After comparing the uncertainty that surrounds the departure of the Virgin with the unknown fate of Moses' body, the preacher reminds his hearers that even St. John, who cared for the Virgin

[1] *P.L.* cxxiii. 202.　　　　[2] *P.L.* cxxiv. 365.
[3] *P.L.* xcvi. 266.　　　　[4] *Sermo CCVIII, P.L.* xxxix. 2130.

in her old age, has nothing to say on the subject:[1] 'It remains therefore that no man should, in lying fashion, invent as true what God wished to remain hid'.

Such scruples had little chance of prevailing over the general eagerness to enjoy a clear-cut, attractive picture of the Falling-asleep of the Virgin—*advocata nostra*, around whose every action was woven a shimmering web of mystery. Moreover, the enthusiasm of popular devotion gradually hardened into dogmatic definition, so that, by the thirteenth century, such scholastic philosophers as Albertus Magnus could declare: 'It is obvious that the most blessed mother of God was assumed in flesh and spirit; and we believe this to be true in every respect'.[2]

From time to time, however, controversy revived. In the middle of the seventeenth century, for instance, the canons of Paris split into two factions, the subject of vehement dispute being whether the passage from Usuard or some homily rather more positive concerning the mystery of the day should be used on August 15th. Canon Claude Joly, with the support of others, demanded the restoration of the Usuard passage which 'in no way detracts from the honour of the blessed Virgin and is not opposed to her corporeal Assumption but merely refrains from affirming it'.[3] 'We ought not', Joly continued, 'to make rash statements, lest we offend the most holy Virgin, the mother of Him who is the way, the *truth* and the life. For this reason she takes no pleasure in statements made about her which either add to or detract from *truth*.' The rival canons, led by Jacques Gaudin and Nicolas Billiard, protested that they could not 'remain silent, while old-established and seemly devotion to the mother of God and thus of all Christians is torn in pieces'.[4] Pleading the numerous voices raised on behalf of the doctrine and the need for certainty in such matters, Gaudin expressed his horror that, if the tradition of the corporeal assumption had to be attacked, this impious work should be carried out by a canon of Paris. The learned Tillemont, a little later, inclined towards Joly's view, but preferred to remain silent on a subject of widespread and popular belief.

A number of influences, therefore, seem to have operated in favour of the doctrine of the Assumption. First and foremost comes that love of the miraculous which characterizes the 'mediaeval' outlook; secondly there is the impatience felt at the silences of Scripture and the Fathers

---

[1] This presents a contrast with the plea made at the Vatican Council of 1870 that the Assumption should be defined dogmatically because it was an 'apostolic tradition, based on a divine revelation with which the apostle John had, perhaps, been favoured'. Martin, 'Les Travaux du concile du Vatican', quoted in *Dictionnaire de théologie catholique*, i. 2. 2140.

[2] *Opera* (Lyons, 1651), xx, p. 87.   [3] *De verbis Usuardi* (Sens, 1669), p. 154.

[4] J. Gaudin, *Assumptio Mariae Virginis vindicatae* (Paris, 1670), p. 415.

which would not allow of a neat and clear-cut picture of the Virgin. Then again, love of parallelism drew men on to attribute to the Virgin experiences which reproduced, in a minor key, those of her Son; so that the Assumption provided an appropriate counterpart to the Ascension. To such reasons may perhaps be added ecclesiastical rivalry, whereby Jerusalem and Ephesus were both impelled to claim the empty tomb where the Virgin had lain. There were also genuine misunderstandings of an author's meaning, and such misunderstandings seem to have occurred in the artistic as well as in the literary field.

The conventional manner in which Christian artists represented the human soul was to show it as a diminutive, childish figure wrapped in swaddling bands, and it is as such that the Virgin's soul is depicted in the first illustrations of her Falling-asleep. The earliest examples were destroyed in the course of the Iconoclastic controversy, but the primitive form of the picture was carefully retained for centuries, and spread widely from the East, where it originated, to the West. As displayed, for instance, in the mosaics of Daphni[1] or of the Martorana at Palermo,[2] it shows the Apostles ranged in two groups, at the head and at the feet of the Virgin as she lies on her bed. Christ stands behind the bed, holding the swathed and mummy-like figure of the soul with both hands, while overhead two large angels hover. A striking example of this *motif*, worked out with the vigorous and expressive realism of thirteenth-century Gothic sculpture, occurs in the porch of the south transept of Strasbourg Cathedral. Here the angels are not shown, but, instead, Mary Magdalene is introduced, crouching at the bedside and wringing her hands in dismay, while, on the other side of the couch, Christ raises his right hand in blessing while his left hand supports the figure of a graceful child which represents the Virgin's soul.[3] Sometimes the illustration, while preserving the traditional form, is modified, as on an ivory preserved in the Musée Cluny at Paris, in that two scenes are shown simultaneously. The grouping is exactly the same but one of the two angels has changed his posture and is flying away clasping a soul similar to that which Christ holds. Christ, in fact, is receiving the Virgin's soul at her death, while an angel bears it off to Heaven.[4]

[1] C. Diehl, *Manuel d'art byzantin*, ii, pp. 524 ff.
[2] O. Demus, *The Mosaics of Norman Sicily*, pp. 78 ff., pl. 56.
[3] E. H. Gombrich, *The Story of Art*, p. 138.
[4] K. Künstle, *Ikonographie der christlichen Kunst*, i, p. 567. In thirteenth-century glass at Chartres Cathedral, the soul of St. Martin is shown as a figure, naked except for his mitre, ascending to Heaven in an aureole of light. Similarly a relief in the church of S. Gregorio at Rome shows the soul of the monk Justus, depicted as a fully grown man, being raised up to Heaven by angels in response to Gregory's prayers. Künstle, *op. cit.* i, p. 494.

In such pictures, the soul is often a close replica, in miniature, of the body of the Virgin. An observer might therefore be excused for interpreting the Virgin's departure to Heaven as a bodily ascension, which, indeed, it clearly becomes when the scene is remodelled by the ingenuity of western artists. The first stage of variation is marked by the removal of Christ from the bedside. He is shown instead as enclosed in a mandorla of light and bearing on his knees a round medallion in which the Virgin is depicted as an *Orans* while an attendant angel hovers at each side.[1] This form of the picture exhibits a natural development when, as in an eleventh-century sacramentary from Augsburg,[2] the Virgin appears alone, full-length in a mandorla of light, being raised up to Heaven by four angels. Here, the Assumption is set forth in a manner closely comparable with that which had earlier been used to depict the Ascension of Christ, for, in the church of S. Clemente at Rome, a wall-painting which dates from the time of Pope Leo IV (A.D. 847–855) shows Christ in a mandorla being borne heavenwards by angels,[3] an art-form of Syrian origin which appears in the Gospels of Rabula[4] (A.D. 586). Similar parallelism is to be noted in the early and unusual example provided by an ivory ascribed to Tutilo of St. Gallen (c. A.D. 900) where, under an inscription *Ascensio Sce Marie*, the Virgin is shown as an *Orans* standing with two angels on each side of her in a grouping elsewhere used of Christ's Ascension.[5]

The early illustrations of the death of the Virgin thus display two tendencies of the primitive and mediaeval Church—the desire to assimilate the history of the Virgin to the events recorded of her Son, and, in particular, the pious eagerness to convert metaphor, or reverie, into concrete fact.

Moreover, the doctrine of the Assumption grew up in a world where miraculous translations were an accepted sign of God's especial favour and a mark of pre-eminent holiness. Examples of this belief occur both in the Graeco-Roman and in the Jewish tradition. The story of Heracles, in its later form,[6] records that the hero, tormented by the poison prepared for him by Deianira, climbed up the slopes of Mount Oeta and, under the instructions of Apollo, built his own funeral pyre with the wood of beech and fir trees. He then lay upon the pyre, in full armour,

---

[1] As in a Reichenau manuscript, preserved at Munich. Künstle, *op. cit.* i, p. 568.
[2] British Museum, Harl. 2908.
[3] Wilpert, *Die römischen Mosaiken und Malereien*, ii. 528.
[4] Illustrated in Diehl, *op. cit.* i. 251.   [5] Shown in Künstle, *op. cit.* i, p. 570.
[6] Sophocles, *Trachiniae*; not in the *Odyssey*. Cf. L. R. Farnell, *Greek Hero Cults*, pp. 166 ff., M. P. Nilsson, 'Der Flammentod des Herakles auf dem Oite', in *Archiv für Religionswissenschaft*, 1922, pp. 310 ff.

while Poeas, father of Philoctetes, performed the office of kindling the fire. The wood soon blazed up, but a cloud descended and Heracles was taken up into heaven in a four-horse chariot, with an angelic being, Athena or sometimes Nike, as his companion.[1] No trace could ever be found of his bones or his ashes, for which earth could provide no worthy resting-place.

The Igel monument, near Trèves, shows Heracles in his chariot being greeted by Minerva (Athena) who no longer sits by his side but emerges from the clouds to meet him and extends her hand to draw him within the gates of Heaven, a *motif* which is repeated, with a difference, on later Roman medallions of consecration where the hand of God is stretched out to raise the Christian emperor. But the theme of the assumption of the emperor into Heaven is found long before the days of Constantine. It typifies the divinization which could be conferred by senatorial decree and was linked with cremation, the body being, as it were, snatched away from the pyre and transported heavenwards.

The earliest example of the apotheosis of an emperor is provided by an altar set up by Augustus, that stands in the precincts of the Vatican.[2] The divine Julius is borne aloft in the four-horse chariot to be received by Jupiter, shown within the curving folds of the mantle of the Cosmos. The chariot of the sun also appears in the left upper corner of the monument, while Augustus, who, with other members of the imperial household, witnesses the assumption, raises his hand in a last greeting. The theme of apotheosis is treated in a somewhat similar manner on the Antonine column, where Antoninus Pius and Faustina are shown as Jupiter and Juno being borne aloft on the back of a gigantic winged angel, while, down below, Roma raises her hand in salutation. But the thought of bodily departure to the gods is illustrated even more clearly by an ivory at the British Museum.[3] Here the emperor, who may be Constantius Chlorus, is borne aloft by two winged angels (possibly Sleep and Death) to Heaven where five gods are seated, two of whom stretch out their hands to welcome him as one of their number. Underneath is shown the funeral pyre, and the chariot of the sun with two flying eagles preceding it, while still lower down elephants are shown drawing a funeral chariot which contains the image of the now divinized emperor.[4]

[1] Illustrated by a number of vase-paintings. Daremberg-Saglio, *Dictionnaire des antiquités*, fig. 3778. Cf. Roscher, *Griechische und römische Mythologie*, i. 2240, 2250.

[2] Mrs. A. Strong, *Apotheosis and After-life*, pl. vii.

[3] Strong, *op. cit.* pl. xxxi.

[4] Cf. Justin, *Apology*, i. 21. 3. E. Bickermann, 'Die römische Kaiserapotheose', *Archiv für Religionswissenschaft*, 1929.

APPENDIX

Pictures produced under this inspiration began again in the seventeenth century, when Rubens illustrated the apotheosis of King Henry IV of France. Ingres, in his designs for the painted ceiling of the Hôtel de Ville at Paris, kept even closer to his classical models. For Napoleon is shown as being borne aloft in a four-horse chariot while Nike, his companion, crowns him and an eagle flies overhead. Below, an empty throne takes the place of the funeral pyre, and Paris, represented by a female figure in deep mourning, gazes upwards as she waves her hand in a last salute. A remarkable combination of classical and mediaeval forms is provided by the carving,[1] executed by G. Schadow in 1811, of the apotheosis of Queen Luise. Here, as the queen floats upwards from the globe of earth, she is attended by the Virtues, while the seven stars more commonly associated with the Virgin Mary shine over her head.

The idea that persons of especial sanctity were appropriately delivered by God from the shock of death and the humiliation of the tomb was congenial to Hebrew thought also. The temporary assumption of the prophet Ezekiel whom 'the spirit lifted up between the earth and the heaven'[2] for the purpose of revelation is probably not intended to be understood any more literally than St. Paul's description of himself as being 'caught up into Paradise',[3] but the mind of man has a natural tendency to objectify metaphorical language, and the story of Habakkuk being snatched away to Babylon 'by the hair of his head'[4] is told with naïve realism.

According to some accounts, both Abraham[5] and Isaiah[6] were, during their lifetime, whirled up to the heights of Heaven to enjoy supernatural revelations, and similar stories were told of Mohammed. But this was a case of transient experiences only; and the three classic[7] examples of translation at death were provided by Enoch, Elijah and Moses. According to the book of Genesis,[8] 'Enoch walked with (LXX. 'pleased') God: and he was not: for God took him', words which may

[1] At Paretz. Cf. O. Schmitt, *Reallexicon zur deutschen Kunstgeschichte, s.v.* Apotheose.
[2] Ezek. viii. 3.
[3] II Cor. xii. 4. The newly discovered Coptic *Ascension of Paul* (H. C. Puech in *Coptic Studies presented to W. E. Crum*), however, gives certain details of Paul's ascent and purports to explain the nature of the 'ineffable words'. Cf. Epiphanius, *adv. Haer.*: xxxviii. 2. 5.
[4] *Bel and the Dragon*, 36.
[5] *Apocalypse of Abraham*, ch. xv. ff. (ed. G. H. Box, S.P.C.K. 1919).
[6] *Ascension of Isaiah*, vi–xi, ed. R. H. Charles.
[7] But not the only ones. Others included Ezra (II Esdras viii. 19) and Baruch (*Apocalypse of Baruch*).
[8] v. 24. Cf. Livy's notice about Romulus (i. 16), 'he was not thenceforth on earth'.

mean no more than that Enoch died after a life that was, by patriarchal standards, a short one but marked by happy communion with God. This notice was, however, developed along two lines. The *Book of Enoch* consists largely of visions which it was Enoch's high privilege to receive and communicate to men, while the Slavonic *Apocalypse of Enoch* introduces the idea of bodily translation: 'The angels hasted and took Enoch and carried him into the highest heaven, where the Lord received him'. This is in accord with the predominant tradition of the Scriptures. In the Septuagint version of Genesis, it is stated that Enoch 'was not found, for God translated him', while the author of Ecclesiasticus is still more explicit: 'Enoch pleased the Lord and was translated': 'upon the earth was no man created like Enoch; for he was taken up from the earth'.[1] This belief is echoed in the Epistle to the Hebrews:[2] 'By faith Enoch was translated that he should not see death; and was not found, because God had translated him'.

Elijah is similarly favoured. According to the '*Apocalypse of Elijah*', he, too, enjoyed heavenly visions; while the Second Book of Kings[3] relates that Elijah was parted from Elisha by the appearance of a chariot and horses of fire, whereat 'Elijah went up by a whirlwind into heaven'. Later versions of the story make Elijah depart in the chariot of fire itself: he was 'taken up in a whirlwind of fire, and in a chariot of fiery horses'.[4] The exceptional nature of the reward is stressed in the First Book of Maccabees:[5] 'Elijah, for that he was exceeding zealous for the law, was taken up into heaven'.

Later traditions about Moses were no less dramatic, and were based on the Biblical statements, 'Moses went up into the mount and the cloud covered the mount'[6] and 'he was buried . . . in the land of Moab over against Bethpeor; but no man knoweth his sepulchre unto this day'.[7] The former passage was held to justify an apocalypse of visions accorded to Moses, the second forms the basis of the belief that he was taken up bodily into Heaven. Josephus cautiously observes: 'As he was saying goodbye to Eleazar and Joshua and conversing with them still, a cloud suddenly encompassed him and he disappeared in a ravine. The writer in the Holy Scriptures recorded that he died, for fear that, by reason of their very great affection for him, they might venture to say

[1] Ecclus. xliv. 16, xlix. 14.
[2] xi. 5. Josephus (*Ant.* i. 3. 4) says of Enoch: 'He lived for 365 years and then departed to Heaven; for which reason they have written up nothing about the end of his life'.
[3] ii. 11.
[4] Ecclus. xlviii. 9. Christian tradition identified Enoch and Elijah with the 'two witnesses' of Rev. xi who 'ascended up to heaven in a cloud'.
[5] ii. 58.   [6] Exod. xxiv. 15.   [7] Deut. xxxiv. 6.

that he had departed to heaven.'[1] The first-century *Assumption of Moses*[2] appears to have been far more colourful and definite, though, the text being defective, the details of the narrative have to be gathered from scattered references in the Epistle of Jude,[3] Clement of Alexandria[4] and Origen.[5] The picture that may be drawn from these sources is as follows: Michael receives the commission to bury Moses, but is opposed in this task by Satan who claims the body on the ground that he is the lord of matter. This claim Michael rebuts, with the reply that God created the world and is therefore lord of matter, and he adds the countercharge that it was Satan who malevolently inspired the serpent to tempt Adam and Eve. Opposition being thus overcome, the departure of Moses follows, and Joshua and Caleb observe its twofold aspect. Moses 'living in the spirit' is raised up to Heaven, while Moses 'dead in the body' is buried secretly in the recesses of the mountains.

The influence of such narratives in forming the legend of the Assumption is not hard to trace, and the interpretation of the Falling-asleep of the Virgin in terms of the Falling-asleep of Moses is particularly noticeable in a Syriac poem[6] written by Jacob of Serug, at the end of the fifth century, for a monophysite council assembled at Nisibis. According to this account, a veil of bright cloud descended upon the Mount of Olives, and the Virgin's death occurred in the presence of Christ, his angels and a gathering of souls of Old Testament worthies. Christ thereupon carried the body of his mother to the mountain-top, and the author notes that the burial of Mary on the summit of a mountain of Galilee (identified with the Mount of Olives) resembles that of Moses, in that it was carried out by God. The body is placed by St. John in the tomb, while the soul is borne heavenwards by the hierarchy of angels amidst the jubilations of nature. For Jacob of Serug, the location of the grave of Mary, like that of Moses, was unknown. Even though the monophysite school of thought, to which he belonged, was inclined to press the veneration due to Mary, the general picture as presented by Jacob of Serug is that Mary's body is committed to the silence of the grave while her soul is taken up to Heaven to enjoy fellowship with her son. That this Palestinian form of the story did not entirely yield to the Transitus-texts and the great name of Dionysius the Areopagite is shown by a liturgical poem of some antiquity incorporated by the emperor Theodore Lascaris II into the late Byzantine Great Office of

---

[1] *Antiquities*, iv. 326.   [2] Ed. R. H. Charles (1897).
[3] Verse 9.   [4] *Stromateis*, vi. 15. 132.
[5] *De Principiis*, iii. 2. 1. *Hom. in Iosuam*, ii. 1. Charles notes other patristic references, *op. cit.* pp. 108–110.   [6] Baumstark in *Oriens Christianus*, iv.

intercession addressed to the most-holy Mother of God.[1] In this poem the Virgin entrusts her body to the Apostles for burial while 'her Son and God' is asked to receive her soul. So, in the pictures of the standard Byzantine type, it is with the soul of his mother rather than with her body that Christ concerns Himself.

On the mediaeval view of things the Virgin Mary was not the only New Testament figure who was honoured by a corporeal assumption into Heaven. Of John the Evangelist it had been said, 'If I will that he tarry till I come, what is that to thee?'[2] and this enigmatic saying formed the basis of a tradition that he was spared the humiliation of normal death. St. Ambrose, when commenting on the necessity for all who wish to enter Paradise to be tested by fire, notes concerning St. John: 'Some have had doubts regarding his death, but we can have no doubt that he passed through fire; for he is in Heaven and not separated from Christ'.[3] St. Augustine somewhat hesitantly mentions[4] the tradition that he slumbered beneath the earth, which moved with his breath; but more widely acceptable was the account, based on some versions of the second-century Acts of John[5] and illustrated in the windows of Chartres, Bourges and Rheims cathedrals, of the manner in which he arranged his own burial at Ephesus. Having received the command of Christ: 'Come, my friend to me; for it is time that thou came. Eat and be fed at my table with thy brethren',[6] he ordered a pit to be dug and, bidding his friends farewell, descended into it, whereupon a blinding light flashed all around and, when the people were able to see the grave again, they discovered that it contained nothing but manna. The *Golden Legend* continues: 'Some say and affirm that he died without pain of death, and that he was in that clearness borne into heaven body and soul, whereof God knoweth the certainty'.

A comparable tradition about Mary Magdalene arose later and was less widespread. The *Golden Legend*[7] is content to state that she was 'every day lift up by the hands of angels into the air' and that her dead body exhaled a sweet fragrance for seven days after her death. But, from the fifteenth century onwards, Mary Magdalene, borrowing from the legends of both the Virgin Mary and Mary of Egypt, is shown not infrequently as a naked woman, clad in little save her own hair, being raised up to heaven by a choir of angels. Early examples are provided by

---

[1] ‘Ωρολόγιον τὸ μέγα (Venice, 1884), p. 457.

’Απόστολοι, ἐκ περάτων συναθροισθέντες ἐνθάδε Γεθσημανῇ τῷ χωρίῳ, κηδεύσατέ μου τὸ σῶμα· καὶ σύ, Υἱὲ καὶ Θεέ μου, παράλαβέ μου τὸ πνεῦμα.

[2] John xxi. 22.   [3] *Expositio in Psalmum CXVIII, P.L.* xv. 1487.

[4] *In Ioannem,* 124. 2.   [5] M. R. James, *Apocryphal New Testament,* p. 270.

[6] *Golden Legend* (ed. F. S. Ellis), ii. 173.   [7] *Op. cit.* iv. 84.

a stone-screen at Thorn, by a wood-carving in the Marienkirche at Danzĭg,[1] and by a panel of Swiss glass[2] by Hans Fries, of Fribourg, now preserved in the Victoria and Albert Museum, while remarkable illustrations of the same theme are offered by Riemenschneider and Donatello.

It was, then, natural enough that men should be drawn on to foster legends like that of the Assumption. Apart from other impulses to such a course, there was the strong desire to let the imagination play around the well-loved figure of the Virgin and affectionately to fill in such details of her life as would make her stand out even more distinctly from the mists of time long past. On those engaged in this agreeable task no limits were imposed by any nice scrupulosity concerning historical facts, or, as Coulton put it, 'if the early Christians had known more about the Mother of the Lord, the mediaeval mind would have known far less'.[3]

The longing to entwine the figure of the Virgin with a garland of fantasy is illustrated by the Coptic discourses, probably of fourth- or fifth-century date, that pass under the names of Cyril of Jerusalem, the mythical Demetrius of Antioch, Epiphanius of Salamis and Cyril of Alexandria.[4] 'Cyril of Jerusalem' starts off in a mood of self-conscious rectitude: 'We are wholly unable to follow the fictitious statements which are found in the fabulous lives of the Virgin, and which resemble the writings of the Greek poets, who in their works on theology relate mere myths about their gods; neither will we invent lives of her in order to gratify her'. However, the impulse to tell a satisfying story about her is never very far away, and 'Cyril' declares: 'There is no trouble whatsoever in discussing the queen, who became the mother of the King, and he who listeneth is not wearied by her history. It is like unto one who goeth to draw water from a spring; as soon as he stretcheth forth his hand to draw therefrom, the spring sendeth water in great abundance. And this is my own case when I begin to describe the life of the Virgin, for the fountain of my speech bubbleth up abundantly.'[5] 'Cyril's' is the kind of world wherein lack of miracles implies lack of any exceptional holiness, where, for instance, as the Holy Family go down into Egypt, 'the Child rode upon the light cloud that transporteth those who are without sin. And the mountains and the rocks levelled

[1] Künstle, *Ikonographie der christlichen Kunst*, ii. 432. Cf. Braun, *Tracht und Attribute der Heiligen*, p. 498, where an illustration is given of a carved figure at Tiefenbronn, dated 1525.

[2] About A.D. 1500. B. Rackham, *A Guide to the Collections of Stained Glass*, pl. 53.

[3] Coulton, *Five Centuries of Religion*, I, p. 155.

[4] E. A. Wallis Budge, *Miscellaneous Coptic Texts*, pp. 626 ff.

[5] Budge, *op. cit.* p. 642.

themselves before them, and smooth roads whereon they could walk easily made themselves ready for their feet, and they crossed rivers and streams without the help of ship or sailor.' So also with the life of the Virgin: 'She was in the Temple before the gift of the Lord was given unto her, and there was no limit to her beauty, and the Temple was wont to be filled with angels because of her sweet fragrance, and they used to come to visit her for the sake of her conversation'. With this atmosphere of miracle and devotion the remarkable stories which 'Cyril' adds concerning the Virgin's birth on the one hand and her death and assumption on the other are in complete harmony.

Some of the details given in these encomiums of the Virgin are no more than reflective word-painting, as the writer sets before his eyes the scene at Bethlehem or Nazareth. Thus Cyril of Alexandria describes in an attractive manner how 'Mary used to take hold of Jesus' hand and lead Him along the roads, saying "My sweet Son, walk a little way", in the same manner as all other babes are taught to walk. And He, Jesus, the very God, followed after her untroubled, as He clung to her with his little fingers. He stopped from time to time and hung on the skirts of Mary his mother,—He upon whom the whole universe hangs.' But 'Demetrius' and Epiphanius carry their interest in the Virgin's ancestry to the point of concocting spurious genealogical lore, and picturesque marvels are never far away: 'And Mary sat in Joseph's house for three years, and his sons ministered unto her, and the angels were round about her at all times, for they earnestly desired to remain with her because of her purity, and they were in the form of doves or some other kind of holy bird. They flew about her in the place where she used to sit working at her handicraft, and they would alight upon the window of her room, and they longed to hear her holy voice, which was sweet and pretty and holy.'

This type of imaginative novel-writing not seldom took the specialized form of apocalypse, perhaps the most influential of these compositions, though its fourth-century date makes it a fairly late one, being the *Apocalypse of Paul*. Condemned by a decree of Pope Gelasius and viewed askance by the established writers of orthodoxy, its popularity was nevertheless widespread and persistent, and it is echoed even by Dante.[1] The author, who draws freely on the much earlier *Apocalypse of Peter*, tells with considerable gusto of the various punishments which, in St. Paul's sight, were inflicted on the malefactors in Hell. Those who were jealous for the Virgin's honour felt impelled to include her also in the small and distinguished circle of those who had been allowed to wit-

[1] *Inferno*, ii. 28, where there is an allusion to the visit to Hell paid by the 'chosen vessel'.

ness the torments of the damned; so the *Apocalypse of Paul* was rewritten around the figure of the Virgin, and Mary, no less than certain chosen Apostles, views the varied tribulation of those whose 'worm dieth not' in the 'place of gnashing of teeth'.[1] Still more certainly was it due to Mary's pre-eminent holiness that she should be included with Enoch and Elijah and such other of the patriarchs as had been by God's especial favour taken, body and soul, into Heaven without having to wait for the general Resurrection. Of Moses it was related, by the beginning of the Christian era, that no place upon earth was fit to receive his body. 'And now,' says Joshua, 'what place shall receive thee? Or what shall be the sign that marks thy sepulchre? Or who will dare to move thy body thence as that of a mere man from place to place? For all men when they die have according to their age their sepulchres upon earth; but thy sepulchre is from the rising to the setting sun, and from the south to the confines of the north: all the world is thy sepulchre.'[2] In a similar spirit, but with greater exuberance, Christian writers from the eighth century onwards wrote of the exceptional honours rightly accorded to the 'Queen and lady of all'. Thus Theodore of Studium calls on all the world to celebrate with joy the 'funeral and translation of Mary mother of God. For she passes from this earth and approaches the heavenly mountains, the true mount Zion where it has pleased God to dwell.'[3] After relating the story of the Assumption in terms of the Transitus-texts, Theodore goes on to ask: 'Who ever saw such a translation as that of which the mother of my Lord was found worthy? And rightly so. For no one has ever ranked higher: she is greater than all.' The emperor Leo VI presses the point that bodily incorruption is to be expected as a part of the Virgin's high privilege: 'Those hands, whereby everything is held together, receive your blameless soul, and your pure, spotless body was translated to be in the realms of complete purity. Because thou didst bear God clothed in flesh, thou art borne by the hands of God now that thou hast put off the flesh.'[4] About the same time as Leo's oration, the preacher of a Latin sermon on the Assumption of the Blessed Virgin Mary spoke to similar effect: 'I cannot imagine

---

[1] The (Ethiopic) *Apocalypse of the Virgin.* M. R. James, *op. cit.* 563.

[2] R. H. Charles, *op. cit.* p. 45. This extract is from the writing that usually goes under the name of *Assumption of Moses* but is, in fact, a cognate work, the *Testament of Moses,* with which the *Assumption of Moses* was combined at an early date.

[3] P.G. xcix. 720. Theodore lived A.D. 759–826.

[4] P.G. cvii. 162. χειρῶν μὲν ἐκείνων, αἷς πάντα συνέχεται, τὴν πανάμωμον δεχομένων ψυχήν· τοῦ δὲ καθαροῦ καὶ ἀσπίλου σώματος ἐν καθαρωτάτοις μεθισταμένου χωρίοις. ὅτι ἐβάστασας Θεὸν σάρκα ἠμφιεσμένον, βαστάζῃ Θεοῦ παλάμαις ἀπαμφιασαμένη τὴν σάρκα. Leo VI reigned A.D. 886–912.

that most holy body, from which Christ took flesh thus uniting divine with human nature, delivered over as a prey to worms, as also I shrink from saying that it is subject to the common lot of corruption and dust'.[1] By this time, use was being made of new arguments, based not on history or pretended history but on what was deemed appropriate, a principle which was later summed up in the Scholastic maxim 'potuit; decuit; ergo fecit'—God has the power, the action was fitting; therefore He must have done it.[2] But reflection on the fallibility of human knowledge and perceptions might well cause the theologian to hesitate before pronouncing what God must have done in an exceptional and mysterious case. And the historian will perhaps display his reverence rather by presenting a record, often imperfect and incomplete, of events that he has collected and arranged to the best of his ability than by allowing fantasy, however pious, to masquerade as fact and thus to weaken the firm foundation of truth.

[1] P.L. xl. 1146.

[2] The view that the unique position of the Virgin demands unique honour was stated thus by Cardinal Newman (Discourses to Mixed Congregations, xviii.): 'It was becoming that she should be taken up into heaven and not lie in the grave until Christ's second coming, who had passed a life of sanctity and miracle such as hers'. The theological arguments are clearly and concisely summarized by V. Bennett and R. Winch, The Assumption of Our Lady and Catholic Theology (S.P.C.K., 1950), where the historical evidence also is reviewed.

NOTES

1. *Discours sur l'histoire universelle* (avant-propos).
2. Cf. Cicero, *De or.* ii. 9. 36.
3. Bolingbroke, *On the Study and Use of History*, letter 2, 'I have read somewhere or other, in Dionysius of Halicarnassus, I think, that History is Philosophy teaching by examples'.

4. *Ad Fam.* v. 12.   5. *Letters*, Feb. 5th, 1750.
6. i. 21.   7. *Annales*, iii. 65.
8. Address given at Cambridge, 1895.
9. Ordericus Vitalis, *Hist. eccl.* vi. 1.
10. *Lecture on Steele.*   11. *Pericles and Aspasia*, cxli.
12. *The Muse of History.*   13. *Expansion of England*, p. 174.
14. Matthew Arnold, *Literature and Dogma*, ch. i. 5.
15. i. 1.   16. i. 14.
17. *De or.* ii. 15. 62.   18. *De or.* ii. 9. 36.
19. *Ad Fam.* v. 12.   20. *Brutus*, 11. 42.
21. *Ep.* xlix. 13.
22. *De la connaissance de Dieu et de soi-même, Œuvres*, xxxiv (1818), p. 115.
23. F. M. Powicke; quoted by Burleigh, *The City of God*, pp. 19, 192.
24. So Quintilian x. 2. 21: 'Id quoque vitandum, in quo magna pars errat, ne in oratione poetas nobis et historicos, in illis operibus oratores aut declamatores imitandos putemus. sua cuique proposita lex, suus decor est'. Cf. Pliny, *Ep.* v. 8. Cicero's declaration that the composition of history is *oratorium maxime* (*De leg.* i. 2. 5) may be interpreted along the lines of Augustine's argument (*De doctr. chr.* iv. 2. 3): 'cum per artem rhetoricam et vera suadeantur et falsa, quis audeat dicere adversus mendacium in defensoribus suis inermem debere consistere veritatem?'
25. xii. 25b.   26. *De doctr. chr.* ii. 28.
27. *Ap.* Gellius, v. 18. 8.
28. Tr. C. Cotton (1743), ii. 97. Cf. Polybius, xii. 25 g: 'Neither is it possible for a man who possesses no experience of military affairs to write well about what happens in war, nor can one write well of political matters who has had no experience of public affairs'.
29. Milton, *Paradise Regained*, iv. 327.
30. *The Causal and the Casual in History* (Rede lecture, 1929).
31. *Childe Harold*, IV. lxxxii.

32. *Institutio oratoria*, x. 1. 31. Aristides (*Or.* 49) calls historians 'those who are midway between poets and orators'. Cf. Norden, *Antike Kunstprosa*.

33. *Bibl. hist.* i. 1. 3, and i. 2. 2.

34. Deut. vi. 4.   35. Gen. xi. 1-9.

36. Cf. Acts xvii. 26.   37. Eph. i. 10.

38. *Carm.* 12. 31.   39. Eccles. i. 9.

40. Mark iv. 12.   41. Amos v. 11.

42. Eccles. ii. 18.   43. Bossuet, *Discours*, iii, ch. 1.

44. Inaugural address given at Cambridge in 1903.

45. Dr. Inge, however, says of this statement made in 1912: 'I don't think I should write that now'.

46. Cf. H. G. Wood, *Christianity and the Nature of History*, p. 17.

47. *Analogy*, part II, ch. VII, ii. 2.

48. Shotwell, *Introduction to the History of History*, p. 128.

49. J. Skinner, *Kings* (Century Bible), pp. 6 and 15.

50. *Contra Apionem*, i. 15.   51. *Contra Apionem*, i. 27.

52. *B.J.* vi. 241.   53. *Chron.* ii. 30.

54. xx. 31.

55. Berdyaev, *Meaning of History*, p. 21.

56. i. 1.   57. Exod. xv. 11.

58. *Annales*, vi. 22.   59. *Œuvres*, x. 70.

60. Quoted and commented on by W. Nigg, *Die Kirchengeschichtsschreibung*, p. 239.

61. *Coningsby* (Everyman ed.), p. 43.

62. W. G. de Burgh, *Hibbert Journal*, October 1936.

63. T. S. Eliot, *Little Gidding*.   64. i. praef. 10.

65. viii. 40.

66. Pichon, *Histoire de la littérature latine*, p. 316. Livy's attitude is illustrated, with perhaps a touch of exaggeration, in the debate which he is made to carry through with Asinius Pollio in Robert Graves' novel, *I Claudius*:

LIVY: Do you mean that I mustn't write a history with an epic theme because that's a prerogative of poetry, or put worthy eve-of-battle speeches in the mouths of my generals, because to compose such speeches is the prerogative of oratory?

ASINIUS POLLIO: That is precisely what I do mean. History is a true record of what happened, how people lived and died, what they said; an epic theme merely distorts the record. As for your generals' speeches, they are admirable as oratory but damnably unhistorical.

LIVY: Any legendary episode from early historical writings which bears on my theme of the ancient greatness of Rome I gladly incorporate in the story: though it may not be true in factual detail it is true in spirit.

67. xxi-xxx.   68. *Charles V* (1857), ii. p. 60.

69. Address given at Cambridge, 1895.

70. *Roman History*, i. 1.

71. For quotations illustrating Hume's attitude towards history cf. J. W. Thompson, *A History of Historical Writing*, II, p. 71.

72. II Macc. ii. 26.

73. Letter written December 14th, 1770.

74. Sanh. 34 *a*.   75. *Comm. in Amos*, I. ii. 1.

76. *Time must have a Stop*, p. 295. G. C. Field, in *Proceedings of the British Academy*, 1938, writes: 'The language and practice of *some* historians has suggested a belief that in some cases some kinds of selection, so far from distorting, positively increase our understanding of what happened, and make it clearer than would a mere reconstruction of all the events that took place. That is to say, the assumption seems sometimes to be made in some historical work that some events are more *important* than others. If we ask, Important for what? the answer would be, Important for understanding what happened.'

77. For this reason, the preservation of 'typical' stories, such as those which have gathered round the name of Dr. W. A. Spooner, may be claimed as an aid to biographical history, even though the authenticity of any one example may be open to doubt.

78. Yet while, as Croce explains (*On History*, tr. Ainslie, p. 190), sympathy is permitted, partisanship deserves censure.

79. *New Yorker*, Feb. 12th, 1949.

80. 'History.' *Edinburgh Review*, May 1828.

81. *Memoirs*, p. 61.

82. Picasso, in his picture of a cockerel, abandoned realism in favour of exaggeration, in order 'to bring out the bird's aggressiveness, its cheek and its stupidity'. E. H. Gombrich, *The Story of Art*, p. 12.

83. Cf. W. Addison, *Worthy Dr. Fuller*, p. 44.

84. Westcott, 'The Relation of Christianity to Art', an appendix to his *Commentary on the Epistles of St. John*, p. 371.

85. *The Meaning of History*, p. 25.

86. L. Halphen, *Introduction à l'histoire*, p. 9.

87. E. Seeberg, 'Paulus', *Zeitschrift für Kirchengeschichte*, 1941. Seeberg adds: 'Geschehen und Deutung gehören zusammen und lassen sich nicht trennen'.

88. *Symbolism and Belief*, p. 380.

89. Aldous Huxley, *Ends and Means*, p. 267.

90. *The Victories of Love.*

91. J. R. Illingworth, *Reason and Revelation*, p. 63. Illingworth, however, uses the word 'actuality' instead of 'reality'.

CHAPTER II

1. I Cor. xv. 4.
2. I Cor. x. 11.
3. Zech. ix. 9.
4. Isa. lvi. 7.
5. Matt. xxi. 15.
6. Isa. liii. 3.
7. Mark x. 45.
8. Hos. vi. 2.
9. Origen, *in Celsum*, iv. 23.
10. Cf. Isa. lxvi. 18.
11. Cf. Deut. xiv. 2.
12. Rom. ch. xi. Cf. Jer. xi. 16 and Hos. xiv. 6.
13. *Epistle of Barnabas*, ed. K. Lake. *Apostolic Fathers*, I (Loeb, 1925), ii. 6.
14. *Op. cit.* v. 11.
15. *Op. cit.* iv. 7.
16. *Op. cit.* xiii. 7; based on Gen. xvii. 4 and Rom. iv. 12.
17. *Op. cit.* xiv. 4.
18. Cf. Luke i. 4.
19. Isa. xlix. 6.
20. *Didache*, x.
21. *Adv. Haer.* i. 3.
22. Mark i. 22.
23. *Acts of John*, 97, tr. M. R. James, *The Apocryphal New Testament*, p. 254.
24. Ignatius, *To the Smyrnaeans*, ii.
25. *Op. cit.* v.
26. A. E. Taylor, *The Faith of a Moralist*, i, p. 28.
27. *The First Epistle of Clement*, xix. 1. Cf. iv. Convenient text and translation in *Apostolic Fathers*, I (ed. K. Lake, Loeb).
28. *Op. cit.* xi. 2.
29. *Op. cit.* v.
30. *Op. cit.* lv. 1.
31. Henry of Huntingdon, *Historia Anglorum*, praef.
32. *History of the World*, preface, iv.
33. *I Clement*, iii. 1.
34. Deut. xxxii. 15.
35. *I Clement*, xlv. 2.
36. Ezek. xxxix. 21.
37. Polybius, xii. 25 b.
38. *I Clement*, xiv. 1.
39. *Op. cit.* lvi. 16. Cf. Nahum i. 7.
40. Justin, *Apology*, i. 46.
41. *Apology*, ii. 10.
42. *Apology*, ii. 13.
43. Cowper, *The Task*, ii. 499.
44. Justin, *Dialogus*, 7.
45. *Apology*, i. 44.
46. *Dialogus*, 7. Cf. *Ad Graecos*, 8.
47. *Dialogus*, 9.
48. *Apology*, i. 2.
49. *Fra Lippo Lippi*, 313.
50. *Apology*, i. 59.
51. Deut. xxxii. 22.

52. Justin, *Apology*, i, 60.   53. *Dialogus*, 134.
54. *Apology*, ii. 4.   55. *Dialogus*, 19.
56. Dan. ix. 16.
57. Tennyson, *In Memoriam*, fin.   58. II Cor. iv. 6.
59. *History of Ancient Greek Literature*, p. 404.
60. Sophocles, *Antigone*, 333.   61. *Dial.* i. 4. 16.
62. *I Clement*, xlii.   63. Isa. lx. 17.
64. *Adv. Haereses*, iii. 3. 1.
65. *Adv. Haereses*, iii. 3. 3. Cf. iv. 26. 2.
66. Tertullian, *De praescriptionibus*, 32.
67. *Adv. Marcionem*, i. 21. Cf. iv. 5.
68. Hegesippus, *Memorabilia*, ap. Eusebius, *H.E.* iv. 22. Cf. Caspar, *Die älteste römische Bischofsliste*, and *Geschichte des Papsttums*, 6 ff.
69. Or, at any rate, the determined rival of Pope Callistus.
70. Heb. xi. 13.

CHAPTER III

1. *Philocalia*, ii. 5.
2. Wordsworth, *Lines composed a few Miles above Tintern Abbey*, 95.
3. These words are attributed to W. H. Auden.
4. H. St. L. B. Moss, *The Birth of the Middle Ages*, p. 258.
5. *Hom. in Gen.* ix. 7.   6. *Ode on a Grecian Urn*.
7. *Opera* (ed. Dutens), vi. p. 297.
8. *Ep. ad Gregorium.* (*Philocalia*, xiii. 2.)
9. *Comm. in Mat.* x. 14.   10. *De princ.* iv. 26.
11. *Div. Inst., P.L.* lxx. 1107.   12. *Hom. in Gen.* ii. 6.
13. *De princ.* iv. 23 (Curtailed.)
14. For his painstaking construction of the Hexapla, a conspectus of five parallel versions with a transliteration of the Hebrew, cf. Eusebius, *Ecclesiastical History*, vi. 16.
15. Review in *The Times Literary Supplement*, Sept. 22nd, 1945.
16. *De princ.* iv. 11.   17. *Edinburgh Review*, May 1828.
18. Leibniz. A letter written in 1692. Cf. E. Bodemann, *Zt. des hist. Vereins der Niedersachsen*, 1885.
19. *Comm. ser. in Mat.* 77.   20. *De princ.* iv. 9.
21. *Comm. ser. in Mat.* 138.
22. Origen's interpretations are often to be classed as 'symbolic' or 'typological' rather than as 'allegorical' in the strict sense. Julius Held in Schmitt's *Reallexicon* distinguishes symbol from allegory thus: 'Symbolik in ihrer reinsten Form sehen wir da, wo einfache, meist

dingliche Formen auf Grund einer angenommenen, rational nicht fass-
baren Wesensverwandschaft einen höheren und allgemeineren Inhalt
vertreten'. Of allegory, on the other hand, it may be said: 'Eine Darstel-
lung, in der ein unanschaulicher, begrifflicher oder gedanklicher Vor-
stellungsgehalt (z.B. "Ungerechtigkeit" oder "Huldigung der Künste
an einen Fürsten") durch bildliche Mittel vollständig zum Ausdruck
gebracht wird'.

23. Eusebius, *H.E.* ii. 18.

24. J. E. Sandys, *A History of Classical Scholarship*, I, p. 29.

25. Heraclitus, *Quaestiones Homericae*, cap. 22.   Cf. Edmund Stein,
Die allegorische Exegese des Philo aus Alexandria, Beihefte zur *Z.A.T.W.*,
1929.

26. *De Providentia*, ii. 40.   Cf. Varro *ap.* Aug. *De civ. Dei* vi. 5.

27. *Leg. All.* ii. 7.	28. *Leg. All.* i. 14.
29. *Leg. All.* i. 19.	30. *Leg. All.* ii. 18.
31. Num. xxi. 6.	32. Wisdom, xvi. 5-7.

33. Philo, *De vita contemplativa*, 78, *ap.* Eusebius, *H.E.* ii. 17. 20.

34. Lev. xi.	35. II Cor. iv. 7.
36. I Cor. ix. 9.	37. I Cor. x. 4.
38. *De princ.* iv. 13.	39. *De princ.* iv. 7.
40. *De princ.* iv. 7.	41. *De princ.* iv. 9.
42. *Ap.* Eusebius, *H.E.* vi. 19.	43. *De princ.* iv. 18.
44. Jerome, *In Cant.*, praef.	45. Song of Songs, ii. 9.

46. *In Cant.* iii (Baehrens, 220). The Song of Songs seems regularly
to have induced commentators to abandon the literal sense and to rely
on allegory. Bede, in speaking of this work, says: 'nil carnale et iuxta
litteram resonat'. (*Opp.* ix. 365.)

47. Heb. ix. 24.	48. *In Cant.* ii. (Baehrens, 160).

49. *De Princ.* iv. 19.

50. *The Authority of the Bible*, p. 260.

51. *In Celsum*, i. 42.	52. *Hom. in Lev.* vii. 5.
53. *Comm. in Ioann.* i. 4.	54. *Comm. in Ioann.* x. 5.

55. *Comm. ser. in Mat.* 77.

56. ἡ κατὰ τὴν ἱστορίαν ἀσυμφωνία.   *Comm. in Ioann.* x. 3. 14.

57. *Philocalia*, vi. 2.	58. *Hom. in Ier.* xxxix.

59. Sanday, *Inspiration*, p. 421.

60. *Allegoriae quaedam sacrae Scripturae*, 2. 5. 158. 163.

61. 'Littera gesta docet, quid credas allegoria.' Cf. É. Mâle, *L'Art
religieux en France*, ii. 139-141.

62. *Opp.* (ed. J. A. Giles, 1844), vii. 159, 173.

63. *Opp.* vii. 164.   64. *Opp.* vii. 297.

65. *Opp.* viii. 435.   66. *Opp.* v. 39.
67. *Historia ecclesiastica*, iv. 23.   68. *Opp.* xi. 2.
69. *Opp.* vii. 3. Most of these examples from Bede, along with many others, are noted in C. Plummer's introduction to his edition of Bede's *Ecclesiastical History*, lvi–lxii.
70. *Hom. in Num.* xxvi. 3. Cf. *Hom. in Ier.* xii. 1.
71. *Ap.* Augustine *Conf.* vi. 4. 6.
72. *De princ.* iv. 9.
73. *Comm. in Rom.* ii. 11, *P.G.* xiv. 898.
74. *De princ.* i, praef. 2.
75. 'Facile investigata plerumque vilescunt.' *De doctr. chr.* ii. 6.
76. *De princ.* iv. 15.

CHAPTER IV

1. Wisdom of Sol. ii. 15.   2. Tacitus, *Annales*, xv. 44.
3. *On History* (tr. Ainslie), p. 206.
4. Acts x. 44.   5. *H.E.* ii. 2.
6. Isa. iii. 8.
7. *Demonstratio evangelica*, viii. 3. 10, viii. 3. 12.
8. *D.E.* vi. 7. 5. Cf. Neubauer, *Géographie du Talmud*, p. 96.
9. *Martyrs of Palestine*, 7. 4.   10. *Mart. Pal.* 11. 1.
11. *Vita Pamphili*, ap. Jerome, *Contra Rufinum*, i. 9.
12. *Mart. Pal.* 11. 1.
13. *Mart. Pal.* 7. 4.   14. *H.E.* viii. 7-9.
15. Such, at any rate, is the deduction of Photius, 118.
16. The writing of these books was probably not completed before A.D. 311. Book viii adheres more closely to the first seven than to the last two. Cf. E. Schwartz, *Eusebius Werke*, ii. 3, pp. lv ff., Lawlor and Oulton, *Eusebius' Ecclesiastical History*, ii, pp. 2 ff.
17. *Werke* (Insel-Ausgabe, 1921), iv, p. 637.
18. *H.E.* vii. 32. 32.
19. Suidas, *Lex. s.v.* Africanus, ed. Adler, I, p. 433.
20. Acts xvii. 26.
21. The saying is attributed to Eduard Meyer.
22. The standard work on Julius Africanus is by H. Gelzer, *Sextus Julius Africanus und die byzantinische Chronographie*. Cf. Bardenhewer, ii, pp. 264 ff.
23. *H.E.* vi. 31. 2.   24. *Chronicorum prooemium*.
25. Cecil Woodham-Smith, *Florence Nightingale*, p. 336.
26. E. R. Thiele, *Journal of Near Eastern Studies*, iii (1944), p. 137.

27. *Chron. prooem.* 1.

28. The original Greek version is no longer extant, though portions of it occur in the work of such later chronologists as the Byzantine writer George Syncellus. Jerome's Latin translation, to which he made certain additions (*P.L.* xxvii. 34 ff.), may be compared with the Armenian version, edited and translated by Josef Karst (Leipzig, 1911). Cf. C. H. Turner in *Journal of Theological Studies*, 1900, pp. 181-200.

29. Hipler, *Die christliche Geschichtsauffassung* (Cologne, 1884).

30. *H.E.* i. 1. 6.

31. Later on in the work (*H.E.* iii. 3) he added, as another proposed theme, the use of the Scriptures made by the 'orthodox writers in each period' and how some books gained acceptance as canonical while others were rejected or looked on as doubtful.

32. *H.E.* i. 1. 33. *H.E.* i. 4. 2.

34. *H.E.* i. 2. 1. 35. *B.J.* i. 1.

36. *Antiq.* ii. 9. 37. *Antiq.* i. 22.

38. *De Thuc.* 34.

39. *Dictionary of Christian Biography*, ii, p. 345.

40. *E.g.* by Jakob Burckhardt. Cf. W. Nigg, *Die Kirchengeschichtsschreibung* (Munich, 1934), pp. 7 ff.

41. Mark Pattison, *Isaac Casaubon* (1892), p. 448.

42. Thucydides, v. 47. Cf. M. N. Tod, *Greek Historical Inscriptions*, No. 72.

43. *C.I.L.* iii. 12132, 13625 b. Cf. Eusebius, *H.E.* ix. 7.

44. i. 22. 45. Polybius, ix. 9.

46. Polybius, xii. 25 e 6. 47. *Historia Anglorum*, praef.

48. In the preface to his edition of Thucydides, vol. iii.

49. *H.E.* viii. 2. 3. 50. *Decline and Fall*, ch. xvi.

51. Isa. xxx. 10.

52. *Zeitschrift für Kirchengeschichte*, 1897.

53. *Vita Constantini*, i. 8. 54. *V.C.* iii. 10. 3.

55. *Ecclesiastical History*, i. 1.

56. *V.C.* i. 10. Eusebius was concerned to demonstrate the relation which existed between Emperor and Church. Christ and Augustus had been contemporaries, and the way had been prepared for the Incarnation by the peaceful and orderly rule which characterized the early years of the Roman Empire (Cf. Origen, *in Celsum*, ii. 39). The interest which Eusebius took in the various emperors was largely confined to the question whether they were well or ill disposed towards the Church, which seemed, at the beginning of the fourth century, to be about to flourish without constraint since in Constantine a truly enlightened

Augustus had appeared as patron and protector of the Christians. See H. Eger, 'Kaiser und Kirche in der Geschichtstheologie Eusebs von Cäsarea', in *Zeitschrift für Neutestamentliche Wissenschaft*, 1929.

57. *V.C.* iv. 54.   58. *V.C.* iv. 15.

59. *H.E.* i. 13.

60. *H.E.* iv. 13. So Eusebius understands it, but the title is really that of Marcus Aurelius.

61. *Martyrdom of Polycarp*, xv. The traditional date is perhaps to be retained in spite of H. Grégoire in *Analecta Bollandiana*, 1951.

62. περιστερὰ καί, emended to *e.g.* περὶ στύρακα. Cf. J. B. Lightfoot, *The Apostolic Fathers*, second part, ii. 2. 974.

63. *V.C.* i. 28.   64. *V.C.* ii. 5.

65. *V.C.* ii. 9.   66. *H.E.* i. 4. 2.

67. *H.E.* v, praef.   68. *Vita Malchi*, init.

69. *H.E.* x. 4. 32.   70. Isa. xxxv. 1 (LXX. text).

71. *H.E.* iv. 7. 2.   72. *H.E.* ix. 9. 1.

73. *H.E.* x. 4. 60.   74. *H.E.* ix. 9. 12.

75. *H.E.* x. 8. 6.   76. *H.E.* x. 8. 13.

77. *H.E.* x. 8. 8.   78. *V.C.* i. 55.

79. W. Nigg, *Die Kirchengeschichtsschreibung*, p. 24.

80. R. Laqueur, *Eusebius als Historiker seiner Zeit*, p. 221.

81. Nigg, *op. cit.* p. 26.   82. Amos ix. 7.

83. Ps. xxxiv. 15, 16.   84. Prov. xiv. 34.

85. *V.C.* ii. 66.

86. *V.C.* iv. 12. On the letter, see N. H. Baynes, *Constantine the Great and the Christian Church*, p. 26.

87. *Short Studies in Great Subjects*, first series, p. 21.

88. *The Golden Sequence*, p. 13.

89. Quoted from Mme. de Witt's *Monsieur Guizot in Private Life* by Karl Hillebrand in *Contemporary Review*, xxxix (1881), p. 488.

90. Letter 7 to his brother Heinrich. *Werke*, liii, p. 89.

CHAPTER V

1. 'The Muse of History', *Collected Essays* (1922), p. 38.

2. *The Decline and Fall*, ch. 3. (ed. Bury), vol. i. p. 84.

3. W. B. Yeats, *The Countess Cathleen*, act iv.

4. *De div. quaest.* i. 53. 2.   5. *De catech. rudibus*, ix.

6. *De cons. evangelistarum*, ii. 52.   7. *Conf.* vii. 21.

8. *De cons. ev.* 128.   9. *De cons. ev.* 128.

10. The principle of *synecdoche*, *De doctr. chr.* iii. 35.

11. *De doctr. chr.* iii. 36.   12. *De cons. ev.* i. 9.

13. *Noten zum West-O. Divans.*   14. *De doctr. chr.* i. 33 ff.

15. Ps. xcix. 1.

16. *De civ. Dei,* xvii. 3. But Augustine was not always quite so careful. Cf. Trench, *Exposition of the Sermon on the Mount, drawn from the Writings of St. Augustine,* Introductory essay, ch. iv.

17. *Ep.* cxcvii. 5. Cf. *De Gen. ad litt.* viii: 'melius est dubitare de occultis quam litigare de incertis'.

18. Matthew Arnold, *Literature and Dogma,* i. 5.

19. Ps. xii. 9 (LXX version).

20. Bodin, ap. Croce, *On History* (tr. Ainslie), p. 237.

21. Marcus Aurelius xi. 2. Justin, *Apology,* I. 20. Seneca, *Ep. ad Lucil.* xxiv. 26.

22. *De civ. Dei,* xii. 13.

23. *Ep.* cxcix, *Ad Hesychium de fine saeculi.* Cf. *Ep.* cxcvii.

24. II Pet. iii. 8.

25. *De Gen. contra Manichaeos,* i. 23.

26. The number 6 also has a certain perfection, *De civ. Dei,* xi. 33.

27. Bossuet, *Discours,* part I, ch. xii.

28. Jas. iv. 6 and I Pet. v. 5; from Prov. iii. 34.

29. Bossuet, *op. cit.* part III, ch. 1, 'faithfully Englished' (1703).

30. *Ep.* lx. 16. 3.

31. *Ep.* cxxiii. 16. 4. Cf. Lucan, v. 274.

32. *Ep.* cxxvii. 12.   33. *Aeneid,* ii. 363.

34. Ps. lxxix. 1.   35. *Relatio,* iii. 9.

36. *Ep.* lvii. 3   37. *De civ. Dei,* iii. fin.

38. *De civ. Dei,* iii. 15.   39. *De civ. Dei,* iii. 18.

40. The pagan historian Ammianus Marcellinus makes the same kind of point: 'Those who are ignorant of ancient records say that the state was never before overshadowed by such dark clouds of misfortune, but they deceive themselves by yielding to the horror which recent disasters have caused them to feel. For, if they examine earlier ages or even times not long past, they will find that such gloomy upheavals have often occurred' (xxxi. 5. 10).

41. *De civ. Dei,* i. 7.   42. *De civ. Dei,* iii. 31.

43. *Ep.* cxi. 2.   44. *Sermo,* cv. 9.

45. *Sermo,* lxxxi. 9. For all this, Augustine's hope of the restoration of Rome was never very far away. *De civ. Dei,* iv. 7: 'quamquam Romanum imperium afflictum est potius quam mutatum; quod et aliis ante Christi nomen temporibus ei contigit, et ab illa est afflictione recreatum; quod nec istis temporibus desperandum est. quis enim de hac

re novit voluntatem Dei?' Cf. Rutilius Namatianus' hope that Rome, unlike other cities will thrive by rising superior to her misfortunes: 'ordo
renascendi est, crescere posse malis' (*De reditu suo*, i. 140).

46. *De civ. Dei*, v. 11.
47. I Macc. iii. 18, 60.
48. Ps. i. 7.
49. *De civ. Dei*, iv. 34.
50. *Ep*. xviii. 34.
51. Zeph. i. 12.
52. Matthew Arnold, *Mycerinus*, 53.
53. *De civ. Dei*, iv. 1.
54. *De civ. Dei*, i. 33.
55. *De civ. Dei*, i. 34.
56. *As You Like It*, act ii, scene 1.
57. Isa. xix. 22.
58. *De civ. Dei*, i. 8.
59. *De civ. Dei*, i. 10.
60. Moore, *Judaism*, ii. 256.
61. John xvi. 33.
62. *Discours*, part II, ch. 1.
63. *Tract. in Ioann*. xiii. 5.
64. *De civ. Dei*, v. 21.
65. *Faith and History*, p. 150.
66. Luke xiii. 3.
67. *De civ. Dei*, i. 35.
68. *Commonitorium*, i. Cf. Augustine, *Ep*. clxvi. 2; *Ep*. clxix. 13.
69. i, prol. 9. 10. Cf. Gennadius, *De vir. ill*. 39.
70. iii, praef. 2. Cf. Horace, *A.P.* 26.
71. *Theaetetus*, 176 A.
72. Cf. Löwith, *Meaning in History*, p. 318 f.
73. *Clementissimae admonitiones*, i. 6. 5.
74. ii. 1.
75. Orosius, C.S.E.L. v, ed. C. Zangemeister (1882), appendix II.
76. iv, praef. 4-11.
77. vii. 39.
78. vii. 43. 16-18.
79. vii. 39. 18.
80. vii. 41. 8.
81. *Ineffabilia*, vii. 41. 10.
82. ps-Prosper, *Ad uxorem*. P.L. li. 611.
83. Prosper Tiro, *Carmen de ingratis*, 39 ff.
84. 'Tres res convenit habere narrationem, ut brevis, ut dilucida, ut
verisimilis sit.' Cicero, *Ad Her*. i. 9. 14.
85. Pope, *An Essay on Man*, Epistle i. 267.
86. *De gubernatione Dei*, iii. 1.
87. i. 6.
88. I Thessalonians iii. 3.
89. viii. 1.
90. ii. 1.
91. i. 9.
92. v. 5.
93. vi. 4.
94. vi. 7.
95. iv. 13.
96. iii. 11 and iv. 17.
97. v. 3.
98. Isa. xiv. 23.
99. *De gub. Dei*, iii. 4.

CHAPTER VI

1. This is the thesis of the *Magdeburg Centuries*.

2. F. Wirth, *Römische Wandmalerei* (1934). G. Rodenwaldt, 'Über den Stilwandel in der antoninischen Kunst' (*Abh. Berl.*, 1935), and 'Zur Kunstgeschichte der Jahre 220–270' (*Jahrb. des Deutsch. Archäolog. Inst.* 1936).

3. The frequency of the scenes most commonly shown is computed by Wilpert (*Die Malereien der Katakomben Roms*, I) as follows: Old Testament: Moses striking the rock 68, Jonah 57, Daniel in the lion's den 39, Noah and the Ark 32, sacrifice of Isaac 22, the young men in the fiery furnace 17. New Testament: Raising of Lazarus 53, feeding of the five thousand (or four thousand) 35, healing of the paralytic 20. The figure of the Good Shepherd occurs 114 times.

4. *Apostolic Constitutions*, v. 7. The same motif appears in the litany for the dying in the *commendatio animae* (*Rituale Romanum*, tit. v, cap. vii): 'Libera, Domine, animam servi tui ex omnibus periculis inferni et de laqueis poenarum et ex omnibus tribulationibus. Amen.

'Libera, Domine, animam servi tui, sicut liberasti Henoch et Eliam de communi morte mundi. Amen.

'Libera, Domine, animam servi tui, sicut liberasti Abraham de Ur Chaldaeorum.

'Libera, Domine, animam servi tui, sicut liberasti Iob de passionibus suis.

'Libera, Domine, animam servi tui, sicut liberasti Isaac de hostia et de manu patris sui Abrahae.

'Libera, Domine, animam servi tui, sicut liberasti Lot de Sodomis et de flamma ignis.

'Libera, Domine, animam servi tui, sicut liberasti Moysen de manu Pharaonis.

'Libera, Domine, animam servi tui, sicut liberasti Danielem de lacu leonum.

'Libera, Domine, animam servi tui, sicut liberasti tres pueros de camino ignis ardentis et de manu regis iniqui.

'Libera, Domine, animam servi tui, sicut liberasti Susannam de falso crimine.

'Libera, Domine, animam servi tui, sicut liberasti David de manu regis Saul et de manu Goliae.

'Libera, Domine, animam servi tui, sicut liberasti Petrum et Paulum de carceribus.

'Libera, Domine, animam servi tui, sicut beatissimam Theclam virginem liberasti de tribus atrocissimis tormentis.'

5. Cf. Ignatius, *Ephesians*, xx; based on such teaching as John vi. 54 and 58.

6. A. E. Housman, *A Shropshire Lad*, lv.

7. Ps. xxxiv. 22   8. I Sam. xvii. 37.

9. 'The Paintings in the Christian Chapel', by P. V. C. Baur, in *Preliminary Report of fifth Season of Work of the Excavations at Dura-Europus, conducted by Yale University and the French Academy of Inscriptions and Letters*, pp. 254-283. Cf. M. I. Rostovtzeff, *Dura-Europus and its Art*.

10. Cf. the Mosaic of Yakto, which shows six combats with wild beasts. Narcissus thrusts at a lion, Tiresias at a panther, Actaeon at a bear, Meleager at a tigress, Adonis at a boar and Hippolytus at an animal which has disappeared where the mosaic is broken.

11. I. A. Richmond, *Archaeology and the After-life in Pagan and Christian Imagery* (Riddell Memorial Lectures, 1950), pp. 29-40. Cf. the changed emphasis in the story of the Niobids. A. Rumpf, 95. *Berliner Winckelmannsprogramm*, 1935.

12. Jas. i. 10.   13. Cyprian, *De mortalitate*, xix.

14. Wilpert, *I sarcofagi cristiani antichi*, pl. lxvi. 3.

15. Ps. xxii. 21.

16. Cyprian, *De mortalitate*, xxvi.

17. Tertullian, *Apology*, xlvi. 2-5.

18. Wilpert, *op. cit.* pl. i. 1. Gerke, *Die christlichen Sarkophage der vorkonstantinischen Zeit*, pl. 51, pp. 295 ff. The sarcophagus was in a damaged condition and two of the heads, along with certain other pieces, have been restored.

19. Wilpert, *op. cit.* pl. ix. Gerke, *op. cit.* pl. I, pp. 38 ff.

20. Gen. xix. Gerke, however, thinks that the reference is to some incident in the life of Moses, *op. cit.* p. 38.

21. Künstle, *Ikonographie der christlichen Kunst*, i. 12.

22. Num. xxiv. 3 and 15.

23. William Blake alludes to this interpretative faculty, whereby nature and imagination are happily fused into one impact of Reality: 'I know that this world is a world of imagination and vision. I see everything I paint in this world, but everybody does not see alike. To the eye of a miser a guinea is far more beautiful than the sun, and a bag worn with the use of money has more beautiful proportions than a vine filled with grapes. The tree which moves some to tears of joy is in the eyes of others only a green thing which stands in the way. Some see Nature all ridicule and deformity, and by these I shall not regulate my proportions; and some scarce see Nature at all. . . . As a man is, so he sees. As the eye is formed, such are its powers' (*Letters of William Blake*, p. 62).

24. *Paedagogus*, iii. 11.

25. Such as the Cubiculum of Lucina. Cf. M. Vloberg, *L'Eucharistie dans l'art*, pp. 12-17.

26. Paulinus of Nola, *Ep.* xiii. 11, to Pammachius.

Origen, *Comm. in Matt.* xviii. 10, describes Christ as ὁ τροπικῶς λεγό-μενος ἰχθύς. The *Epitaphium Abercii* (*Monumenta minora saeculi secundi*, ed. G. Rauschen (Bonn, 1914), pp. 38-40) refers to the 'huge, pure fish from the fountain which faith provides as food' and the *Epitaphium Pectorii* (*op. cit.* pp. 42-43) instructs Christians to eat the Saviour's honey-sweet food, 'clasping the Fish in your hands'. Cf. Augustine, *Confessions*, xiii. 21: 'quamvis piscem manducet levatum de profundo in ea mensa quam parasti in conspectu credentium; ideo enim de profundo levatus est, ut alat aridam'. So in certain Byzantine pictures of the Eucharist, as well as in a few Western mediaeval representations, a fish is shown as the main food provided at the table. E. Dobbert, *Das Abendmahl Christi in der bildenden Kunst* and J. Dölger, ΙΧΘΥΣ, *Das Fischsymbol im frühchristlichen Zeit*.

27. Augustine, *De civ. Dei*, xviii. 23, after a reference to the acrostic, adds an explanatory note: 'ἰχθύς, id est piscis, in quo nomine mystice intelligitur Christus, eo quod in huius mortalitatis abysso velut in aquarum profunditate vivus, hoc est sine peccato, esse potuerit'.

28. *De baptismo*, i.

29. The mosaic in the diaconicon of the church built by Bishop Dumetios at Nicopolis (J.-S. Pelekanidis, 'Die Symbolik der frühbyzantinischen Fussbodenmosaiken Griechenlands', *Z.K.G.*, 1940) shows three symbolic pictures. First there is a fish-catching, or baptism, then a hunting-scene, representing the battle against evil, and lastly a group of saints, indicative of the holy life completed in mystical union with God.

30. *E.g.* Augustine, *Enarratio in Ps.* ciii. i. 14.

31. *Mart. Pol.* iv.   32. I Pet. iii. 15.

33. Nahum i. 3.   34. Ps. xxxvii, 39, 40.

35. John iii. 14. Cf. viii. 28 and xii. 32.   36. Mat. xii. 40.

37. Gal. iv. 22 ff. Cf. his reference to the 'spiritual rock' in I Cor. x. 4.

38. *Comm. in Exod.* 73. Cf. *De civ. Dei*, xvi. 26: 'quid enim quod dicitur Testamentum Vetus nisi Novi occultatio? et quid est aliud quod dicitur Novum nisi Veteris revelatio?'

39. *Ep.* xxxii. 5.

'Lex antiqua novam firmat, veterem nova complet:
   In veteri spes est, in novitate fides,
   Sed vetus atque novum coniungit gratia Christi.'

Cf. Vincent of Beauvais, *Spec. moral*, i. 2, dist. 8: 'sic igitur est lex nova in veteri sicut fructus in spica; omnia enim quae credenda traduntur in novo testamento explicite et aperte, traduntur in veteri testamento, sed implicite sub figura'.

40. *Sermo II*, 6, with reference to Gal. iv. 22, 24.

The doctrine of significant correspondences between the two Testaments came to be a prime favourite in the Middle Ages, when the influence of such works as Honorius of Autun's *Speculum Ecclesiae* was widespread. It receives typical expression in one of the medallions of stained glass introduced into the church of St. Denis by the abbot Suger. Here Christ is shown standing between two female figures representing the Church and the Synagogue. With his right hand He is crowning the Church, while with his left hand He tears away the veil with which the Synagogue has covered her face. A Latin inscription points the moral: 'Quod Moyses velat Christi doctrina revelat'. Mâle, *L'Art religieux en France*, I, p. 166. (The inscription is now jumbled and partly missing.)

41. *Ep.* xxxii. *Carm.* xxvii.

42. Wilpert, *Die römischen Mosaiken und Malereien der kirchlichen Bauten*, pp. 423 ff., pls. 8-28.

43. Gen. xiv. 18-20. Jos. ix. 16-27.

44. Gen. xviii.

45. *L'Art religieux en France*, II, p. 153.

46. E. von Dobschütz, *Christusbilder* (*Texte und Untersuchungen*, xviii). Künstle, *op. cit.* I, pp. 589 ff.

47. Irenaeus, *Adv. Haer.* i. 25. 6. Hippolytus, *Refutatio*, vii. 32.

48. *Vita* by Lampridius in *Historia Augusta*, xxix. 2.

49. P. Vignon, *Le Saint-Suaire de Turin* (Paris, 1938). Cf. A. Grabar, *La Sainte Face de Laon* (Prague, 1931).

50. Eusebius, *H.E.* i. 13.

51. Künstle, *op. cit.* I, pp. 589-592.

52. *P.G.* xcvii. 1304.   53. *Adv. Hermogenem*, i.

54. *Protrepticus*, iv. 62. *Stromateis*, v. 5. 28.

55. *Ep. ad Constantiam Augustam*, *P.G.* xx. 1545.

56. *P.L.* xxii. 526. But the letter to John of Jerusalem in which this story occurs is not above suspicion.

57. Isa. liii. 2.

58. *Paedagogus*, iii. 1. Cf. Tertullian, *De carne Christi*, ix.

59. *Contra Celsum*, vi. 75.

60. *Contra Celsum*, vi. 77. *Comm. ser. in Matt.* 100.

61. Tertullian, *Adv. Marcionem*, iii. 17.

62. *Ep.* lxv.

63. Antoninus of Placentia. Geyer, *Itinera Hierosolymitana*, p. 175, P.P.T.S. ii. 20.

64. II Cor. v. 16.   65. Ezek. xxxiv. 23.

66. Isa. xl. 11.   67. John x. 15.

68. Wilpert, *Die Malereien der Katakomben Roms*, pp. 311 ff. pl. 45.

69. It is sometimes impossible to tell whether the diminutive figure shown, in wall-paintings or•on sarcophagi, as receiving baptism is intended to represent Christ or the Christian neophyte. C. F. Rogers, *Baptism and Christian Archaeology*.

70. I Sam. xvi. 12; xvii. 42.

71. *Passio S. Perpetuae*, xii. E. C. E. Owen, *Some Authentic Acts of the Early Martyrs*, p. 86.

72. Notable pictures in this dignified and impressive style are provided by the mosaic at S. Pudenziana, in Rome (Wilpert, *Die römischen Mosaiken*, pls. 42-46: the mosaics have, however, been extensively restored), and the painting in the catacomb of SS. Peter and Marcellinus (Wilpert, *Die Malereien*, pls. 252 and 253). F. Gerke's *Die christlichen Sarkophagen der vorkonstantinischen Zeit* and his *Christus in der spätantiken Plastik* give numerous illustrations of the two contrasted ways in which Christ is shown on the sarcophagi.

73. Wilpert, *Die römischen Mosaiken*, iii, pls. 97-100. E. W. Anthony, *A History of Mosaics*, pp. 91 ff.

74. Künstle, *op. cit.* I, pp. 25-29, where references are given to other literature on the subject of the *nimbus*.

75. J. Carcopino in *Museum Helveticum*, 1948.

76. *De corona militis*, iii.

77. *E.g. Inscr. Chr. Rom.* i. 201, n. 463. *Monumenta Asiae Minoris Antiqua*, i. 213.

78. Col. i. 20.

79. H. Leclercq in *D.A.C.L.* xxix, col. 3048 ff. The mocking crucifix with the ass's head, found on the Palatine and probably of third-century date, is illustrated also. Fig. 3359.

80. J. Neuss, 'Die Oranten in der altchr. Kunst' in *Festschrift Clemen*.

81. G. Jerphanion, 'La représentation de la Croix et du Crucifix aux origines de l'art chrétien' in *La Voix des monuments* (1930), pp. 138 ff.

82. C. R. Morey, *Early Christian Art* (Princeton, 1942), pp. 116 ff., pl. 126. Diehl, *Manuel de l'art byzantin*, I, pp. 253-254.

83. Morey, *op. cit.* pl. 203. Wilpert, *Die römischen Mosaiken und Malereien*, iv, pl. 180.

CHAPTER VII

1. *Prelude*, book xiv. l. 189.

2. Saint-Simon, ed. Pléiade, i. 377.

3. Sifrè, *Deuteronomy*, 49. Cf. G. F. Moore, *Judaism*, i, pp. 161 ff.

4. *Book of Jubilees*, chs. xi-xii. R. H. Charles, *Apocrypha and Pseudepigrapha of the Old Testament*, p. 30.

5. *On History*.

6. T. R. Glover, *Life and Letters in the Fourth Century*, p. 361.

7. J. W. Thompson, *A History of Historical Writing*, i, p. 108.

8. Book of Common Prayer. *Concerning the Services of the Church*.

9. J. W. Thompson, *op. cit.* i, p. 131.

10. Matt. xvii. 24-27.   11. xxvii. 19.

12. xxvii. 51-53.

13. *Acta Apostolorum apocrypha* (R. A. Lipsius and M. Bonnet, 1898), pp. 117 ff. Cf. M. R. James, *The Apocryphal New Testament*, pp. 458-460.

14. *Acta Apostolorum apocrypha* (R. A. Lipsius and M. Bonnet, 1903), pp. 39 ff. Cf. M. R. James, *op. cit.* pp. 439 ff. E. Peterson, 'Zum Messalianismus der Philippus-Akten' in *Oriens Christianus*, 1932.

15. *P.G.* xxxiv. 772.

16. Schmidt in *Sitzungsberichte der Akademie der Wissenschaften zu Berlin*, xxxi, pp. 705-711.

17. See the allegorical explanation, in the same document, of the wise and foolish virgins. The wise are Faith, Love, Grace, Peace and Hope, while the first two foolish ones are Knowledge and Wisdom (γνῶσις and σοφία).

18. Ignatius, *To the Trallians*, vi.

19. Ignatius, *To the Smyrnaeans*, iii.

20. *Gospel of Bartholomew.* Greek texts in *Revue Biblique*, 1913 (Wilmart and Tisserant), and in *Revue Biblique*, 1921 (Moricca). M. R. James, *op. cit.* pp. 167 ff., for English translation.

21. Rosa Söder, *Die apokryphen Apostelgeschichten und die romanhafte Literatur der Antike* (Stuttgart, 1932). But see also the contrasting views of M. Blumenthal, *Formen und Motive in der apokryphen Apostelgeschichten* (T. und U., 1933).

22. *De arte praedicatoria*, i.

23. Crane, *Exempla of Jacques de Vitry* (1890), p. xx.

24. Delehaye, *Les Légendes hagiographiques*, p. 76.

25. *Acts of Peter* (Vercelli text), xiii.

26. *Icaromenippus; Philopseudes*, 13, where one Cleodemus records that he saw a Hyperborean in flight; *The Cock*, 23; *Eicones*, 21.

27. *Acts of Andrew and Matthias*, 17.

28. *Acts of Paul* (The Martyrdom, v).

29. *The Martyrdom of Matthew*, 23 ff.

30. Delehaye, *Les Légendes hagiographiques*, 32. Cf. Pausanias, ix. 23.2; Cicero, *De div.* i. 36; Olympiodorus, *Vita Platonis*.

31. Diogenes Laertius, viii. 62.	32. *Acts of Thomas*, 106, Cf. 129.
33. *Acts of John*, 27.	34. ii. 33. Müller, 5. 86.
35. *Acts of Peter*, 9.	36. *Acts of Thomas*, 78.

37. As shown on the roodscreens at Cawston and Gateley, Norfolk.

38. Shown on a carved bench-end at Dennington, Suffolk.

39. *Acts of Paul and Thecla*, 5.   40. *Acts of Thomas*, 51.

41. Told in the *Acts of Nereus and Achilleus*, two of Peter's converts.

42. The fourth-century sarcophagus at St. Engracia's, Saragossa, has been adduced as an exception to this rule. Here, amidst the usual miracles of healing, exemplified by a blind man and the woman with the issue of blood, occurs a female figure, whose right hand is grasped by the hand of God from above, while a man stands at either side of her and supports her by the elbows. (*D.A.C.L.* I, part ii, fig. 1025.) Some have thought that this scene indicates the assumption of the Virgin, but it is more likely that the sculptor intended to show another miracle of healing. Pictures of the Assumption are otherwise quite unknown till the end of the eighth or beginning of the ninth century, the earliest being probably a fragment of woven material, preserved at Sens, which displays a repeated medallion of the Virgin ascending between two angels while the Apostles salute her from below. An inscription explains the scene: 'cum transisset Maria mater Domini de Apostolis' (*D.A.C.L.* I, part ii, fig. 1022).

43. Tischendorf's text in *Evangelia apocrypha* (1876). More recent texts and notes by E. Amann (1910) and by Michel and Peeters in *Évangiles apocryphes*, i (1911). Translation, somewhat curtailed, by M. R. James, *The Apocryphal New Testament*, pp. 39 ff.

44. *The Golden Legend* (ed. F. S. Ellis, *Temple Classics*), iv. p. 234. Other versions of the story describe the Virgin as sixty years old.

45. However, the idea of Mary as a crowned queen is considerably older. In the sixth-century mosaics of S. Apollinare Nuovo at Ravenna she is seated in regal splendour on a jewelled throne, but here she is plainly dressed, and it is at Rome, in the choir of S. Maria Antiqua, that she is first shown, about A.D. 590, wearing a high crown and richly bejewelled robe. (M. Lawrence, 'Maria Regina', *The Art Bulletin*, VII.)

Perhaps more significantly, the Benedictional of Ethelwold (*c.* A.D. 980) offers an early picture of the Assumption, in which the Virgin reclines on her bed which is being raised heavenwards while, between four angels coming down to greet her, the hand of God is seen clasping the crown which is soon to be hers. The Triumph of the Virgin, where she sits crowned on a throne at Christ's right hand, is splendidly illustrated in the mosaics of Ss. Maria in Trastevere, at Rome (A.D. 1148). This theme failed for some reason to gain favour in Italy, but the growing veneration of the Virgin which characterized the period of the Crusades led to its adoption at several places in France, of which the tympanum of Senlis Cathedral is the best-known example, as well as in England, where the twelfth-century tympanum of Quenington church, Gloucestershire, illustrates, with rude but powerful symmetry, the moment when Christ sets the crown on the Virgin's head. (G. Zarnecki, *Journal of the Warburg Institute*, xiii.)

46. *Spec. hist.* vii. lxxix.

47. Mâle, *op. cit.* ii, p. 248.

48. Leclercq in *D.A.C.L.* (*s.v.* Marie), x, part ii, col. 2019.

49. Heb. xi. 5.

50. *Encomium on the Falling-asleep of the God-bearer*, *P.G.* lxxxvi. 3312.

51. *Sermo in dormitionem Mariae*, ii, *P.G.* xcvii, 1081.

52. But the influential *Second Homily on the Falling-asleep of the Blessed Virgin Mary* is of very doubtful authenticity. (Bardenhewer, v. 81.)

53. *P.L.* lxxi. 708.

54. Texts in Tischendorf, *Apocalypses Apocryphae* (1866). Translation and short notes in M. R. James, *The Apocryphal New Testament*, pp. 194 ff.

55. *Eastern Churches Quarterly*, summer 1951.

56. B. Capelle, *Nouvelle Rev. Théol.*, Dec. 1950.

57. Rom. xi. 33.

58. Pohle-Preuss, *Dogmatic Theology*, vi. pp. 105 ff.

59. S. Radhakrishnan, in *Proceedings of the British Academy*, 1938, p. 149

60. 'Ubi historiam non inveni, aut qualiter eorum vita fuisset . . . illorum vitam composui et credo non mentitum esse, quia et oratores fuerunt, castique et eleemosynarii et Deo animas [*sic*] hominum adquisitores.' *Vita S. Exuperantii*, *P.L.* cvi. 525.

This Agnellus, abbot of S. Maria ad Blachernas at Ravenna in the ninth century, is not to be confused with Agnellus, bishop of Ravenna, A.D. 553-566.

CHAPTER VIII

1. L. Halphen, *Introduction à l'histoire*, p. 59.
2. *The Muse of History*, in *Essays and Addresses* (1922), vol. iii. p. 47.
3. W. R. Matthews, *God, in Christian Thought and Experience*, p. 152.
4. *Instit.* i. xvii.
5. Halphen (*op. cit.* p. 56) quotes the saying of Fustel de Coulanges: 'pour un jour de synthèse il faut des années d'analyse', and then adds the comment: 'Synthèse et analyse doivent donc cheminer de compagnie, s'épaulant l'une l'autre, se perfectionnant l'une l'autre'.
6. *Short Treatise*, pt. i, ch. iv; pt. ii, ch. xxiv.
7. J. A. Froude, *A Bishop of the Twelfth Century*.
8. Socrates, *Ecclesiastical History*, v. praef.
9. i. 1. Eusebius' *Life of Constantine* incurs sharp criticism.
10. v, praef.   11. vii. 32.
12. Bright's introduction to Hussey's edition of Socrates (1893), pp. xxiii-xxiv.
13. i. 1.   14. Sozomen, i. 1.
15. G. Schoo, *Die Quellen des Kirchenhistorikers Sozomenos* (Berlin, 1911).
16. Cf. L. Parmentier's introduction to his masterly edition (Leipzig, 1911).
17. Socrates, i. 18.   18. *E.g.* Theodoret, i. 2.
19. Ps. xxxvii. 25.
20. This is the judgement of W. Nigg, *Die Kirchengeschichtsschreibung* (Munich, 1934), p. 35.
21. i. 1.
22. Aristotle, *Nic. Eth.* viii., 1. 6. Hippolytus, *Refutatio*, ix. 9.
23. *On History* (tr. Ainslie), p. 205.
24. C. A.D. 363-420.   25. *P.L.* xx. 81.
26. Amos ix. 7.   27. *Chron.* i. 1.
28. *P.L.* xx. 159 ff.
29. Sulpicius Severus is thus described by Paulinus of Périgueux who, about A.D. 460, wrote a versified life of St. Martin which was to a large extent based on Sulpicius' narrative. *P.L.* lxi. 1009.
30. Ammianus Marcellinus, xvi. 1. 3. It is not quite so easy to include Theodoret in this group.
31. H. H. Milman, in a note to his edition of Gibbon's *Decline and Fall*, ii. 285.
32. *Epistle*, xxviii. 4.   33. *The Way to write History*, 39.
34. R. Graves, *I Claudius*, p. 137.

35. *Discours*, part III, ch. 8.   36. iii. 7. 6.

37. vi. 9. 10.   38. xxix. 21.

39. xxxvi. 17. 15.   40. Ps. ciii. 19.

41. In his inaugural address, delivered at Cambridge in 1903.

42. *Geschichten der röm. und germ. Völker* (1824), Vorrede.

43. Sybel, *Gedächtnisrede auf Ranke* (1887), p. 6. The anecdote about the bishop is quoted by Acton, *The Study of History* (1895), from Cherbuliez, *Revue des Deux Mondes* (1872), i, p. 537.

44. Quoted by J. W. Thompson, *A History of Historical Writing*, II, p. 179.

45. P. 50 in the 1885 edition.

46. *Religio Medici* (Everyman ed.), p. 51.

47. John Smith, *Select Discourses* (1821 ed.), p. 406.

48. *De doctr. chr.* iii. 5.   49. *Sermo II, 6, P.L.* xxxviii. 30.

50. Prov. xx. 24.

51. *Eastern Churches Quarterly*, spring 1953.

52. E. H. Gombrich, 'Icones symbolicae' in *Journal of the Warburg Institute*, xi.

53. John xv. 1.

54. Berdyaev, quoted by J. W. Buckham in *Hibbert Journal*, October 1936. Buckham adds: 'Idealization, instead of distorting, tends to normalize selfhood, bringing out the finer qualities which, after all, constitute its essence. . . . Idealization serves to make perduring persons more real, more themselves.'

55. 'The Relation of Christianity to Art.' Appendix to *The Epistles of St. John*, pp. 371 ff.

56. Rom. xii. 15.

57. Cf. Hazlitt's remarks on Crabbe and Cowper. *The Spirit of the Age*, p. 201.

58. P. B. Deknatel, *Edvard Munch*, p. 20. Cf. 'Anxiety', p. 24. An illustration of 'The Shout' is given also in E. H. Gombrich's *The Story of Art*, p. 423.

59. G. C. Field in *Proceedings of the British Academy*, 1938, p. 81.

60. Jos. x. 12.

61. *Book of James*, xviii. 2, tr. M. R. James, *The Apocryphal New Testament*, p. 46.

62. Matt. xxvii. 45. The somewhat confused narrative of the Apocalypse of Moses records that the sun, moon and stars were darkened for seven days after Adam's death.

63. 'Some Problems in Modern Historiography', in *Proceedings of the British Academy*, 1932, p. 174.

64. *Symbolism and Belief*, p. 278.
65. *Op. cit.* p. 370.
66. *Pensées*, No. 233 (ed. Brunschvicg).
67. Preface to his *History of the Exchequer*.
68. II Cor. iv. 7.
69. Bridges, *Testament of Beauty*, II, 506-508.
70. Anaxagoras, *ap.* Diogenes Laertius, ii. 6.
71. Wordsworth, *The Excursion*.
72. Origen, *De principiis*, ii. 11. 4.

INDEX

Aaron, 107
Abel, 51, 93, 136
Abgar of Edessa, 68, 109
Abraham, 24, 28, 31, 45, 59, 60, 80, 81, 97, 107 ff., 118 ff., 168, 185
Acton, 2, 15
Acts of the Apostles, 6, 10, 24, 25, 128, 133, 161
Adam, 43, 80, 81, 100
Adamnan, 178
Ado, 180
Agnellus, 140
Aijalon, valley of, 158
Alaric, 82, 90
Albertus Magnus, 181
Alexander, 67, 92, 131
Alexander of Abonuteichos, 131
Alexander Polyhistor, 34
Alexander Severus, 109
Alexandria, 34, 42, 55, 138
Allegory, 24, 42 ff., 78, 125
Ambrose, St., 52, 82, 84, 110, 130, 137, 161, 188
Ambrosius Aupertus, 180
Ammianus Marcellinus, 71, 150
Amos, 72
Anatomists, compared with Biblical critics, 50
Anaxagoras, 160
Andrew, St., the Apostle, 126, 129
Andrew of Crete, 109, 137, 174 f.
Anicetus, 36
Anne, Queen, 159
Anne, St., 133, 168
Annunciation, the, 18, 168
Antichrist, 89
Antoninus Pius, 68, 184
Antony of Egypt, 145
Apocalyptic, Jewish, 156
Apollo, 112, 183
Apollonius of Tyana, 120
Apostles, the, 26, 35 ff., 53, 61, 76, 113, 126, 129 ff., 135 ff., 161 ff.
Apotheosis, 184 f.
Arabs, the, 99
Arculf, 178
Aretalogy, 129 ff., 149

Arnold, Thomas, 17, 65
Arycanda, inscription of, 64
Ascension, the, 25, 98, 140, 182, 183
Asceticism, 132, 145
Assumption, the, 136 ff., 161 ff.
Athena, 184
Athens, 7, 59, 64, 69, 147
Augsburg, 183
Augustan History, 71
Augustine, St., 5, 74 ff., 107, 150, 155 f., 162, 180, 188
Augustus, 112, 184

Babel, tower of, 6
Babylon, 185
Balaam, 104
Baptism, 98, 105
Barnabas, Epistle of, 24, 44, 79
Bartholomew, St., 124, 127
Baur, F. C., 62
Beauvais, Vincent of, 136
Bede, 51, 52, 61, 178
Berdyaev, 19
Bethlehem, 176, 190
Bevan, Edwyn, 19, 155, 159
Billiard, Nicolas, 181
Birrell, Augustine, 2, 74, 142
Blachernae, church at, 176
Boarium, Forum, 14
Bordeaux, pilgrim of, 176
Bossuet, 1, 4, 81, 86, 151
Botanists, compared with Biblical critics, 50
Bourges, 188
Breviary, the Roman, 175, 179
Bridges, Robert, 160
Browne, Sir Thomas, 154
Browning, Robert, 32
Buchan, John, 6
Buddha, the, 140
Burgundians, 91
Bury, J. B., 8, 152
Butler, bishop, 8, 38
Byron, 6

Caesar, 10, 184
Cain, 28

215

Faustina, 184
Fish-symbol, the, 105
Five Thousand, the feeding of the, 105
Flacius, Mathias, 97
Fortunata, Passion of St., 128
Frederick the Great, 11
Freising, Otto of, 97
Fribourg, 189
Froude, J. A., 72, 143
Fuller, Thomas, 17

Gabriel, 18, 135, 170
Galatians, the Epistle to the, 45, 150
Gallican calendars, 172
Gaudin, Jacques, 181
Gelasius I, pope, 138, 171, 190
Genesis, 118, 185, 186
Gentiles, the, 22, 25, 54, 80, 87
George, St., 174
Germanus, patriarch of Constantinople, 175
Gethsemane, 137, 168, 173, 175, 177
Gibbon, Edward, 65, 74
Gibeon, 158
Gnostics, the, 26, 27, 36, 40, 109, 110, 127, 132, 171
Goethe, 57, 77
Golden Legend, the, 134, 136, 138, 188
Gospels, apocryphal, 68, 158
Gospels, the Four, 7, 10, 18, 21, 48, 83, 106, 113, 121, 122, 136, 157
Gothic Missal, 138, 172
Gratian, 84
Gregory of Nazianzus, 7
Gregory Thaumaturgus, 40
Gregory of Tours, 138, 162, 171, 172

Habakkuk, 185
Haggadah, 118, 127
Halphen, L., 19
Hannibal, 82
Hebrew monotheism, 6
Hebrews, the Epistle to the, 107, 186
Hegesippus, 36
Helen, St., 176
Heracles, 183, 184
Heraclitus, 31, 147
Herbert, George, 86

Hermes, 111
Herod, 18, 54
Herodotus, 1, 7, 54, 62, 147
Hesiod, 43
Hilarion, 145
Hippolytus, 37
Homer, 43, 129, 131
Hosea, 22
Housman, A. E., 98
Hügel, F. von, 28
Humboldt, Wilhelm von, 11, 12
Hume, 15, 17
Huns, the, 91
Huntingdon, Henry of, 65
Huxley, Aldous, 16, 19
Hyginus, 36

Icarus, 130
Ichthys, the, 105
Iconoclastic controversy, 182
Igel monument, the, 184
Ignatius, bishop of Antioch, 27
Ildefonsus, bishop of Toledo, 180
Illingworth, J. R., 20
Impressionism, 104
Incarnation, the, 23, 26, 48
Inge, W. R., 8
Ingres, 185
Irenaeus, 26, 35, 36, 70
Isaac, 107, 114, 168
Isaiah, 30, 35, 70, 85, 110, 111, 185
Ishmael, 107
Isidore, bishop of Seville, 50, 51, 130
Israel, 25, 32, 38, 43, 45, 59, 72, 80, 87
Israel, the New, 6, 25, 29

Jacob, 24, 28, 33, 41, 168
Jacob of Serug, 187
James, Protevangelium of, 133, 158
Jehoshaphat, valley of, 135, 166, 170, 177 ff.
Jephonias, 167, 168
Jeremiah, Origen's Homily on, 50
Jerome, St., 3, 16, 47, 59, 70, 81, 82, 88, 110, 134, 150, 176, 179
Jerusalem, 25, 27, 54, 55, 82, 107, 133, 137, 161, 176, 182
Jewish historians, 8, 9
Joachim, 133, 174

John, Acts of, 26, 188
John, bishop of Thessalonica, 173
John, Origen's commentary on the
    Gospel of, 49
John, St., 7, 10, 18, 26, 68, 77, 109, 111,
    115, 116, 131, 135, 162, 166 ff., 180,
    187, 188
John the Baptist, 168, 177
John Chrysostom, 110, 145
John Damascene, 138, 175, 176
Joly, Claude, 181
Jonah, 98, 103, 106
Joseph, 24
Joseph, St., 134, 190
Josephus, 9, 10, 62, 186
Joshua, 108, 186, 187, 191
Jovian, 84, 147
Jubilees, Book of, 118, 119, 127
Judas, 177
Judas Maccabaeus, 84
Jude, Epistle of, 187
Judgement, Divine, 7, 87 ff.
Julian, the emperor, 147
Juno, 184
Jupiter, 184
Justin Martyr, 31 ff., 44, 63, 78
Juvenal, bishop of Jerusalem, 175

Keats, John, 39
Keble, John, 39
Kings, the Books of, 8, 108

Laban, 33
Landor, W. S., 2
Lateran Museum, the, 102, 103, 105
Law, the, 46, 52, 118
Lazarus, 98, 103, 111, 112
Lebanon, 135
Leclercq, Henri, 137
Leibniz, 39
Leo VI, the emperor, 191
Leviticus, Origen's Homily on, 48
Licinius, 69, 70
Lightfoot, J. B., 63
Lille, Alain de, 128
Linus, 36
Lion-hunt, on sarcophagi, 100 ff.
Livy, 6, 13, 14
Logos, 34

Longinus, 115, 116
Lot's wife, 28
Louis XV, 94
Louvre, the, 101
Loyola, Ignatius, 15
Lucian, 130, 151
Lucina, crypt of, 101, 111
Lucius Lucceius, 3
Luke, St., 25, 77, 79, 109, 161
Lycomedes, 131

Macarius, 125
Macaulay, 17, 42, 154
Maccabees, the Book of, 186
Macchiavelli, 154
Macedon, 152
Madox, Thomas, 159
Mâle, Émile, 108, 136
Manichees, the, 168
Maran Atha, 26
Marcian, the emperor, 175, 176
Marcion, 52
Maria Antiqua, church of S., 115
Maria Maggiore, church of S., 108
Mariamne, 124
Martha, 125
Martin, St., of Tours, 148 ff., 162
Martyrs, Acts of the, 119 ff.
Mary, St., of Egypt, 188
Mary, St., the Virgin, 109, 115, 125,
    133 ff., 161 ff.
Mary Magdalene, St., 125, 182, 188
Matthew, Acts of, 130
Matthew, Gospel of St., 22, 40, 49,
    77, 79, 121, 180
Matthews, W. R., 142
Maurice, the emperor, 177
Maximin, 64
Melchizedek, 107, 108
Melito, bishop of Sardis, 138, 168, 171
Messiah, the, 4, 22, 80, 101, 106, 141
Michael, the Archangel, 135, 165, 170,
    187
Millennium, the, 79
Moab, land of, 186
Modestus, bishop of Jerusalem, 137,
    173
Mohammed, 185
Montaigne, 5

Moses, 24, 27, 28, 33, 35, 44 ff., 51, 58, 62, 67, 81, 97, 98, 103, 106, 118, 127, 180, 185, 186, 191
Moses, the Assumption of, 187
Munch, Edvard, 157
Murray, Gilbert, 33
Myth, 22, 43, 118 ff., 154, 163 ff.

Napoleon, 185
Nazareth, 190
Neoplatonists, the, 102
Nero, 90
Nestorius, 144, 163
Nicaea, Councils of, 67, 144, 175
Nicholas, St., 174
Niebuhr, Reinhold, 87
Nightingale, Florence, 58
Nineveh, 103
Nisibis, 187
Noah, 28, 80, 81, 95, 103, 108
Nogent, Guibert de, 96
Numbers, the Book of, 43
Numbers, Origen's Homily on, 52

Objectivity in history-writing, 12, 19, VIII *passim*
Oeta, Mount, 183
Olives, Mount of, 27, 135, 187
Olympiads, 59
Onesiphorus, 122 ff.
Orans, the, 101 ff., 114
Origen, 23, III *passim*, 55, 75, 133, 155, 187
Orosius, 74, 88 ff.
Orpheus, 109

Palermo, 182
Pamphilus, 55, 56
Paris, 181, 182, 185
Pascal, 41, 159
Patmore, Coventry, 20
Patriarchs, the, 23, 37
Pattison, Mark, 17, 64
Paul, St., 7, 21 ff., 28, 30, 45, 54, 82, 87, 93, 95, 106, 111, 114, 130, 150, 167, 185, 190
Paul, Apocalypse of, 190, 191
Paula, 179
Paulinus of Nola, 107, 108, 148

Pelagians, the, 88, 148
Pentateuch, the, 43, 108
Pentecost, 6, 137
Perpetua, St., 112
Persia, shah of, 13
Persians, the, 99, 152
Peter, Acts of, 129 f.
Peter, Apocalypse of, 190
Peter, St., 25, 28, 82, 90, 99, 122 f., 126, 129 f., 150, 167
Peter, Second Epistle of St., 79
Peter and Andrew, Acts of, 122 f.
Peter and Marcellinus, catacomb of, 111
Petronilla, 132
Pharisees, the, 21, 40, 118
Philip, Acts of, 124 f.
Philip, St., the Apostle, 123, 124 f.
Philip the Evangelist, 54
Philo, 42 ff.
Philoctetes, 184
Philostratus, 120
Photius, 173
Piacenza, 177
Pilgrims, 164, 176, 177
Pindar, 130
Pistis Sophia, 171
Pius XII, pope, 139
Plato, 33, 47, 89, 130, 151
Plotinus, 102, 121
Plutarch, 120
Poeas, 184
Pohle, Joseph, 140
Polybius, 3, 5, 10, 11, 13, 14, 30, 65, 151, 152
Polycarp, 68, 105
Polyphemus, 131
Pontius Pilate, 47, 87, 109, 111, 113, 121, 123
Porphyry, 46
Potammon, 56
Priscilla, catacomb of, 111
Proclus, bishop of Cyzicus, 163
Progress, idea of, 89
Prophecy, 4, 7, 21 ff., 31, 32, 37, 95, 126
Prosper of Aquitaine, 92
Proverbs, Book of, 156
Psalmist, the, 38, 74, 78, 79, 82, 99, 136, 146, 166